T0318464

Judith Butler and Organization Theory

The year 2020 marks thirty years since the first publication of Judith Butler's ground-breaking book *Gender Trouble*. Here, and in subsequent work, Butler argues that gender and other forms of identity can best be understood as performative acts. These acts are what bring our subjectivities into existence, enabling us to be recognized as viable, employable social beings, worthy of rights, responsibilities and respect. The three decades since the publication of *Gender Trouble* have witnessed Butler become one of the most widely cited and controversial figures in contemporary feminist thinking. While it is only in her most recent work that Butler has engaged directly with themes such as work and organization, her writing has profound implications for thinking, and acting, on the relationship between power, recognition and organization. Whilst her ideas have made important inroads into work, organization and gender studies that are discussed here, there is considerable scope to explore further avenues that her concepts and theories open up. These inroads and avenues are the focus of this book.

Judith Butler and Organization Theory makes a substantial contribution to the analysis of gender, work and organization. It not only covers central issues in Butler's work but also offers a close reading of the complexities and nuances in her thought. It does so by 'reading' Butler as a theorist of organization, whose work resonates with scholars, practitioners and activists concerned to understand and engage with organizational life, organization and organizing. Drawing from a range of illustrative examples, the book examines key texts or 'moments' in the development of Butler's writing to date, positing her as a thinker concerned to understand and address the ways in which our most basic desire for recognition comes to be organized within the context of contemporary labour markets and workplaces. It examines insights from Butler's work, and the philosophical ideas she draws on, considering the impact of these on work, organization and management studies thus far; it also explores some of the many ways in which her thinking might be mobilized in future, considering what scope there is for a non-violent ethics of organization, and for a (re)assembling of the relationship between vulnerability and resistance within and through organizational politics.

Melissa Tyler is a professor of work and organization studies at Essex Business School, The University of Essex, UK.

Routledge Studies in Gender and Organizations
Series Editor:
Elisabeth K. Kelan

Although still a fairly young field, the study of gender and organizations is increasingly popular and relevant. There are few areas of academic research that are as vibrant and dynamic as the study of gender and organizations. While much earlier research has focused on documenting the imbalances of women and men in organizations, more recently, research on gender and organizations has departed from counting men and women. Instead research in this area sees gender as a process: something that is done rather than something that people are. This perspective is important and meaningful as it takes researchers away from essentialist notions of gender and opens the possibility of analysing the process of how individuals become women and men. This is called 'gendering', 'practising gender', 'doing gender' or 'performing gender' and draws on rich philosophical traditions.

Whilst Routledge Studies in Gender and Organizations has a broad remit, it will be thematically and theoretically committed to exploring gender and organizations from a constructivist perspective. Rather than focusing on specific areas of organizations, the series is to be kept deliberately broad to showcase the most innovative research in this field. It is anticipated that the books in this series will make a theoretical contribution to the field of gender and organization based on rigorous empirical explorations.

Gender and the Professions
International and Contemporary Perspectives
Edited by Kaye Broadbent, Glenda Strachan, and Geraldine Healy

Postfeminism and Organization
Edited by Patricia Lewis, Yvonne Benschop, and Ruth Simpson

Women and Careers
Transnational Studies in Public Policy and Employment Equity
Marilee Reimer

Gender, Age and Inequality in the Professions
Edited by Marta Choroszewicz and Tracey L. Adams

Judith Butler and Organization Theory
Melissa Tyler

Judith Butler and Organization Theory

Melissa Tyler

Routledge
Taylor & Francis Group

LONDON AND NEW YORK

First published 2020 by Routledge

2 Park Square, Milton Park, Abingdon, Oxon, OX14 4RN
605 Third Avenue, New York, NY 10017

Routledge is an imprint of the Taylor & Francis Group, an informa business

First issued in paperback 2020

Library of Congress Cataloging-in-Publication Data
A catalog record for this book has been requested

ISBN: 978-1-138-04834-8 (hbk)
ISBN: 978-0-367-74747-3 (pbk)

Typeset in Sabon
by Apex CoVantage, LLC

For Ellis—with love, and the hope that you will continue to always be audacious

Contents

Preface   ix

Introduction   1

1 Making Trouble: Organizational Performativity
   and Parody   29

2 The Organizational 'Matter' of Bodies at Work   60

3 Un/Doing Organization—Coherence at the Cost
   of Complexity   85

4 Accounting for/in Organization: Giving and
   Working an Account of One's Self   109

5 Organized Dispossession: The Organizational
   Politics of Precarity   140

6 Organizational (re)Assemblage: Towards a Plural
   Performativity   165

   Postscript   197

   References   206
   Index   215

Preface

The year 2020 marks thirty years since the first publication of Judith Butler's book, *Gender Trouble*. The three decades since have witnessed Butler becoming one of the most widely cited yet controversial figures in contemporary feminist thinking. Her performative ontology of gender has led many to worship at the altar of 'St Jude' with a fanzine in the 1990s and now various social media groups devoted to her. In Buenos Aires in 2019, queues formed outside the hall where Butler was speaking more than seven hours ahead of the scheduled start time such was her popularity, while in Brazil in 2017, she was burned in effigy by Far Right protestors who had interpreted her work as 'anti-family'.

Butler has been hailed as 'a genius for insubordination' (Fraser, 1995a: 65), celebrated as a public intellectual whose work reaches well beyond the confines of academia (Fischer, 2016), yet she is also the notorious winner of a 'bad writer' award (see Butler, 1999) and has been derided as a 'professor of parody' who is capable of little more than setting the feminist movement back through her 'hip defeatism' (Nussbaum, 1999: 37).

Responses to Butler's work from within work and organization studies have tended to sit somewhere between these extremes. A growing number of scholars, practitioners and activists have drawn on her ideas and have applied and developed her insights, often re-framing her thinking through an organizational lens where her writing, particularly her earliest work, tended to lack this substantive focus. As Butler's own thinking about organizational lives and contexts continues to evolve so too do the possibilities, as well as the challenges and limitations, of drawing her work into a dialogue with organizational scholarship, activism and practice.

Butler's performative theory of gender in particular has made a significant contribution to work and organization studies in the years since the first publication of *Gender Trouble*. As Lloyd (2007) notes, it is this aspect of her thinking for which Butler continues to be best known, and it is her performative ontology of gender, in particular, that has been the most influential aspect of her writing for organizational scholars. Kenny's (2019: 33) book on whistleblowers is a notable exception, drawing together insights and ideas from across the full breadth of Butler's work noting 'its elegance in analyzing, critiquing and destabilizing what we take for granted' in organizational life.

I began drawing on Butler's ideas when I was a PhD student in the mid-1990s, encountering her work largely by tracing threads of De Beauvoir's (2011 [1949]) writing where they had been taken up by contemporary feminist thinkers, and reading Hegel's (1977 [1807]) philosophy of inter-subjectivity through Butler's, and in turn De Beauvoir's, analytical lens. It has become a bit of a standing joke with collaborators since that I rarely write anything that does not make reference to Butler's work. This does not make me an 'expert' by any stretch of the imagination, simply someone who has a long-standing interest. My reading is always provisional and partial; it is also quite personal, as themes in her writing resonate with my everyday life. This being the case, there are many people to thank.

Most obviously (and at the risk of being trite), I am grateful to Butler for providing such a rich and continually evolving body of ideas on which to draw. I have been informed and inspired by the work of many academic friends, colleagues and collaborators over the years, whose own thoughts on Butler have also provided a wealth of material from which I have been able to learn a great deal. There are too many to thank everyone individually, but of most significance have been the following: Joanna Brewis, Leanne Cutcher, Karen Dale, Philip Hancock, Nancy Harding, Kate Kenny, David Knights, Patricia Lewis, Martin Parker, Alison Pullen, Kat Riach, Carl Rhodes, Nick Rumens, Ruth Simpson, Katie Sullivan, Torkild Thanem and Sheena Vachhani. I am also very grateful to Talila (Tilly) Milroy, for kindly granting permission for me to draw from material developed in work co-authored with Leanne Cutcher and I on her grandmother, Bigali Hanlon. Not only did Tilly generously share details of her grandmother's life story with us, both she and Leanne also kindly agreed to me citing it here as an example of what happens to people when they are called to account for themselves in ways that organizational regimes make impossible.

Several texts have been constant reference points for me, notably Vicki Kirby's (2006) book *Judith Butler: Live Theory* and Moya Lloyd's (2007) *Judith Butler*. Although Butler has written a great deal since the publication of both texts, their insights continue to illuminate her complex body of ideas, and in both cases, anticipated subsequent developments in her thinking, not least the evolution of her more social scientific and politically engaged recent work that arguably speaks much more directly to organization theorists, practitioners and activists. For anyone with an interest in the full depth of Butler's writing and the breadth of her theoretical, ethical and political concerns, both Kirby and Lloyd's books are the best reference points I can think of, and I am grateful to both authors for providing the opportunity for me to draw on their extensive knowledge and expertise.

On that note, I am very grateful to Continuum books; John Wiley & Sons; Polity press and Sage Publications for kindly granting permission for me to draw from material previously published in the following articles and books: Hancock, P. and Tyler, M. (2007) 'Un/doing Gender and the Aesthetics of Organizational Performance', *Gender, Work and Organization*. 14(6): 512–533; Kirby, V. (2006) *Judith Butler: Live Theory*. London: Continuum; Lloyd, M. (2007) *Judith Butler*. Cambridge: Polity; Milroy, T., Cutcher, L. and Tyler, M. (2019) 'Stopped in our Tracks: From "Giving an Account" to an Ethics of Recognition in Feminist Praxis', *Gender, Work and Organization* (online early); Riach, K., Rumens, N. and Tyler, M. (2014) 'Un/doing Chronormativity: Negotiating Ageing, Gender and Sexuality in Organizational Life', *Organization Studies*. 35(11): 1677–1698; Riach, K., Rumens, N. and Tyler, M. (2016) 'Towards a Butlerian Methodology: Undoing Organizational Performativity Through Anti-narrative Research', *Human Relations*. 69(11): 2069–2089; Tyler, M. (2019) 'Reassembling Difference? Rethinking Inclusion Through/As Embodied Ethics', *Human Relations*. 72(1): 48–68. And I am extremely grateful to everyone at Routledge, including the series editors, for their support.

Most of all, I am very grateful to my family, particularly Philip, Ellis and William. Philip, our ongoing conversations about recognition have always fascinated me and given me so much to think about. Butler's writing is often criticized for being overly abstract, esoteric and divorced from the social struggles she writes about. My engagement with her work is no 'academic' project in the traditional sense of the word; for me, it speaks to how we live our daily lives, continually mindful of the themes that most concern her: bodily vulnerability, the desire for recognition, the impact of normative violence, and the ensuing temptations of accommodation to injurious ways of being, as well as the need to constantly give an account of ourselves, especially of our difference. But perhaps most of all, we are also aware of the ethical and political capacity of assembly, of the possibilities attached to the audacity of appearing in conceptual and physical spaces where we are made to feel that we don't belong, or have no right to be. We have a strong sense of the power of simply standing together; of giving the world, each day that we venture into it, the chance to be better than it is. Ellis, you have taught me more about the risks and rewards attached to recognition and relationality than any book ever could; this one is just for you.

Introduction

Judith Butler is perhaps the most widely cited contemporary feminist philosopher. Although her work emanates from the United States, she holds a number of international academic posts; her writing has global resonance and has been translated into at least twenty languages. It draws from and speaks to a range of empirical 'problems', philosophical and political, contemporary and historical, and engages a complex and rich variety of theoretical traditions. A recent article in the *New York Times* magazine cited her performative theory of gender as recognizable to an audience well beyond academia, albeit in a popularized form (Fischer, 2016).[1] As Vicki Kirby (2006) has noted, Butler's writing is a valuable illustration of how to read critically and generously, unfettered by disciplinary boundaries whilst at the same time being painstakingly respectful of intellectual traditions and dialogues. The latter has often led to criticisms of Butler's work as being overly and unnecessarily complex,[2] yet it is a significant scholarly template, one that connects academic and activist concerns, and which shows what is possible when we write and think about mutual recognition[3] as a textual as well as a thematic preoccupation, as both an ethical and a political imperative. It is the latter, in particular, that connects Butler's evolving intellectual interests and growing body of work over the past thirty years or so, and that is the focus of this book.

Underpinning Butler's (2004a: 31) writing is the conviction that 'to persist in one's own being is only possible on the condition that we are engaged in receiving and offering recognition'; this premise is considered here as both an organizational process and problem.[4] If, as Butler puts it, our identities are 'impossible ideals' that compel 'a daily mime' that can, by definition, never succeed in its effort to approximate that ideal, whether at an individual, group or corporate level, we need to 'account for the complex and divergent ways in which these impossible ideals are *manufactured and sustained*' (Butler, 1995b: 142, *emphasis added*), a task that converges Butler's preoccupations and those of organization theorists concerned to understand—and address—the ways of being that our workplaces and organizational lifeworlds both compel and constrain. A further important aspect of convergence is the performative basis of Butler's critique of this, namely her contention that 'what passes for necessary and unalterable' is contingent and performatively constructed. From Butler's perspective, power inheres in the naturalization, in the rendering as pre-social (or pre-organizational) and hence reification, of what is socially produced. A third important area of overlap lies in the ethical and political concerns of organization theorists and those articulated in Butler's writing on the struggle between attachment and differentiation (Butler, 2008: 109). If the latter is, as she puts it, 'coextensive with being human', what this means for how organizations are configured, experienced, managed and resisted as, at least in part, encounters with difference seems to be an increasingly urgent task for organizational scholars, practitioners and activists.

Butler has been an extremely influential figure in the social sciences and humanities since the publication in 1990 of her innovating book, and the work for which she continues to be best known, *Gender Trouble*. Here, and in subsequent writing, Butler argues that gender identities can best be understood as performative acts. These acts are what bring gender subjectivities into existence, enabling us to be recognized as viable social beings, worthy of rights and responsibilities. This insight inspired and popularized what Slavoj Žižek (2000: 132, n.30) calls the 'anti-identarian turn' that has come to be associated particularly with queer theory and politics, and it is not too much of a stretch to say that it 'rocked the foundations' of feminist thinking.[5]

While it is only in her most recent writing that Butler has engaged directly with themes such as work and organization in any sustained way, her thinking has profound implications for critical management scholars and sociologists of work focusing as it does, on the relationship between power, recognition and organization. Butler herself acknowledges this in various works, when she says, for instance, that

> It is simply not a strong enough claim to say that the 'I' is situated; the 'I', this 'I' is constituted by positions that are not merely theoretical products, but *fully embedded organizing principles of material practices and institutional arrangements*, those matrices of power and discourse that produce me as a viable 'subject'.
>
> (Butler, 1995a: 42, *emphasis added*)

While her writing has made many important inroads into work and organization studies that will be discussed here, there is considerable scope to expand Butler's readership within the field and to further explore the significance of her concepts and ideas for the analysis of work and organization. These include, but are not limited to, a critique of the ways in which organizational processes both produce and preclude viable subjectivities through organizing principles, material practices, institutional arrangements and 'matrices of power and discourse'. These inroads and the avenues noted so far are the focus of this book. In this sense, the book continues work begun by Janet Borgerson (2005) who was one of the first scholars within the field of management and organization studies to advocate the adoption of a Butlerian approach, arguing that Butler's writing opens up the range of questions and modes of engagement with/through organization that are possible, not least in challenging both ontologies of organization and the organization of ontologies. The former are taken here to refer to the ways in which we think about and study organizations as empirical phenomena, most commonly as places of work. The latter refers more broadly to the social processes through which particular phenomena come into being in organizationally recognizable, economically viable forms. One of the most widely cited examples of organizing ontologies in Butler's work is that of the heterosexual matrix—an ontological, epistemic schema through which a normative—binary, hierarchical and linear—relationship between sex, gender and sexuality is sustained. In Butler's writing, as discussed later, the heterosexual matrix is an organization of ontology—a structured, sense-making process that serves to compel and constrain particular ways of being, conferring or denying recognition, and allocating access to rights, responsibilities and resources accordingly; it is the mechanism through which 'the *organization* of gender comes to function as a presupposition about how the world is structured' (Butler, 2004b: 215, *emphasis added*).

The focus of this book is on how these two ways of thinking about organization—as social entities and as processes, or to put it more grammatically, as nouns and as verbs, interrelate. It draws heavily on the work of those who have already begun this analysis, connecting insights from Butler's own writing to a critique of work organizations and organizing processes.

This is no easy task, however Butler's writing is complex and wide-ranging—she does not routinely 'translate' her theories or illustrate her ideas with reference to particular contexts, and this perhaps explains both its appeal and the sense of frustration that is sometimes associated with her work. As Kelan (2010: 50) has put it, 'Butler's theories are largely elaborated at a very abstract level', which potentially leads to difficulties concerning how the processes she outlines can be studied empirically or how the politics she urges us to take up might be enacted.

Butler's writing on gender and on feminist theory and politics is perhaps the one notable exception to this, at least in her earlier work (Butler, 1988, 1990/2000a, 1993, 2004b). Drawing from her most formative texts and considering gender performativity within/through organizational contexts and processes provides an interesting way of examining how certain ways of being come to take the form they do, and come to 'matter' more than others, and of what different subjectivities and points of identification mean to those who embody, experience and enact them.

If gender performances are shaped by social (and organizational) regulatory norms, there is a need to think about, and to engage critically and reflexively, with those rules and the contexts within which they are situated, enforced and challenged. Butler herself suggests the importance of this in some of her earliest publications on gender and feminist theory in which she argues that scholarship ought to interrogate the ways in which 'the life-world of gender relations is constituted, at least partially, through . . . concrete and historically mediated acts' (Butler, 1988: 523). As Butler's concern is to understand how individuals and bodies are gendered through constitutive, concrete acts or doings, we might surmise that these include organizational processes and practices and their underlying imperatives.

Despite the emergence of a wealth of organizational literature over the past three decades or so that draws on Butler, there is as yet no collated reference point for organizational scholars, or sociologists of work, who would like to engage with her thinking. This book aims to fill that gap, introducing insights from Butler's work to those new to her writing, mapping out the impact of her concepts and ideas on work and organization studies thus far and exploring some of the many ways in which her ideas might be mobilized within the field in future. The coverage is by no means all encompassing, and the reading is particular. For those already familiar with Butler's writing, the book will gradually build the argument that Butler can be thought of as an organization theorist, or at least as a theorist of organization, given the ways in which each of the chapters outlined below weave together a concern to understand the organization of the desire for recognition—a central theme in Butler's texts.

Butler's writing on performativity—the starting point for any engagement with her work—has significant implications for the way in which we think about the performativity of organizational life but also performativity as a process of organization in and of itself. With this idea in mind, the aim of this book is to provide a 'way in' to Butler as well as a way of reading Butler into management, work and organization studies that appeals to a wide readership, yet which does not lose sight of the sophistication and complexity in her thinking and writing. To this end, the main chapters follow a similar structure, designed to consider what Butler's writing and organization theory bring to each other. This means that the first part of each chapter focuses on the depth and detail of Butler's writing through an organizational lens, before moving on, in the second part, to explore more concretely organizational phenomena from the perspective of Butler's work.

In this sense, the book has three specific aims: (i) to provide an introduction to Butler's writing and ideas for work, organization and management scholars; (ii) to summarize the inroads that her work has made within the field to date; and (iii) to explore some of the ways in which Butler's writing might be developed further within organizational scholarship, or taken up by practitioners and activists, in the future. Amounting to something of an emergent 'performative turn' (Gond et al., 2016: 457), the inroads that Butler's writing has made thus far into the field focus largely on her theory of performativity, which is arguably the ontological starting point for all of her major works, as noted above.

Although, as Gond et al. (2016: 441) have observed, 'discussions of how organizations are performed and how performativity is organized remain embryonic', several currents within organization studies established fertile ground for the favourable reception of Butler's theory of performativity during the 1990s. These include, first, an upsurge of scholars interested in the 'linguistic turn' in the humanities and social sciences, sharing the view that discourse does not merely describe a pre-existing social reality, but actively constitutes it. This non-representational view of language is central to Austin's (1955) concept of performativity on which Butler draws. As Gond et al. (2016) note, Austin's thesis has had a significant impact on management and organization studies, through narrative and storytelling based approaches (Boje, 1995), and, in particular, via the widespread influence of Fairclough's (2013) work on critical discourse analysis. Second, a 'doing' ontology as the basis of what has been called a 'practice turn' has been particularly influential, articulated largely through an emphasis on 'becoming' as an interactive, social (organizational) process. Third, a 'process turn' has seen a sustained interest in thinking about organization/s as a process, and organizational phenomena as multiple and fluid. Finally, a 'socio-material turn' inspired largely by phenomenology has brought a post-dualistic interest in the intertwined nature of meaning and materiality to the fore, highlighting the material effects of discursive practices and vice versa, and bringing embodied ways of thinking about organizational life to prominence. Taken together, these various strands of theoretical influence and orientation make important connections between different ways of thinking about performativity and its relationship to performance and served to set the scene for a relatively enthusiastic reception for Butler's work from the 1990s onwards.

Performativity and Performance

The term 'performativity' refers to the idea that what we perceive and experience is the outcome of a process of social construction through which particular phenomena come to be enacted or are brought into being in such a way as to make them recognizable and meaningful. In its simplest form, performativity is the attribution of particular sets of meanings to phenomena that bring those phenomena into being in order for them to be perceived as credible and viable and understood in specific ways.

In linguistics, the term derives largely from John L. Austin (1955) who described 'speech acts' as the capacity of speech to performatively enact or engender particular entities; for Austin, performativity is the capacity of language to 'do things with words'. As he put it, a performative utterance is one in which 'to *say* something is to *do* something; or in which *by* saying something we are doing something' (Austin, 1955: 12, *original emphasis*). As Gond et al. (2016: 443) have summed it up, Austin's performatives 'bring about what they say'. One of the clearest examples that Austin gives is that of a wedding ceremony in which two people are proclaimed (in the case of a heterosexual coupling) to be 'husband and wife'. Through this pronouncement, two people who have not necessarily changed in their material form have come to mean something different to themselves and others. This is not to deny their materiality but to suggest that the meanings and perceptions attached to that materiality have somehow changed as a result of this ceremonial pronouncement, or speech act.

While Austin himself did not use the term 'performativity', he referred to instances such as these as 'performative utterances' to emphasize situations in which speech *does* something rather than simply reports or describes the world around us. Performative utterances bring about what they say. In *How to Do Things with Words* Austin (1955) distinguished between three different forms of speech: *locution* (actual words spoken), *illocutionary force* (the intent of the locution) and *perlocutionary effect* (the actual effect of the speaker or speech, intended or not). To illustrate, if a speech act is an attempt to chastise someone, the illocutionary force is the intent to reprimand (the 'telling off') and the perlocutionary effect is the experience or sense of being caught out or brought to account. As part of a wider linguistic turn in the humanities and social sciences, Austin's analysis of speech acts provides a useful method for studying the performative effects of ordinary language use, and is one that Butler takes up in her own theory of gender performativity (Butler, 1990/2000a).

In addition to Austin's concept of 'speech acts', Michel Foucault's writing on the discursive constitution of subjectivity was a major influence on the development of Butler's thinking on performativity. For Foucault (2002: 54), discourses are practices that governmentally 'form the objects of which they speak'. Foucault's concern to develop a critical analysis of the interplay between power and knowledge is widely drawn on by researchers who take a performative approach to understanding the ways in which language, rather than reflecting or representing a pre-existing reality, constitutes that reality through discursive practices and effects embedded within power relations.

In another important reference point for Butler, Jacques Derrida (1979) developed Austin's performative analysis of speech acts, emphasizing the significance of what he called citationality and iterability in the circulation of signs. In Derrida's reading, Austin (1955) argued that the force of performatives derives from the intentions of the speaker and the context of the utterances. But Derrida stressed that all signs (visual or textual symbols) must be *citational*. By this he meant that, for instance, in opening a meeting, launching a ship or making a marriage pronouncement performatives must conform to 'an iterable model' (Derrida, 1979: 92) in order to be recognized; in other words, they are compelled, through the citation of recognized reference points, to perform in a particular way.

As Gond et al. (2016) note, Butler develops a material version of this emphasis on iterability in Derrida's work, highlighting how 'the reiterative power of discourse . . . produce[s] the phenomena that it regulates and constrains' (Butler, 1993: 3).

In a footnote in *The Postmodern Condition*, another widely cited contributor to the theoretical analysis of performativity, Jean-François Lyotard (1984 [1979]) connects his more systemic understanding of performativity as the optimization or calculation of input and outputs with Austin's concept of performative speech acts. In making this connection, Lyotard argues that knowledge not only reports, it 'does' something and in doing so is required to realize optimal outcomes. Thus, Lyotard outlines how the funding, conduct, articulation and evaluation of knowledge production is highly performative, measured according to expectations that not only represent a pre-existing reality but which bring that reality into being through the pursuit of efficiency and effectiveness. In moving away from Austin's original linguistic conception of performativity, Lyotard develops it as a way of understanding optimization. As Gond et al. (2016) note, the 'performance' of a company is a metaphor that is widely used to refer to its efficiency or profitability.[6] And Lyotard (1984: 88) himself notes the connection between his own concept of performativity as a system of efficiency measured according to input/output ratios and speech acts: 'the two meanings are not far apart. Austin's performative realizes the optimal performance.' Where Lyotard moved away from Austin, and arguably where Butler reunites them, is in thinking about performativity as an organized system.

Butler's Performative Ontology of Gender

A concern with performativity has been a sustained focus of Butler's work since the publication of her foundational article on gender constitution in which she sets out her performative ontology of gender as a series of stylized acts of repetition (Butler, 1988). Here, and in her book *Gender Trouble* (Butler, 1990/2000a), Butler argues that gender identities can best be understood as performative acts of constitution. She draws from Derrida and Foucault in her understanding of what she calls 'the reiterative power of discourse', emphasizing how performativity 'produces the phenomena that it regulates and constrains' (Butler, 1993: 3). For Butler, gender comes to exist in the form that it does as a result of performative acts that continuously recite the normative expectations governing gender identity in any given context. Gender is not something that we have or are; it is what we do.[7] And we 'do' gender in such a way as to make us socially and culturally intelligible.

In Butler's account of performativity, intelligibility is the perceptual framework or field that shapes the ways in which the desire for recognition comes to be organized; it is the 'normative framework that conditions who can be recognized as a legitimate subject' (Lloyd, 2007: 33). At the risk of oversimplification, 'intelligibility' can perhaps best be understood as the cultural corollary or condition of recognition, it is the organizing mechanism through which we perceive one another as viable, social beings if, as Butler emphasizes throughout her work, 'without recognition from one another, we cannot be a subject' (Harding et al., 2017: 1211).

Butler's critique of the conditions shaping intelligibility is inherently linked to her political aim of revealing the possibilities attached to a liveable life; that is, to a life that will be recognized as having value, as opposed to those deemed to be 'illegible, unrealizable, unreal and illegitimate' (Butler, 2000a: viii). It is a commitment to understanding—in order to change—the relationship between normative violence, cultural intelligibility and the parameters governing who/what counts as a liveable life that drives Butler's writing, connecting its philosophy, theory and politics. As Lloyd (2007: 36) puts it, 'the primary political aim of *Gender Trouble* is to make life possible for those who, within the terms of the dominant heteronormative regime, are presently unintelligible'.

In *Gender Trouble*, Butler (1990/2000a) maps out how cultural intelligibility functions as a binary, hierarchical form of categorization through what she calls the 'heterosexual matrix'.[8] According to the terms of this matrix, intelligible and therefore recognizable and liveable genders are those which cohere a continuous, even causal relationship between sex, gender and sexual desire; this relationship and its normalizing effects, Butler maintains, are not natural or pre-social but have the constitutive *effect* of being so.

In her theory of how (and why) this takes place, Butler develops Austin's concept of speech acts by arguing that gender is instantiated through acts of citation that bring men and women into being in specific ways that conform to the dominant norms shaping the heterosexual matrix. The latter is an ontological-epistemic schema governing what is deemed, in any given social context, to be 'normal' and 'natural' in the configuration of sex, gender and sexuality. This ideological framing privileges masculinity through the organization of gender in binary and hierarchical terms. Drawing on this concept, Butler's critique emphasizes how the recitation of particular gender norms is necessary in order to be accorded recognition as a viable subject. Hence, performances recognized as successful are those that conform to the binary and hierarchical terms of heteronormativity. The matrices of cultural intelligibility that shape social life therefore govern gender as a 'performative accomplishment' (Butler, 2000a: 179) by compelling certain subjectivities (those that conform to normative expectations), at the same time as foreclosing others.

Butler's performative theory of gender also draws on the concept of interpellation as it is developed in Louis Althusser's (2001) discussion of the ideological processes through which particular subject positions are 'hailed' into being, a concept she refers to throughout much of her work (see Butler, 2016). For Althusser, it is through the process of hailing (being beckoned into a response) that individuals become 'interpellated' into subject positions that are continually re-enacted. To illustrate this process, Althusser makes reference to a police officer commanding, 'Hey! You there!'. In the combined act of calling out, acknowledging and responding, the police officer and the person being hailed effect the latter as a 'suspect', someone who is required to account for him- or herself (e.g. their actions or presence). Through this process, even fleetingly, a particular subject position is taken up.

The same interpellatory process can be identified in the proclamation: 'It's a girl/boy,' when a baby is born. Butler argues that the presumption of subject positions such as these serve to perpetuate the idea that the division of humanity into two sexes is somehow normal and natural; rather, she argues, it is the outcome of a social process of interpellation through which gendered subject positions are performatively, continually re-enacted. These performative re-enactments and recitations give the impression that something socially constructed is pre-social or essential. Illustrative examples of such performative enactments include the sex-based classification of competitors by Olympic committees who administer hormone testing, or intersex babies being routinely 'sexed' at birth or shortly afterwards. Practices such as these mean that, for Butler, performativity 'must be understood not as a singular or deliberate "act" but, rather, as the reiterative practice by which discourse produces the effects that it names' (Butler, 1993: 2). It is not simply this process that is of concern to her, but the normative conditions or governmental regimes compelling or constraining that process.

To reiterate, for Butler, gender performativity is driven largely by the desire for recognition of ourselves as viable, intelligible subjects. In other words, underpinning our performance of gender is the desire to project a coherent and compelling identity, one that is recognized and valorized by others, but one that in Butler's terms, produces its coherence at the cost of its own complexity. Arguing that 'this repetition is not performed by a subject', but rather 'is what enables a subject' (Butler, 1993: 95), Butler emphasizes that subject positions are continually evoked through stylized acts of repetition, through mundane acts of gesture and inflection that, if performed in accordance with the social norms governing the conferral of recognition, result in the attribution of viable subjectivity. In one sense, therefore, Butler conceptualizes subjectivity as an act of 'doing' but, crucially, 'not a doing by a subject who might be said to pre-exist the deed' (Butler, 2000a: 33). In other words, she argues against a notion of the subject as the originator of action, in favour of understanding how the doer (or 'subject') is the outcome of a performative process rather than the basis of it, so that 'the doing itself is everything' (Butler, 2000a: 25).

This bifurcation of agency and subjectivity has led Butler to be accused of reducing the latter to a discursive effect, disavowing the capacity of the subject to exist beyond discourse (see Butler, 1993). However, this separation is crucial to understanding how, for Butler, subjectivity is effectively the outcome of a process through which certain performative acts come to be recognized as viable subject positions, while others are not.

But for Butler (2004b), just as gender is always a process of doing, so too is it simultaneously an 'undoing'. Here, Butler plays on the term 'undoing' as referring to both an unravelling of the subject as well as to the subject's capacity to challenge and resist this unravelling. By this she means that we are both 'undone' by the need to perform coherent, recognizable identities. Yet at the same time, the performative nature of gender means that it can be 'undone' more proactively, critically and reflexively in order for it to be re-enacted differently; in other words, as we effectively create ourselves, so we can recreate ourselves. To illustrate how this 'un/doing' is performatively enacted, Butler references drag artists who reveal, she argues, the extent to which all gender performances are citational enactments, undertaken in the hope of being recognized by an appreciative audience.

With reference to the film *Paris is Burning*, she highlights the psychic harm done by this undoing and by the need to perform ourselves in ways designed to make us socially acceptable, and therefore viable, at the same time as showing how this harm might be challenged and resisted by individuals and within communities that strive to undo the psychic and physical harm to which they are subject. In her earlier writing, Butler focused largely on performativity at the level of the individual (Butler, 1988, 1990/2000a, 1993, 2004b), but in her recent work she has considered performativity as a more collective endeavour (Butler, 2015a, 2016; Butler and Athanasiou, 2013; Butler et al., 2016), reflecting on the extent to which, while our desire for recognition renders us all precarious in an existential sense, the socially situated, contextual nature of this desire and the terms governing recognition mean that some individuals and groups are more precarious and vulnerable than others. Her writing frames this as an organizational process, as well as positing organizational practices and modes of resistance as possible means of addressing the unequal distribution of vulnerability.

In *Giving an Account of Oneself*, Butler (2005) considers the self as a narrative composition, considering the ways in which our existential vulnerability, socially and economically induced precarity and subjection to processes that 'undo' us require us to cohere a version of ourselves designed to elicit recognition and to secure the rights and opportunities that recognition of one's social (and organizational viability) potentially brings. Here 'accounting' for oneself involves not simply telling a story about oneself, but providing a convincing ethical defence of one's claim to recognition, particularly when that claim involves accounting for one's difference. Butler's (2005) view of narrative, developed most fully in her discussion of how and why the self is continually called to 'account', provides a performative lens through which to understand how narratives operate in the process of becoming a subject, including within and through organizational subjectivities and settings (Riach et al., 2014, 2016). In particular, Butler's largely phenomenological understanding locates narrative, as an attempt to cohere and convey a liveable life, within the context of the desire for recognition of oneself as a viable subject; as she puts it: 'I come into being as a reflexive subject only in the context of establishing a narrative account of myself' (Butler, 2005: 15). Framed in this way, narrative is not simply telling one's life story but rather the response we are compelled to provide when being 'held to account' for ourselves (Butler, 2005: 12), or being 'hailed' in Althusser's terms.

Important criticisms have been levelled against Butler's concept of performativity. One of the most significant for organization theory is that it focuses too much on individual performativity and does not sufficiently take other factors such as collectivity and context into consideration. As noted earlier, Butler turns to this issue in some of her more recent writing, considering how performativity might be collectively enacted (see Chapters 5 and 6). In her *Notes Towards a Performative Theory of Assembly* (Butler, 2015a), she explores the dynamics of public assembly, understanding assemblies as plural—organized—forms of performative action. Here she extends her theory of performativity to argue that precarity (the destruction of the conditions of subjective relationality) has been a galvanizing force in contemporary social protest. In this sense, Butler broadens her analysis of performativity, moving beyond speech acts in her discussion of the politics of the performative (Butler, 1997a) to argue for the significance of collective assemblies of bodies. For her, when bodies assemble they are exercising 'a plural and performative right to appear', one that delivers 'a bodily demand . . . for a more liveable set of economic, social and political conditions no longer afflicted by induced forms of precarity' (Butler, 2015a: 11).

To put it succinctly, Butler's thinking owes much to the critical thinking about subjectivity that shaped French theory since the mid-1960s, and which became particularly popular in work and organization studies in the early 1990s. Connections in her writing on poststructuralism and feminist thinking make important contributions to feminist debates about subjectivity and to developments within queer theory and LGBTQ politics (Lloyd, 2007). For Butler, *difference* feminism's denouncement of the very possibility of a discernible feminist subject puts at risk the political imperative of feminism as an emancipatory endeavour. However, Butler herself has been accused of adhering too much to this position, on the premise that her performative theory of subjectivity undermines the capacity of feminism to seek to emancipate women as a group, leaving feminist politics with no discernible stable subject to liberate, or speak on behalf of. A notable proponent of the latter view is Seyla Benhabib (1995a: 20), who has argued that a performatively constituted subject, reduced to the status of a linguistic effect, lacks the capacity for 'intentionality, accountability, self-reflexivity, and autonomy'. In Benhabib's view, Butler's discursive 'dissolution' of the subject is incompatible with the critical, emancipatory goals of feminism, for

> The subject that is but another position in language can no longer master and create that distance between itself and the chain of significations in which it is immersed such that it can reflect upon them and creatively alter them.
>
> (Benhabib, 1995a: 20)

Yet at the same time, Butler's writing is premised upon a critique of the totalizing effects of categorical thinking that imposes coherence, even tactically so, on complex lived experiences and identities. In many ways, as Lloyd (2007: 7) notes, one of the reasons why Butler's writing has perhaps been so influential in feminist thinking, including within work and organization studies, is that it not only recognizes and responds to this problematic within feminist theory and politics, but 'it was pivotal in shifting the terms of that debate away from a unified conception of women towards an alternative understanding of subjectivity'. This ontological development, one that combines insights from Foucault, Hegel, Merleau Ponty and many others (see Butler, 2015b), made a significant contribution to the evolution, from the early 1990s onwards, both to feminism and to queer politics;[9] it has yet to influence the way in which we think about organizations to quite the same extent, but it is beginning to make significant inroads in this direction, including through queer organization theory (Rumens, 2018).

Although Butler has described herself first and foremost as a feminist thinker, there is no doubt, as Lloyd (2007: 10) puts it, 'that her work has been seen as central to the advent of queer theory, with *Gender Trouble* regarded as one of its foundational texts'. Her ontology is arguably one of the many reasons for this, emphasizing that power relations not only limit but also enable possibilities of political engagement by a subject that is not determined, but constituted within and through those relations. Butler's Hegelian influences lead her to insist on this constitution as a never-ending process grounded in constant repetition and recitation of cultural norms that is at once discursive and material. Performativity is a citational enactment involving a constant reiteration that is 'contingent on convention' (Lloyd, 2007: 63), but dialectically rather than determinedly so. This continual 'recycling of conventions' (Butler, 1993: 107) over time, and in specific social situations, is embedded in power relations shaping the conferral or disavowal of recognition, a situation that queer thinking, including within organization scholarship and activism, seeks to unsettle.

As well as a critical engagement with Austin, Foucault and Derrida, Butler's writing on performativity is also indebted to Goffman's (1956, 1963, 1967) performance-based understanding of identity (although some have claimed that performativity 'has nothing to do with . . . Goffman's sociology' as it shifts the focus from epistemology to ontology—see Law, 2008: 624). Butler herself contests the claim that she is simply recycling Goffman, arguing that this is a misunderstanding of her work (see Butler, 1995b: 134 and Chapter 1).

For clarification, Goffman argued that performance, in the form of social interaction, is crucial to the symbolic order as it maintains the relationship between individuals and audiences, to whom individuals perform and who, in turn, interpret those performances. For Goffman (1956: 252–253, *emphasis added*), 'the self is a performed character . . . *the peg on which something of a collaborative manufacture will be hung for a time*'. Behind Goffman's self as a 'performed character' therefore lies an actor who takes on particular, socially appropriate *roles* within the dramaturgical context of social interaction.

Butler replaces or rather adapts two basic premises of Goffman's approach to the performing self—first, she rethinks the relationship between agency and subjectivity as a performative one, and second, she shifts the analytical emphasis from roles to acts. Through both moves, she emphasizes that there is no 'doer behind the deed', rather, the subject emerges through repeated acts of constitution. To argue that subjectivities emerge through/from social relations, contexts and processes opens up intriguing possibilities for organizational researchers, as well as some important challenges considered throughout this book, particularly in terms of the critical analysis of how the relationship between agency and subjectivity comes to be organized, through what processes, and on whose terms.

Butler explicitly rejects theatrical notions of performance (see Butler, 1993: 12). In her book *Excitable Speech* (1997a), she examined performativity with reference to rhetorical and political acts, considering not only the speech act itself (discussed earlier) but also the context and consequences of such acts. She drew on Austin's discussion of 'utterances' noted above that distinguishes between speech acts that are illocutionary (doing what they say in the process of saying) and perlocutionary (producing certain effects as a result of the circumstances of the speech act).

Butler argued here that language can engender vulnerability (through hate speech, name calling and so on), causing psychic harm, but that linguistic agency can also emerge from shared recognition of this vulnerability. That speech acts require certain circumstances and venues of power to be effective reinforces the need to consider their material contexts and effects including their organizational locations (see Kenny, 2019), with reference to what Butler calls the 'institutional conditions of utterance' (Butler, 1997a: 13). As she put it,

> The speech act, as a rite of institution, is one whose contexts are never fully determined in advance, [so] that the possibility for the speech act to take on a non-ordinary meaning, to function in contexts where it has not belonged, is precisely *the political promise of the performative.*
>
> (Butler, 1997a: 161, *emphasis added*)

Butler wove this way of thinking about speech acts into her performative ontology, arguing that

> If a word . . . might be said to 'do' a thing, then it appears that the word not only signifies a thing, but that this signification will also be an enactment of the thing. It seems here that *the meaning of a performative act is to be found in this apparent coincidence of signifying and enacting.*
>
> (Butler, 1995c: 198, *emphasis added*)

The bifurcation of agency and subjectivity in her theory of performativity, and her focus on the 'apparent coincidence' of signification and action, causes confusion, particularly revolving around a presumed disavowal of agency in her thinking. But while Butler does not work with any notion of a foundational or pre-discursive subject, a 'peg' on which different performances rest, as Goffman puts it, she does (can) not dispense with agency all together; rather it is subjectivity that emerges through performativity, as a citation that produces intelligible subjects.

Further, Butler understands discourse as powerful but not all pervasive. Following Austin and Foucault, discourse is multiple and often contradictory, but always productive, or rather performative in her terms. Discourse produces particular effects, and herein lies its power. In Butler's writing, performativity means that discourse disciplines subjects as it constitutes them.

As a dialectical way of thinking about agency and subjectivity, discourse and materiality, signification and action, Butler's theory of performativity does not align itself with the extremes of voluntarism or determinism, but draws from elements of both, the result being a theoretical and political 'troubling' of the reification of social, including organizational, categories. As Gregson and Rose (2000: 438) have noted, emphasizing the critical capacity of her thinking for studies of work and organization in this respect, Butler's 'radical anti-foundationalism provides a crucial critical tool for denaturalizing social categories and for destabilising dominant forms of social reproduction'.

Butler (2010: 147) herself hints at this in her discussion of performative agency, drawing parallels between a performative gender ontology and the ways in which we might think about the state or the economy. To recap, she argues that performativity unsettles the presumption that gender is a metaphysical substance that precludes its expression, problematizing but not evading or disavowing gendered effects or the hold they have on us. Similarly, she argues, the state or the economy only becomes singular and/or monolithic as a consequence of certain limiting processes and practices that produce the 'effect' of a knowable unified economy as a clearly definable entity. The implication of this way of thinking, she contends, is threefold. First, it counters lingering positivistic ways of understanding certain entities as pre-socially determined. Second, it draws critical attention to mechanisms of social construction, or the attribution of social meanings to particular phenomena. Finally, it also subjects to critique those 'sets of processes that produce ontological effects; that is, that work to bring into being certain kinds of realities or, . . . that lead to certain kinds of socially binding consequences', including we might argue, organizational ones.

Gond et al. (2016: 447) have picked up on this very point, arguing that this way of thinking about performativity as an organizing system central to, but beyond gender, 'offers the possibility of understanding organizations, management and work as "knowable effects" produced by converging processes and practices that performatively constitute the "effect" of organizations'. This is not to deny their materiality; on the contrary, it is to emphasize the significance of the *organization* of that materiality into meaningful phenomena through the convergence of particular processes, practices and, we might add, perceptions. Crucial to Butler's understanding of how and why this is undertaken is her view that underpinning the organization of social relations, material phenomena and the processes that constitute the social world is the desire for recognition.

Recognition—Putting Hegel to Work

If performativity is the ontological starting point for Butler, then recognition is arguably its philosophical premise. This aspect of her thinking takes Hegel's (1977 [1807]) philosophy of inter-subjectivity, articulated most clearly through his narration of the dialectical relationship between the Lord and Bondsman, as its origins. As Butler herself notes, in many respects, all of her work 'remains within the orbit of a certain set of Hegelian questions' (Butler, 1999: xiv). As Lloyd (2007: 14) puts it, Butler is in many ways a critic of Hegel, but 'a friendly and responsive one' in so far as her work bears what we might think of as a dialectical relation to Hegel's; her writing is indebted to Hegel, although Butler's reading of his work is shaped by her engagement with many other thinkers as well. At the same time, Hegel's writing forms the basis of her own distinctive analysis of recognition as a dialectical phenomenon, one that is *socially situated* in the dynamics of power and cultural intelligibility.

In Butler's hands, Hegel's philosophy of inter-subjectivity is woven through De Beauvoir's (2011 [1948]) critique of women's Otherness, articulated in *The Second Sex* and developed into her own distinctive account of the gendered organization of the desire for recognition. In feminist hands, largely following De Beauvoir, recognition is understood as 'the embodied, practical and cooperative character of the self-other relation' and is framed as 'dialogical, situated in cultural and social contexts and generated through embodied practice' (Harding et al., 2013: 57).

Central to Butler's writing on recognition, developed initially in *Subjects of Desire* (Butler, 1987) and then woven through (arguably all of) her subsequent work in one form or another, is a Hegelian understanding of recognition as a process through which Self and Other come to a mutual understanding of each as reflected in the other. The title of *Subjects of Desire*, based largely on her doctoral thesis, emphasizes Butler's understanding of the constitutive relationship between desire and subjectivity. Her close reading of Hegel highlights how this inter-subjective reflection does not have to result in a collapse of the Self into the Other 'through an *incorporative identification*, . . . or a projection that *annihilates the alterity* of the Other' (Butler, 2000b: 272, *emphasis added*). Nor, she stresses, does the dialectical nature of this encounter have to imply totality or metaphysical closure, as sceptical readings of Hegel tend to emphasize; Butler 'declines to understand the *Phenomenology* as an account of a subject who is progressing neatly from one "ontological place to another"' (Lloyd, 2007: 15). Rather, she emphasizes how the desire for recognition is an 'indefinite movement' (Butler, 1987: 14), always incomplete, and always carrying with it the perpetual risk of negation or misrecognition. Crucially for Butler (following Hegel), it is precisely this risk that needs to be worked through in order to open up and perpetually pursue the possibility of mutual recognition. As she puts it, drawing directly on *Phenomenology* 'as desire, consciousness is outside itself . . . it is always the desire-for-reflection, the pursuit of identity in what appears to be different' (Butler, 1987: 7, *original emphasis*). This means that the subject 'is a reflexive structure', in so far as 'movement out of itself is necessary in order for it to know itself at all' (Butler, 1987: 8).

As Butler puts it, the negative dialectic through which subjectivity is constituted means that the subject 'must suffer its own loss . . . again and again in order to realize its fullest sense of self' (Butler, 1987: 13). This paradox, this 'adventure through alterity' (Butler, 1987: 10) as she puts it, means that thinking about recognition as both a normative ideal to be worked towards and as a template for political activism—as a process of struggle—is crucial to feminist approaches that effectively 'strive for the triumph of recognition over aggression' (Butler, 2000b: 274).[10]

When Hegel introduces the idea of recognition in one of the most frequently quoted passages in the section on Lordship and Bondage in *Phenomenology of Spirit*, he narrates the Self's primary encounter with the Other as one of self-loss. As he puts it,

> Self-consciousness exists in and for itself when, and by the fact that, it so exists for another; that is, it exists only in being acknowledged . . . it has come *out of itself*. This has a two-fold significance: first, it has lost itself, for it finds itself as an *other* being; secondly, in doing so it has superseded the other, for it does not see the other as an essential being, but in the other sees its own self. It must supersede this Otherness of itself. . . . First, it must supersede the *other* independent being in order thereby to become certain of *itself* as the essential being; secondly, in doing so, it proceeds to supersede its *own* self, for this other is itself.
>
> (Hegel, 1977 [1807]: 111, *original emphasis*)

In this same section, Hegel (1977: 112) goes on to emphasize the dialectical nature of this struggle when he says, 'the action has a double significance not only because it is directed against itself as well as against the other, but also because it is indivisibly the action of one as well as of the other'. As well as the dialectical nature of this encounter, what also becomes clear is that the self never returns to itself; in other words, its encounter with the Other becomes reflexively constitutive of the self, a move which gives us the ek-static notion of the self as non-self-identical but relational, a concept that is crucial to Butler's thinking on ethics and politics, as discussed in Chapters 5 and 6.

In Butler's reading of *Phenomenology*, the self that emerges is transformed through its encounter with alterity in irrecoverable ways, so that the self is always outside of oneself. Ek-statis means to be always 'outside oneself, to be Other than oneself' (Butler, 2000b: 286), an ontological predicament that simultaneously opens up the potential for recognition, *and* carries with it the perpetual risk of negation or mis-recognition. In other words, to live always outside of oneself means to live in a state of perpetual, existential precarity and to be constantly at risk of this primary precarity being exploited or appropriated, a theme discussed in Chapter 5. As Butler (1987: 39, *original emphasis*) puts it, this means that the desiring subject lives as a 'negative generativity':

> The intentionality of desire is always also informed by its reflexive project; desire always reveals the desiring agent as intrinsically other

to itself: self-consciousness is an *ek-static* being, outside itself, in search of self-recovery.

Thought of as the permanently precarious outcome of a negative dialectic, the process of becoming a subject is thus a 'dramatization of destruction' (Butler, 1987: 38) through which desire is revealed as a 'negating negativity'. But there is no totalizing progression towards resolution, at least in her reading of Hegel: 'where becoming is not a unilinear but a cyclical process' (Butler, 1987: 18). In a particularly evocative passage in *Subjects of Desire* (one that perhaps hints of the analysis of drag to come in her later work—see Chapter 1), Butler (1987: 20) frames this process of perpetual becoming as a Godot-like burlesque when she says:

> We realize slowly that this subject will not arrive all at once, but will offer choice morsels of himself [*sic*], gestures, shadows, garments strewn along the way, and that this 'waiting for the subject', much like attending to Godot, is the comic, even burlesque, dimension of Hegel's *Phenomenology*.

Here she sums up how, as a generative force, negation articulates desire as a compelling force through which the subject comes to be postulated by *simultaneously* recognizing and continually ridding itself of its own alterity, but by doing so incrementally, through 'hints' of the subject to come. In Butler's (1987: 42, *emphasis added*) summation of this process:

> The mediation of difference is not only the internalization of otherness, but also the externalization of the subject. *These two moments of assimilation and projection are part of the same movement . . .* which, in Hegel's words, 'unifies' subject and 'substance'.

This is the point at which, in Butler's account at least, the notion of desire loses its reified character as an abstract universal ideal and becomes 'situated in terms of an embodied identity' (Butler, 1987: 43). Here Butler builds on Hegel's (1977: 114) own hints at the distinction between human agency and situated self-conscious subjectivity, when he says:

> The individual who has not risked his life may well be recognized as a *person*, but he has not attained to the truth of this recognition as an independent self-consciousness . . . [as] self-consciousness must do more than merely live.

At its simplest, the self in Hegel is therefore conceived of through a primary enthrallment with the Other, one in which the very idea of the self is put at risk, and desire is what initiates the perpetual transition from consciousness to self-consciousness, from One to the Other, as a reflexive movement. Self-consciousness is thus defined by Hegel (1977: 105) as 'the return from Otherness', marking the point at which the subject becomes capable of recognising its own interdependence. The moment when two self-conscious beings encounter one another constitutes a 'life and death struggle', each seeking to annihilate the other in order to 'become certain of itself' as Hegel puts it.[11] For Butler, this certainty is not simply ontological but social and political as well. It is what she frames as intelligibility in phenomenological terms, or liveability when thought about more sociologically; her preoccupation with understanding this as a process through which the desire for recognition comes to be organized is what positions Butler as an organization theorist, or at least, as a theorist of organization. Her concern is with understanding how the desire for recognition comes to be organized, and how recognition comes to be conferred or denied on the basis of organizing and organizational regimes that render some lives intelligible and others not, or less so. This is not simply a philosophical project for Butler; the point is to understand how the desire for recognition is organized in such a way that it compels and constrains particular performativities in order to change it; to broaden the range of possible ways of being—and organizing—that might be deemed viable. This is, in part, why it is so important for her to go back to Hegel in order to establish the significance of recognition, and our desire for it, as shaping our most basic ways of relating to one another, of *organizing* our lives.

In Hegel, the moment of recognition holds destruction in check, as the Self comes to recognize that with the Other's destruction comes the loss of alterity on which self-consciousness depends;[12] the ethical content of the self's relationship to the other is hence to be found in the fundamentally reciprocal state of being 'given over'. This mutual recognition is the opposite of what Butler calls 'incorporation'. Through mutual recognition, or relationality, the self 'does not take the Other in'; on the contrary, 'it finds itself transported outside of itself in an irreversible [ek-static] relation of alterity' (Butler, 2000b: 288).

Understanding this philosophical basis of Butler's thinking helps to address concerns about a disavowal of agency in her work and to begin to make connections between her thinking and the preoccupations of organization theorists and activists. The self, as she sees it, is 'beyond itself from the start and is defined by this ontological ek-statis' (Butler, 2000b: 288), premised upon 'the ontological primary of relationality', one that the desire for recognition, as it comes to be organized (through mechanisms such as the heterosexual matrix, for instance), arrests or appropriates. This ek-static, relational self connects agency and subjectivity in her analysis: it is the link between exertion of individual self-consciousness and the conditions upon which recognition of that self-consciousness, as a socially intelligible being, depends. It also helps us to grasp how, for Butler, the conditions that compel and constrain the form that subjectivity takes neither originate solely within the self, or separate from it, but are embedded within the primary relationality that exists between Self and Other, and within the wider context within which the struggle for recognition is continually played out, not as she puts it, as a presupposition, but as an *achievement*, as something that must be continually worked at or struggled over. A key question for Butler then becomes, what does it mean to recognize one another, understood in this way, 'when it is a question of so much more than the two of us', in other words, when recognition moves beyond individual self-consciousness into the realm of the social, and we might add, organizational.[13]

Butler's reading of the Hegelian struggle not as a conflict to be overcome but as central to social relations underpins her understanding of recognition, and her views on this are worth citing at some length. Borrowing directly from Hegel, she writes:

> Recognition . . . is not the simple presentation of a subject for another that facilitates the recognition of that self-presenting subject by the Other. It is, rather, a *process* that is engaged when subject and Other understand themselves to be reflected in one another, *but where this reflection does not result in a collapse of the one into the Other (through an incorporative identification, for instance) or a projection that annihilates the alterity of the Other.*
>
> (Butler, 2000b: 272, *emphasis added*)[14]

In her discussion of this process, Butler both draws from and differentiates herself from other recognition theorists, notably Jessica Benjamin (1988), Jürgen Habermas (1979a, 1979b) and Axel Honneth (1995, 2008). For Habermas, communicative action becomes both the vehicle for recognition and its evidence base; recognition takes place as communicative action in a way that transforms subjects through the communicative practices in which they are engaged. As Butler notes in her summation of Habermas, 'one can see how this model supplies a norm for both social theory and . . . practice' (Butler, 2000b: 272). Butler partially aligns herself with this position, one that emphasizes how struggle is characterized by a desire to engage in communicative action as an on-going process that, while proffering the possibility of recognition, also poses the risk of destruction. Yet while Hegel referred to negation as the risk that recognition always runs, for Butler (in a position that arguably has more in common with Honneth than Habermas—see Butler, 2008) not all struggle is necessarily destructive or capable of being resolved. The desire for recognition is a complex, on-going and irresolvable process, a point that she illustrates with reference to trans people for whom trans involves not simply moving from 'one' gender to another but rather living beyond gender categorization. Butler's reading therefore sets up recognition as a simultaneously philosophical, political and sociological problem, not least because of its dual grammar, as both 'the norm towards which we invariably strive . . . and the ideal form that communication takes when it becomes a transformative process' (Butler, 2000b: 273).

The challenge Butler sets herself, in her reading of Hegel, is to find a way to recognize difference as a relation of negation ('the Other is not me') that does not, by definition, descend into destruction if, for Hegel, subjectivity founded on recognition is negation that is continually survived—outlived and outsmarted. In Butler's reading, the Hegelian struggle for recognition is 'an achievement, not a presupposition' (Butler, 2000b: 285). Teleological readings of Hegel, she argues, imply that struggle is the process of overcoming destruction, 'once and for all'. But Butler asks, 'Would we trust those who claim to have overcome destructiveness?' if (i) the conditions of recognition are socially situated, embedded as they are in established social structures, cultural norms and power relations (including those that we might call 'organizational'), and (ii) the risk attached to the desire for recognition is 'a *perennial and irresolvable* aspect of human psychic life' (Butler, 2000b: 285, *emphasis added*). Taken together, these two concerns—the one sociological, the other philosophical—raise a political problem that is of particular concern to Butler: any norm that seeks to overcome destructiveness bases itself on a premise that is not only implausible but itself destructive. In this aspect of her thinking, Butler subscribes to what might be called a 'non-synthetic dialectic' (Lloyd, 2007: 19), a position reflected in her engagement with Althusser's notion of hailing and Derrida's writing on iterability (discussed earlier and in Chapter 1), played out perhaps most notably in her critique of the relationship between sex and gender in *Gender Trouble* (Butler, 1990/2000a).

This non-synthetic dialectical lens, and Butler's way of thinking about subjectivity as shaped by a perpetual, irresolvable desire for recognition, raises important questions for organization theory: if to recognize 'is to affirm, validate, acknowledge, know, accept, understand, empathize, take in, appreciate, see, identify with, find familiar . . . love' (Benjamin, 1988: 15–16), we might argue that recognition epitomizes many of the qualities of social relations that we might hope to associate with organizations and organizing. As Ahmed (2000: 22) reminds us, recognition means 'to know again, to acknowledge and to admit', implying a process premised upon a recollection of our basic connections to others and of a sense of collective identification or belonging ('admission'). But because of the conditions attached to an organizational/organized form of recognition, the question becomes 'Does organization make lives more or less recognizable and therefore, liveable?'[15]

Hegel's sense that we are somehow displaced while remaining bound within something, in other words that we (paradoxically and precariously) 'find ourselves' by surrendering to being lost, fascinates Butler, and arguably sets up her sociological interest in the organization of the desire for recognition already noted, positing the ek-static self as an organization of subjectivity, and of the relationality from which it proceeds. The challenge she sets herself in some of her earliest writing on this theme is to consider the existential possibilities attached to what seem to be oppressive conditions and power relations. In other words, her main concern is with the question of the social and cultural norms governing who/what counts as worthy of recognition, a preoccupation that underpins Butler's interest in the differential values applied to particular lives, and deaths. This is a discussion that is embedded, in Hegelian terms, in a philosophical understanding of all lives as precarious, with some being more precarious than others. The question for Butler is why this is the case and with what consequences and, perhaps most importantly: what can we do about it?

As Kirby (2006) notes, Butler's aim in *Subjects of Desire* is a sustained investigation of 'the degree to which opposition keeps desire alive' (Butler, 1987: 15). It is in this sense, to put it simply, that '*Butler puts Hegel to work* to envisage different futures' (Kirby, 2006: 4, *emphasis added*). One of the ways in which she does this, Kirby notes, is in drawing on Hegelian dialectics to consider how differentiation and opposition are not external assaults upon a coherent 'system', hailing from the outside to disrupt some kind of internal integrity; rather, they are expressions of an essential incoherence or complexity that enables any existence or phenomenon to continually 'become' who or what it is. Again, as Kirby (2006: 9) puts it in her account of Butler's reading of Hegel, 'difference isn't "the other" of identity but rather an expression of its own process of becoming, . . . [of] constantly evolving into itself'.

Of importance here is that every entity is constitutively caught up with what it opposes or separates itself from in order to be itself. This means that the transcendence of negativity, or supersession of the Other, in Hegel's terms, the 'negation of the negation', enables the negative Other's continual reappearance. In Butler's reading, if Hegel's argument is that an encounter with an Other is always a form of self-encounter, and by the same token, a negation of the Other is always, also a self-affirmation, then subjectivity is always precarious and contingent. Into what is often presumed to be a totality in Hegel's dialectic, in which the negative is read as a straightforwardly oppositional force subject to a fixed and finite normative regulation, Butler reads openness. This is because in negation she finds the possibility of continual regeneration, of 'redoing' as she puts it (Butler, 2004b). In other words, underpinning her critique of negation is a continual striving to recover this political possibility, in what Kirby (2006) aptly calls the 'precarious foundations' of her reading of Hegel. An important part of this endeavour is Butler's attempt to comprehend how and why alterity comes to be attached to certain phenomena and subject formations rather than others, or as she puts it, to understand 'the effort to annihilate within the context of life' (Butler, 1987: 52). Butler's own attempt to connect this to corporeality also has important resonance for organizational scholars. With reference to Hegel's narration of the Lord and Bondsman, she notes how:

> For the lord, bodily life must be taken care of . . . by an Other, for the body is not part of his *own* project of identity. The lord's identity is essentially beyond the body; he gains illusory confirmation from this view by requiring the Other to *be* the body that he endeavours *not* to be.
>
> (Butler, 1987: 53, *original emphasis*)

We return to this theme in more depth in Chapter 2, but for now it is useful to note that here Butler articulates the premise of much of the feminist critique of women's over-representation in embodied labour and in what sociologists of work call 'body work', pursuing accumulation on behalf of their employers by working on their own and others' bodies in a way that reaffirms their own subjugation, at the same time as rendering their own labour invisible. Arguably this is a classic case of the 'negation of the negation' in Hegelian terms embedded within the inequalities of the labour market and the exploitative appropriations of organizational life.

Butler as/and Organization Theory

Butler's writing has been subject to a number of on-going criticisms over the years. It has been termed hyper-voluntarist for its suggestion that gender can simply be enacted and re-enacted at will; and it has been deemed overly determinist for its implication that nothing exists beyond discourse, and that gender performativity is locked into a rigidly oppressive set of social relations and regulatory regimes. Yet Butler's largely phenomenological understanding of subjectivity as situated, '*conditioned* rather than *determined*' (Lloyd, 2007: 58), offers up interesting and important ways of thinking about, and addressing, social and organizational inequalities, forms of negation and exploitation, and the imperatives by which they are underpinned. It highlights, for instance, the oppressive nature of identity categories within organizations and how they might be 'troubled' (Kenny et al., 2011: 66). It emphasizes the significance of the 'ek-static' self, a concept Butler draws from her Hegelian reading of Heidegger (see Butler, 2000b: 277, n.1) to highlight the struggle for recognition as a process of 'standing outside of oneself', a theme developed within organization studies through, for instance, Kenny's (2010) work on the ek-static subjectification engendered by corporate discourses on ethical living, and in her most recent work, on the treatment of whistleblowers, those who speak out against organizational wrongdoing (Kenny, 2019).

Perhaps most significantly, it highlights how matrices of power and control can lead to organizational subjects being cast out of frames of references and become 'foreclosed from possibility' (Butler, 2004b: 31) as a result. Butler shows how we are 'done' and 'undone' by these matrices and the processes through which they are enacted, as well as the structures they shore up; she highlights how we are often compelled or constrained into unsustainable ways of being and of relating to one another; called by 'injurious names', we are led to embrace ways of working and living that we know to be harmful to ourselves and others because they are the very mechanisms that constitute us as socially and organizationally viable (Butler, 1997a: 104). Idealized templates for working life hold up unattainable ways of existing that negate the complex experiences that make up who we are, as dominant norms undermine the connections we have to one another. As Kenny's (2018, 2019) work on the fate of whistleblowers in the financial services sector shows, these insights provide an important starting point for thinking about what organizations do to and with us. They highlight processes of subjectification lived at the level of individuals, groups and communities, as well as the wider flows and structures of power that pervade organizational life.

Butler shows how casting out subjects that constitute the outside of the domain of subjective recognition is not a one-off 'disaster' (Butler, 1993) but an ongoing process on which organizational ontologies depend; she shows us how the paternalistic forms of power which those designated as 'vulnerable' and in need of protection are subject to accentuates their disenfranchisement (Butler, 2016), further paving the way for corporate exploitation and the epistemic violence enacted by managers and professionals who claim to 'know better'. But she also reminds us how those who are excluded haunt the borders of subjective viability, living and working at the margins as a vital part of a wider 'repudiation by which the subject installs its boundary and constructs the claim to its integrity' (Butler, 1993: 3). In this sense alone, Butler's recognition-based critique of the conditions governing viable subjectivity, lives deemed to 'matter' (Butler, 1993, 2004a, 2009), provides an important reference point for organizational scholars, practitioners and activists. It offers a rich understanding of the ways in which powerful processes and practices permeate the organizational worlds we inhabit, enabling us to critically and reflexively interrogate our vulnerability to these and our submission to them.

For Butler (1987: 21, *emphasis added*), Hegel's narrations of the dialectic of recognition through the encounter of the Lord and Bondsman are 'instructive fictions', or as she puts it, insights into *'ways of organizing the world* which prove to be too limited to satisfy the subject's desire to discover itself as substance'. This opens up important questions for organization theory, highlighting as it does our need to collude with ways of being that we know, to borrow from Butler, effectively do us in.

The chapters that follow explore this theme, reflecting on some of the ways in which Butler's writing has been taken up thus far within work and organization studies, and considering what potential it might have for future research, practice and activism. Each chapter draws on insights from Butler's own work, from commentaries on her writing, from the growing body of literature within work and organization studies that draws on and develops her ideas, as well as some more personal, autobiographical fragments that seek, in part, to 'undo' the traditional analytical frame of reference (Höpfl, 2007).

Throughout each chapter, Butler's dialectical thinking is brought to the fore, aiming in part to reinstate her phenomenological approach to subjectivity, one that has significant implications for how we think about, study and ultimately try to change organizations and what they do to/ with us. Echoing the evolution of Butler's own work, whilst also striving not to retire or overshadow the continuing centrality of her writing on gender and feminism, each chapter also seeks to consider Butler's work 'beyond gender'. This involves exploring how the underlying concerns she has with the connections between performativity, mattering, un/ doing the terms that render lives culturally intelligible, or liveable; with accounting, dispossession and precarity, and with the ethics and politics of assembly, and most recently, a non-violent ethics, are woven together through her evolving preoccupation with the way in which the desire for recognition comes to be organized. In this sense, Butler is explored here as an organization theorist, or rather as suggested earlier, as a theorist of organization in its broadest possible sense.

The titles of each of the key books that have punctuated her intellectual narrative convey the importance of dialectics to her thinking and signify the resonance between Butler's thematic concerns and theoretical preoccupations, and those of organization theorists. Her earliest substantive text, *Subjects of Desire* (Butler, 1987), situates Butler's Hegelian-inspired thinking, emphasizing both the desiring subject and the extent to which becoming a subject involves being *subject to* the regulatory norms governing the desire for recognition. *Gender Trouble* (1990/2000a) highlights the extent to which gender both 'spells trouble' for those subject to it, at the same time as containing within it the capacity to 'make trouble'. This duality is explored in more depth with reference to the linguistic politics of performativity in *Excitable Speech* (Butler, 1997a). *Bodies That Matter* (Butler, 1993) plays with the double meaning of the term 'mattering' as both a process of materialization, and as a recognition of what is important, of what 'counts', a theme developed in *The Psychic Life of Power* (Butler, 1997b) and in *Precarious Life* (Butler, 2004a). *Undoing Gender* (Butler, 2004b) develops her view that gender both 'does us in' at the same time as its performative ontology opens up the possibility of doing gender otherwise, not in order to reinstate a different set of normative expectations, but so as to dismantle the regimes of intelligibility governing who or what counts as a viable subject. *Giving an Account of Oneself* (Butler, 2005) similarly develops her concerns with politics and ethics more specifically, explicating her argument that in order to 'count' (to matter) as subjectively intelligible, we must be able to assume ethical responsibility for ourselves. 'How can we do this if denied the very possibility of "counting" as human' is the troubling question she poses. In *Dispossession*, co-authored with Athena Athanasiou (2013), Butler returns us to her early concerns with the Hegelian idea that in order to assume ethical responsibility for ourselves as viable subjects, we must take the risk attached to living outside of ourselves, in ek-statis (Butler, 1987, see also Butler, 1997b, 2008, 2009, 2015b). Here she considers what this means not simply for us as individuals but collectively.

This focus on performativity as a collective political endeavour is a theme Butler explores in a more sustained way in the most recent of her key texts considered here, *Notes Towards a Performative Theory of Assembly* (Butler, 2015a) and *Vulnerability in Resistance* (Butler, 2016; Butler et al., 2016). In the former, Butler expands on her performative ontology of gender, which hitherto in her writing had been largely explored at the level of the individual, shifting the focus towards (as the title suggests) a performative theory of assembly as a collective undertaking. Once more playing with the agentic associations of the concept of assembling, Butler moves the focus away from doing to being, making the (deceptively simple) point, drawing on Arendt (1958), that refusing not to exist, and doing so *en masse*, is an ontological move that is politically very powerful, perhaps one of the best that we currently have available to us. Simply standing together is, she argues, a political and ethical imperative (Butler, 2016). This is an idea that returns Butler to her earliest philosophical concerns with the non-synthetic Hegelian dialectic, each existing for the other; it is one that has profound implications for how we might rethink what it means to organize the desire for recognition on which we all depend, and it provides the focus for the closing discussion in the chapters that follow.

Notes

1. See also Fotaki and Harding (2017), who note that Butler's work has not only received a considerable number of academic citations but also that her writing is widely respected by many outside of academia, including practitioners and activists.
2. Nancy Fraser, perhaps Butler's most notable critic in this respect, raises concerns about, in particular, the language she uses as both 'deeply anti-humanist' and 'removed from our everyday ways of talking and thinking about ourselves'. Her rhetorical critique, written with reference to Butler's commitment to feminist thinking and politics, is phrased thus: 'Why should we use such a self-distancing idiom? What are its theoretical advantages (and disadvantages)?' Further, she asks, what is the likely political impact of a mode of writing that 'projects an aura of esotericism?' (Fraser, 1995a: 67).
3. Here and throughout, I am using the term 'recognition' as Butler has written about it, namely as grounded specifically in an Hegelian philosophy of intersubjectivity that frames recognition as a mutual awareness (a *re*-cognition, or

remembering) of our primary relationality. While other feminist writers such as Jessica Benjamin (1988: 14) have argued that to recognize is 'to affirm, validate, acknowledge, know, accept, understand, emphasize, take in, tolerate, appreciate, see, identify with, find familiar', it is arguably only these latter two synonyms that closely reflect this specifically Hegelian understanding of recognition, namely as identification and familiarity.

4. Butler herself raises the question of recognition as an organizational one when she reflects on her discussion of drag in *Gender Trouble*. As she puts it, the relation between drag performances and gender performativity is broadly as follows: when a man performs drag as a woman, his performance is generally taken to be an 'imitation' of femininity, but the femininity that he imitates is not in itself taken to be an imitation. Yet if we accept that gender is acquired, and enacted, that it is 'assumed in relation to ideals which are never quite inhabited by anyone', then all gender performances are 'imitations' of ideals that no one can ever embody. Thus drag 'imitates' what is itself always, already an imitation or approximation. Hence, her argument is that drag reveals gender to be an imitation of itself. Reflecting on this performative theory in later writing, Butler notes that however attractive (and influential) this formulation may have been, 'it didn't address the question of how certain forms of disavowal and repudiation *come to organize the performance of gender*' (Butler, 1997b: 145).

5. Žižek (2000) and Segal (1994) both cited in Lloyd (2007: 1–2).

6. As Gond et al. (2016: 451) also note, the idea that Critical Management Studies is 'anti-performative' in this sense has had a considerable impact via the work of Fournier and Grey (2000). Spicer et al. (2009) have challenged this anti-performative stance, advocating a 'critical performativity' instead that seeks to engage critically and reflexively with management practice in a more pragmatic way.

7. Butler makes clear her view that figuring gender as a property, as something that we can 'possess' (or in turn, that we are entirely possessed by) would be 'just a massive mistake' (More, 2016: 294).

8. Butler herself explains the origins of the heterosexual matrix as lying in Gayle Rubin's 'The Traffic in Women' (see Rubin with Butler, 1994), but as Lloyd (2007: 34) points out, it is also conceptually and theoretically indebted to Foucault's (1980) notion of a 'grid' of intelligibility in *The History of Sexuality*.

9. The latter especially were most notably influenced by Foucault's critique of essentialist identity claims in the various volumes of his *History of Sexuality* in which he shows how certain kinds of sexual subjectivities are produced as the discursive effects of power relations, an aspect of his writing that also had a significant impact on Butler's understanding of subjectivity and on organization theory.

10. An ethico-politics of recognition has certainly not been without its critics within feminist thinking, however. Louis McNay (2008b: 294) has argued, for instance, that because recognition theory falsely unifies the diversity of political conflicts through a homogenizing unification of them as a basic ontological struggle, feminist thinking and activism should 'dispense with the idea of recognition' (see also McNay, 2008a).

11. See Hancock and Tyler (2001, 2007) for a more extended discussion of Hegel's relevance to organization theory, particularly the management of subjectivity.

12. As Lloyd (2007: 16) notes, the pursuit of desire as a constant process of negation therefore means that the subject has to repeatedly seek out objects,

an insight that has important implications for the analysis of organizational processes and imperatives.

13. In this aspect of her work, Butler arguably transcends the somewhat stalemate debate between two important recognition theorists: Nancy Fraser and Axel Honneth. As McNay (2008b) summarizes it, Fraser criticizes Honneth for his subjectivist reduction of social oppression to psychic harm, while Fraser embeds misrecognition, understood in her writing as institutionalized patterns of discrimination and inequality, in questions of redistribution. For Honneth, conflicts over economic distribution are variants of a fundamental struggle for three types of recognition: personal, legal and social (that correspond roughly to Hegel's division of society into the family, state and civil society). By focusing her critique on the conditions of possibility shaping recognition as the socially and historically specific effect of a given configuration of power relations, Butler avoids falling into this bifurcation of recognition and redistribution, but sees the two as dialectically related, as an intrinsic part of the power relations in which the self-other dynamic in embedded. For her, the crucial endeavour is to question the conditions of possibility of this dialectical relationship between recognition and redistribution, 'not to take it for granted as an a priori guarantee' (Butler, 1995a: 47).

14. For Butler (2000b: 277), this incorporative identification constitutes an 'over-inclusiveness' that is incapable of becoming 'the condition for recognizing difference'. In practice, this means that, as a 're-avowal of what was disavowed', inclusion becomes a form of ownership that 'allows' otherness a place (Butler, 2000b: 286–287).

15. To paraphrase Spivak (1993), cited in Butler and Athanasiou (2013: 76), inclusion (in the form of employability, for instance) as an organizational form of liberal, market recognition becomes 'that which we cannot not want'.

1 Making Trouble

Organizational Performativity and Parody

Introduction

> Because I am a strong Black woman, people always assume that I am angry. It makes me so angry.

Butler's writing on performativity and undoing is developed across a number of her 'core' texts (1988, 1990/2000a, 1993, 2004a, 2004b, 2005), in particular, *Gender Trouble* (1990) and its anniversary edition (2000a). It is the latter for which Butler is best known, and which remains her most widely cited publication to date. It is in *Gender Trouble* that Butler connects, in a very formative way, her phenomenological account of gender acts (Butler, 1988) to her Hegelian preoccupation with the dialectics of recognition (Butler, 1987). I say 'formative' because it is in this way that Butler sets out the ontological starting point for her subsequent work, namely her theory of performativity as a gendered organization of the desire for recognition. This theory rests on a radical questioning of the idea that intelligible (i.e. coherent and continuous) subjectivity is a pre-social and self-evident given, a presumption that denies both the complexities of social life as it is lived and experienced, and the on-going struggles for recognition on which subjectivity depends. The main target of Butler's critique is the ways in which heteronormativity organizes the relationship between sex, gender and desire, but her insights have much wider resonance and relevance beyond this thematic focus. Kirby (2006: 20, *original emphasis*) notes that underpinning Butler's performative ontology is her aim 'to acknowledge the complex forces that render *any* identity inherently unstable', but more than this, she does so in order to show how within this inherent instability lies the capacity to do things differently, a conviction that connects her theoretical commitment to performativity to her political interest in parody (Butler, 1990/2000a, 1993), and more recently, to her faith in the political capacity of assembly, vulnerability and resistance (Butler, 2015a, 2016; Butler and Athanasiou, 2013).

To put it simply, 'gender performativity' describes Butler's (2000a: xv) view that 'gender is manufactured through a sustained set of acts, posited through the gendered stylization of the body'. While Butler's focus (at least in her earliest expositions of this performative ontology) is largely on gender, performativity is a way of thinking about subject formation that has much wider applicability, particularly for understanding the complexities of organizational life. It is an idea that is indebted to various strands of critical theory, phenomenology, poststructuralism and existentialism; in Butler's hands, these strands are woven together into something distinctive that transcends intellectual boundaries and at the same time interweaves them.

De Beauvoir's *The Second Sex* is particularly vital to her performative theory of gender. For Butler, her theory would have been impossible without two important insights in this work that underpin *Gender Trouble*. First, De Beauvoir's ontological emphasis on gendering as a dynamic, corporeal process summed up in the book's most oft-quoted line: 'One is not born, but rather, *becomes* a woman' (De Beauvoir, 2011: 293),[1] and second, her insistence on understanding this process as embedded within a dialectic of recognition, not as one in which two opposing subjects encounter one another but through which two hierarchically ordered beings engage in a perpetual struggle within which maintenance of the abject status of one is the condition on which the subjective status of the other depends. In De Beauvoir's own words, 'she determines and differentiates herself in relation to man, and he does not in relation to her; she is the inessential in front of the essential. He is the Subject; he is the Absolute. She is the Other' (De Beauvoir, 2011: 6), reducing the other to a perpetual state of alterity. As do so many other aspects of her writing, this issue takes Butler straight to the heart of the question of agency and its relationship to subjectivity (a separation that is crucial to her critique). It is not that those who are Othered lack agency; it is that they lack the capacity to exercise it as the latter is paradoxically both a condition for, and dependent upon, being accorded recognition. Agency is to be found precisely at the junctures where matrices of power are open to 'resignification, redeployment, subversive citation from within, and interruption and inadvertent convergences with other such networks' (Butler, 1995b: 135). Picking up where De Beauvoir left off, it is to the question of how one becomes a woman both as a 'variable cultural accomplishment' (Butler, 2000a: 142) yet at the same time 'always under a cultural compulsion' (Butler, 2000a: 12) that Butler turns, as she asks: 'How does one "become" a gender? What is the moment or *mechanism* of gender construction?' (Butler, 2000a: 143–4, *emphasis added*).

Drawing on both Hegel and De Beauvoir to respond to this question, Butler suggests that agency should be thought of as a capacity that exists within, and which is both contained and compelled by, the desire for recognition as a dialectical endeavour. Her theory of gender performativity illustrates this; as Lloyd (2007: 40) sums it up, for Butler, 'gender norms are culturally conditioned, but in the process of appropriating those norms, space is generated for their transformation'. In becoming gendered through 'a series of acts which are renewed, revised, and consolidated through time' (Butler, 1988: 523), and we might argue, in spaces and settings such as the labour market or workplace, Butler brings to the fore the performative labour involved in sustaining modes of agency, and ways of becoming, that have the potential to elicit recognition. Indeed, Butler (1995b: 136, *emphasis added*) hints at this herself when she notes that 'gender performativity involves the *difficult labour* of deriving agency from the very power regimes which constitute us, and which we oppose'. In contemporary organizational contexts, in which practices reaffirming unequal gender relations and regimes outnumber and outweigh, or unreflexively undermine, those that oppose them, this remains a considerable, 'labour intensive' challenge (Fotaki and Harding, 2017; Ortlieb and Sieben, 2019).

The performative ontology underpinning Butler's work can be discerned most clearly in her widely cited conviction that gender is 'a corporeal style, an act as it were, that is both intentional and performative, where "performative" suggests a dramatic and contingent construction of meaning' (Butler, 2000a: 177). Arguing that 'this repetition is not performed by a subject' but rather 'is what enables a subject' (Butler, 1993: 95), Butler emphasizes that subject positions are continually evoked through stylized acts of repetition, through mundane acts of gesture and inflection that, if performed in accordance with the social norms governing the conferral of recognition, result in the attribution of viable subjectivity. Butler is very clear that her use of the term 'performative' is derived from Austin's (1955) *How to Do Things with Words*, read through Derrida's (1979) 'Signature, Event, Context' in *Limited, Inc* (see Introduction), when she emphasizes that 'a performative act is one which brings into being or enacts that which it names' (Butler, 1995b: 134). She clarifies that the force or efficacy of the performative act derives from its capacity to draw on (to cite) and re-encode the historicity of particular conventions in a present act, but the same can also be said of the settings in which performative acts are undertaken, including (but clearly not limited to) organizational contexts. Again, this slightly blurs her attempt to differentiate between a linguistic and theatrical meaning of performativity,[2] but it is important, especially for those who draw on her work in organization studies, to grasp the extent to which because performativity does not necessarily take place 'on stage', it also does not occur in a social vacuum. As Austin (1955) emphasized, performative acts can be 'infelicitous'; saying 'I do' does not have any performative capacity if the people saying it aren't legally allowed to marry or are unlikely to be recognized as a married couple. To be effective, performative utterances need to be intelligible within the social contexts in which they are enacted and made meaningful. Butler makes this very clear when she says that performative acts are constitutive of social realities

> Not because they reflect the power of an individual's will or intention, but because they draw upon and reengage conventions which have gained their power precisely through a *sedimented iterability*.
>
> (Butler, 1995b: 134, *original emphasis*)

To reiterate, this conceptualizes subjectivity as an act of 'doing' but, crucially, 'not a doing by a subject who might be said to pre-exist the deed' (Butler, 1990: 33). In other words, Butler argues against a notion of the subject as the originator of action, in favour of understanding how the doer (or 'subject') is the outcome of a process of recognition rather than the basis of it, so that 'the doing itself is everything' (Butler, 1990: 25). This bifurcation of agency and subjectivity has led Butler to be accused of reducing the subject to a discursive effect, disavowing the capacity of the subject to exist beyond discourse (see Benhabib, 1995a, 1995b and Butler, 1993 and Introduction).[3] However, this bifurcation is crucial to understanding how, for Butler, subjectivity is effectively the outcome of a process of social organization through which certain performative acts come to be recognized as viable subject positions, while others are disavowed. As she puts it,

> The subject ought to be designated as a linguistic category, a placeholder, *a structure in formation*. Individuals come to occupy the site of the subject (the subject simultaneously emerges as a 'site') and they enjoy intelligibility only to the extent that they are, as it were, first established in language. The subject is the linguistic occasion for the individual to achieve and reproduce intelligibility, the linguistic condition of its existence and agency. No individual becomes a subject without first becoming subjected.
>
> (Butler, 1997b: 10–11, *emphasis added*)

This opening chapter examines Butler's performative ontology of gender, initially through a discussion of her 1988 paper 'Performative Acts and Gender Constitution', and then through a focus on her most widely cited book *Gender Trouble* (Butler, 1990/2000a), arguably Butler's most ground-breaking and influential work to date, albeit one that, for a range of reasons, might now be considered to be outdated (see Fischer, 2016). The focus in the second part of the chapter is on the implications of Butler's performative ontology, and her critique of the conditions shaping the conferment or denial of recognition, for understanding organizational life.

For Butler, gender performativity and its materialization in the form of 'bodies that matter' (see Chapter 2) are driven largely by the desire for recognition of ourselves as viable, intelligible subjects. In other words, underpinning our performance of gender is the desire to project a coherent identity, one that is recognized and valorized by others, but one that in Butler's terms produces its coherence at the cost of its own complexity (see Chapter 3). This way of thinking about gender resonates with performative ontologies of organization based on an understanding of the latter as a process rather than a fixed entity. It also highlights the ways in which performativity is a process of organization, or rather an organizing process, through which certain ways of being are compelled, while others are constrained.

In *Gender Trouble*, Butler emphasizes how the recitation of particular gender norms (and not others) is necessary in order to be accorded recognition as culturally intelligible, or viable. Signification is particularly important in this respect, as a process connecting the terms, or signs, of intelligibility and their repetition through social practice, as what we might think of as an *organizing* process. In gender terms, performances recognized as successful are those that conform to heteronormativity, which Butler (2000a: 185) describes as 'rigid codes of hierarchical binarisms'. The matrices of intelligibility that govern social and, as discussed later, organizational life can therefore be understood as compelling and constraining gender as a 'performative accomplishment' (Butler, 2000a: 179). In her early work, Butler uses the term 'heterosexual matrix' to make conceptual sense of what she describes as 'a self-supporting signifying economy that wields power in the marking off of what can and cannot be thought within the terms of cultural intelligibility' (Butler, 2000a: 99–100). This means that organizing schemas such as the heterosexual matrix enable certain subjectivities—those that conform to normative expectations—to come into being, at the same time as foreclosing or disavowing others. In other words, intelligible subjects are configured 'as a consequence of recognition according to prevailing social norms' (Butler, 2004a: 3) that, in gender terms, are binary and hierarchical. The widespread practice of surgically 'correcting' intersex bodies is but one illustration of this.[4]

Although Butler has moved away from the term in her more recent work, the links between performativity, parody and the heterosexual matrix have been particularly influential in work and organization studies (Borgerson, 2005; de Souza et al., 2016; Ford and Harding, 2011; Hancock and Tyler, 2007; Harding, 2003, 2013; Harding et al., 2013; Hodgson, 2005; Kelan, 2009; Kenny, 2009, 2010; Parker, 2002; Thanem and Wallenberg, 2016; Tyler and Cohen, 2010; Wickert and Schaefer, 2014). To date, however, drawing as she does (particularly in her early work) on Foucault and Derrida, Butler has tended to be read predominantly as a poststructuralist thinker[5] to the extent that other important influences in her writing derived particularly from phenomenology, psychoanalytic thinking and critical theory have been relatively retired.

Performative Acts and Gender Constitution

In one of her earliest papers articulating her theory of gender performativity, subtitled 'Phenomenology and Feminist Theory', Butler (1988: 519, *original emphasis*) explores the relationship between feminist theory and phenomenology, developing a theory of gender 'acts' which seeks to explain 'the mundane way in which social agents *constitute* social reality through language, gesture, and all manner of symbolic social signs'. She argues that

> Gender is in no way a stable identity or locus of agency from which various acts proceed; rather, it is an identity tenuously constituted in time—an identity instituted through a *stylized repetition of acts*. Further, gender is instituted through the stylization of the body and, hence, must be understood as the mundane way in which bodily gestures, movements, and enactments of various kinds constitute the illusion of an abiding gendered self.
>
> (Butler, 1988: 519, *emphasis added*)

Significant in her analysis is that

> if gender is instituted through acts which are internally discontinuous, then the *appearance of substance* is precisely that, a constructed identity, a performative accomplishment which the mundane social audience, including the actors themselves, come to believe and to perform in the mode of belief.
>
> (Butler, 1988: 520, *original emphasis*)

In contrast to her later work on social justice and transformation (see Chapters 5 and 6), Butler's analysis here emphasizes alteration not of the wider context of gender performance, or of the compulsion to perform in a particular way, but rather of the performance itself:

> if the ground of gender identity is the stylized repetition of acts through time, and not a seemingly seamless identity, then the possibilities of gender transformation are to be found in the arbitrary relation between such acts, *in the possibility of a different sort of repeating, in the breaking or subversive repetition of that style*.
>
> (Butler, 1988: 520, *emphasis added*)

Through this conception of gender acts, her analysis emphasizes the ways in which reified and naturalized conceptions of gender might be understood as constructed and hence as capable of being constituted differently—a theme she develops in her later writing on gender as a perpetual un/doing (Butler, 2004b)—see Chapter 3. Butler's argument in this respect is that 'in its very character as performative resides the possibility of contesting its reified status' (Butler, 1988: 520).

An important claim derived largely from phenomenological thinking, most notably Merleau-Ponty (and developed in her later work, particularly Butler, 1993), is that the body

> Is not merely matter but a continual and incessant *materializing* of possibilities. One is not simply a body, but, in some very key sense, one does one's body.
>
> (Butler, 1988: 521, *original emphasis*)

Her emphasis then is on the body 'as an intentionally *organized* materiality' (Butler, 1988: 521, *emphasis added*). This embodied ontology of gender 'as *a corporeal style*, an "act", as it were, which is both intentional and performative' (Butler, 1988: 521–522, *original emphasis*) foregrounds both the agentive capacity of the subject, as well as the constraints that compel or constrain particular forms of subjectivity, be they individual, collective or even organizational—a theme developed in later writing (Butler, 2004b). Rendering its own performance apparently pre-social, Butler argues that 'gender is, thus, a construction that regularly conceals its genesis' (Butler, 1988: 522). This means that the body is conceived in terms of 'the legacy of sedimented acts rather than a predetermined or foreclosed structure, essence or fact, whether natural, cultural or linguistic' (Butler, 1988: 523). Her concern with this process of sedimentation connects her writing to organizational thinking, therefore, as it frames embodiment as an organized process through which certain bodies/subjects come to 'matter' more than others—a theme returned to in Chapter 2.

Introducing a conceptual framing developed in more depth in *Gender Trouble*, Butler (1988) argues that the heterosexual matrix is an ideological system through which compulsory heterosexuality is reproduced and concealed through the cultivation of bodies into two discrete sexes that are normatively attached to two similarly discrete genders and sexualities in a linear way that establishes, *organizes* desire 'as a heterosexual, male prerogative' (Butler, 2000a: 55). As she puts it: 'Which pleasures shall live and which shall die is often a matter of which serve the legitimating practices of identity formation that take place within the matrix of gender norms' (Butler, 2000a: 90). As noted earlier, Butler's early writing on the heterosexual matrix is particularly indebted to Gayle Rubin's 'sex/gender system', a term she uses to describe the regulatory cultural mechanism of transforming biological males and females into hierarchically organized, 'binary reifications' (Butler, 2000a: 160) of gender. Drawing on Rubens, and framing the heterosexual matrix as an ontologically organizing device, Butler argues that

> One needs to read the drama of . . . the institution of sexual difference as a self-supporting signifying economy that wields power in the marking off of what can and cannot be thought within the terms of cultural intelligibility.
>
> (Butler, 2000a: 99–100)

Her theory of gender acts as constitutive emphasizes that 'gender attributes . . . are not expressive but performative' (Butler, 1988: 528)—by this she means that 'gender attributes . . . effectively constitute the identity they are said to express or reveal' (Butler, 2000a: 180)—and in this respect (as discussed in the Introduction), she contrasts her ontology with more sociological writing on gender which, in her view, tends to posit 'a self which assumes and exchanges various roles' within the context of social expectation. Her attempt, then, is to move feminist theory beyond an interactionist, expressive model of gender towards a performative, constitutive one. This move has raised two main criticisms: one focusing on the degree to which this ontological distinction between social constructionist and performative theories of gender is convincing, the other revolving around an apparent disavowal of the 'matter' of gender, and the implied suggestion that gender is a purely discursive construction (where this is taken to mean 'linguistic'), performed at will by free floating agents, disengaged from and unconstrained by the wider social context.[6]

Both concerns link with a recurrent theme in Butler's work, namely her critique of 'woman' as the subject of feminism. In her early writing, Butler (1993: 230) concedes that 'the temporary totalization performed by identity categories is a necessary error'. While she appears to concur with those who have advocated something of a strategic or operational essentialism in order to advance feminist politics (without attributing ontological integrity to the term 'woman'), she clearly maintains some discomfort with this concession, primarily in relation to the ways in which women have been essentialized in certain versions of feminist discourse and politics. As she puts it,

> it is one thing to use the term and know its ontological insufficiency and quite another to articulate a normative vision for feminist theory which celebrates or emancipates an essence, a nature, or a shared cultural reality which cannot be found.
>
> (Butler, 1988: 529)

As she goes on, 'there is . . . nothing about femaleness that is waiting to be expressed' (Butler, 1988: 530). Instead as she puts it, 'regardless of the pervasive character of patriarchy and the prevalence of sexual difference as an operative cultural distinction, there is nothing about a binary gender system that is given' (Butler, 1988: 531). Rather, 'as a corporeal field of cultural play, gender is basically an innovative affair, although it is quite clear that there are strict punishments for contesting the script by performing out of turn or through unwarranted improvisations' (Butler, 1988: 531).

In developing this line of argument, Butler draws from phenomenology her commitment to 'revealing the ways in which the world is produced through the constituting acts of subjective experience' (Butler, 1988:

522). Her focus is particularly on the phenomenological conception of an 'act' as a way of being that is 'both social shared and historically constituted' (Butler, 1988: 530). This is neatly summed up in her claim that gender is 'what is *put on*' (Butler, 1988: 531, *emphasis added*), playing on the idea that gender is simultaneously performatively enacted and exploited ('put upon'), a theme developed further in *Undoing Gender* (Butler, 2004b) and one that has significant relevance for critical analyses of the appropriation of gender in organizational contexts.

Butler also argues that gender is not simply an act, but one that is organized into an 'assignment', again evoking the double meanings of the term.[7] As she puts it, 'to the extent that gender is an assignment, it is an assignment which is never quite carried out according to expectation, whose addressee never quite inhabits the idea s/he is compelled to approximate' (Butler, 1993: 231). In other words, gender is both a strategic expectation imposed upon us, at the same time as it is 'projected' to the extent that its successful completion, in accordance with normative expectations, is always (already) unachievable.

Butler often reminds us that performativity must be understood not as a singular or deliberate 'act' that is somehow socially discrete or complete, it is constantly reiterated and is perpetually elusive as a citational practice through which 'discourse produces the effect that it names' (Butler, 1993: 2). Building on this idea in her discussion of racism and diversity in institutional life, Sara Ahmed (2012) introduces the idea of the organizationally 'non-performative' as a way of thinking critically about the relationship between naming and its effects. Her suggestion is not that the non-performative is a particular type of speech act; rather, borrowing from Butler, she argues that 'non-performatives' are those acts that do *not* produce the effects that they name. By way of illustration, she cites how institutional commitments to equality can operate conservatively:

> In such cases, commitments must be understood as non-performatives: as not bringing into effect what they name. The very appearance of bringing something into effect can be a way of conserving the past, of keeping hold of what has apparently been given up.
>
> (Ahmed, 2012: 126)

Evoking De Beauvoir's (2011) earlier writing on gender as a situated social construction, Butler introduces an important distinction in 'Performative Acts and Gender Constitution' between agency and subjectivity, one that Ahmed draws from but one which has also fuelled on-going criticisms of Butler's work (Kirby, 2006; Lloyd, 2007). She argues that

> there is no 'one' who takes on a gender norm. On the contrary, this citation of the gender norm is necessary in order to qualify as a 'one',

> to become viable as a 'one', *where subject-formation is dependent on the prior operation of legitimating gender norms.*
>
> (Butler, 1993: 232, *emphasis added*)

It is only by becoming appropriately gendered that we are accorded the recognition and rights associated with viable, intelligible subjectivity; that we become a 'one' in De Beauvoir's (2011) terms. Of all the many themes and ideas that Butler (1988) introduces in this paper, it is perhaps this one that she takes forward and develops most fully in *Gender Trouble*.

Gender Trouble: Feminism and the Subversion of Identity

Writing in the tenth anniversary edition of *Gender Trouble*, Butler (2000a: vii) reflects that this work has often been 'cited as one of the founding texts of queer theory'. Indeed, it has often been referred to within work, organization and management studies in this respect (see Rumens, 2018; Rumens et al., 2018). Locating queer in the tradition of immanent critique, Butler argues (in *Bodies That Matter*) that

> If the term 'queer' is to be a site of collective contestation, the point of departure for a set of historical reflections and futural imaginings, it will have to remain that which is, in the present, never fully owned, but always and only redeployed, twisted, queered from a prior usage and in the direction of urgent and expanding political purposes.
>
> (Butler, 1993: 228)

Butler injects this sense of political urgency into *Gender Trouble* by developing her performative theory of gender introduced in her earlier paper (Butler, 1988). Her main opponents (see also later discussions in Butler, 2004b) are the writings of New French feminists such as Kristeva, Irigaray and Cixous whose work she describes as 'sexual difference fundamentalism' (Butler, 2000a: viii). In her critique of Kristeva, in particular, Butler argues that she

> describes the maternal body as bearing a set of meanings that are prior to culture itself. She thereby safeguards the notion of culture as a paternal structure and delimits maternity *as an essentially pre-cultural reality.* Her naturalistic descriptions of the maternal body effectively *reify motherhood and* [in doing so] *preclude an analysis of its cultural construction and variability.*
>
> (Butler, 2000a: 103, *emphasis added*)

As Kirby (2006) notes however, Butler's critique of Kristeva's normative representation of the maternal body does not prevent her from finding subversive potential in other aspects of Kristeva's work, most notably the latter's writing on abjection. In characteristic fashion, Butler reads this through an Hegelian lens that brings to the fore the extent to which abjection is an on-going, perpetually incomplete struggle with difference. In sum, the '*organizing* focus' of Butler's engagement with abjection, as Kirby (2006: 21) puts it, is a critique of the process through which lived complexities, be they individual or those of the larger social body, become · narrow, hierarchically structured frameworks of binary possibility. In this sense, Butler's reflexive critique of 'woman' as the problematic subject of feminism (and by implication, 'man' as the troubled/troubling agent of patriarchy) takes as its reference point De Beauvoir's provocation that 'One is not born but rather, becomes woman' (De Beauvoir, 2011: 293). Indeed, Butler acknowledges the debt that she owes to De Beauvoir, tracing her own preoccupation with the gendered conditions of recognition and the consequences of mis-recognition back to De Beauvoir's dual concern with gender as a productive social process, and with the social conditions compelling and constraining that process. For Butler, this opens up the crucial possibility that 'gender is culturally constructed: hence, gender is neither the causal result of sex nor as seemingly fixed as sex' (Butler, 1990: 6).

As Lloyd (2007: 42) observes, this constitutes what might be regarded as the basis of Butler's radical constructivist theory of gender in so far as not only does it problematize the idea that gender is a cultural expression of a pre-given sex, it reverses this logic; instead of arguing that sex is the origin or basis of gender, Butler postulates instead that gender produces sex, or rather that the two are negatively, dialectically constituted. This is arguably what she means when she says that 'the deed is everything'; sex and gender and the relationship between the two, and the forms of subjectivities they bring about, are all in the doing, or rather the 'undoing' as she puts it (Butler, 2004b)—a theme we return to in Chapter 3.

Developing this into a reflexive critique of the risks attached to becoming and articulating 'woman' as a universal category within feminism, Butler emphasizes her view that identity politics disavows the violent exclusions on which it rests, retiring the normative constraints and compromises demanded by categorical thinking. On this basis, she raises the question of whether the complex, lived realities of men's and women's lives might involve such different experiences that the very assertion, even tenuously or tactically, of a homogeneous, universal identity reinstates what it purports to challenge, namely an oppressive regime of conditional recognition and an annihilation of difference not simply between but within categories of identification. Directing her critique specifically at Irigaray (1985a, 1985b), Butler puts it thus, focusing not only on what she sees as a repetitive act, but an appropriative one that colonizes the Other's radical potential:

> The effort to *include* 'Other' cultures . . . constitutes an appropriative act that risks a repetition of the self-aggrandizing gesture of

phallogocentrism, colonizing under the sign of the same those differences that might otherwise call that totalizing concept into question.
(Butler, 1990: 13, *original emphasis*)

What Butler sees as a residual reliance on a pre-social, dimorphic materiality of anatomical sex, even within feminist thinking that separates sex from gender as the basis of a critique of biological determinism, leads her to what is arguably one of the more controversial aspects of her theory of performativity, namely her view that sex itself is a social, cultural construct that is 'always, already' gendered. As she puts it (resonating with phrasing from Virginia Woolf's *Orlando*):

If the immutable character of sex is contested, perhaps this construct called 'sex' is as culturally constructed as gender; indeed, perhaps it was always already gender, with the consequence that the distinction between sex and gender turns out to be no distinction at all.
(Butler, 1990: 7)

Of simultaneous ontological and political interest to Butler in thinking about the relationship between sex and gender in this way is, in Foucauldian terms, sex's genealogy; in other words, her concern is with understanding—and challenging—the ways in which sex comes to signify a pre-cultural, intransigent anatomical substance that precedes social perception and categorization. As well as Foucauldian and Hegelian strands of thinking here, we can also discern the post-dualist phenomenological ontology associated most notably with Merleau Ponty's (2002 [1945]) emphasis on the 'intertwined' nature of subjectivity as a nexus of 'self-others-things'.

More politically engaged than this ontology, however, Butler's focus is on the conditions of recognition—the organizing structures and imperatives—that generate oppositional and politically implicated differences between sex and gender as dichotomously instantiated (objective and subjective) categories of being.[8] In this aspect of *Gender Trouble*, she takes further inspiration from Monique Wittig's (1992) critique of the 'grammar of gender', by which she means the way in which sex designation within language becomes an 'alibi' as Wittig puts it, for sexual (reproductive) purposes within a repressive system of heteronormativity.

Butler's response to this lies in her conviction that culture has the capacity to produce ontological and epistemological schema (in the form of the heterosexual matrix, for instance) that, through repetition over time, congeal into frames of reference that give the appearance of a pre-social, material reality. But, again, in an approach that invests this ontological point with a political critique, it is not simply the substance of this process that is of concern to Butler, but rather its organizing/organizational imperatives and implications. For her, this apparent pre-sociality lends credibility to the conditions of recognition governing cultural intelligibility so that, for instance, societies might recognize only two, binary and (often) hierarchically organized genders, corresponding to a normative, linear relationship with sex and desire that frames male, masculine heteronormative gender as a socially and politically agentic prerogative, and female, feminine, heteronormative sexual passivity, as 'natural' and pre-social. Butler's concern is with how this comes to be lived—and we might argue, organized and worked—in order to think through how it might be lived differently, reworked or undone (see Chapter 3). In this sense, Butler's entire oeuvre represents, in Kirby's (2006: 27) view, a sustained critique of the (appealing but illusionary) metaphysics of substance.

As noted earlier, Butler (1990: 21) opens herself up to a two-pronged critique (see Chapter 2) when she makes this aspect of her approach explicit, arguing that concepts such as the subject, self and individual 'transform into substances fictitious unities having at the start only a linguistic reality'. Two related issues are problematic in this largely Foucauldian assertion, namely, (i) its apparent disavowal of the significance of materiality 'at the start' and (ii) the implied omnipresence of linguistic power, suggesting the impossibility of finding a transcendent position not simply beneath but beyond it. If this is the case, as Kirby (2006: 28) puts it, 'How are we to proceed?' given what appears to be a problematic recuperation of the very commitments that Butler's work contests. Taken together, both problems suggest that in this aspect of *Gender Trouble* and her theory of performativity, Butler is simultaneously insufficiently deterministic and excessively so. Nevertheless, this ontological conviction is central, as Kirby notes, to Butler's political interest in gender as both a troubling category, and as containing within it the capacity to 'make trouble'.

Her discussion of structuralist analyses of gendered subject formation leads Butler back to her Hegelian take on the Foucauldian conviction that it is from within the dynamics of power and signification that politically subversive possibilities might emerge. As she puts it, in what is perhaps one of the most important passages *in Gender Trouble* in this respect,

This task presumes, of course, that to operate within the matrix of power is not the same as to replicate uncritically relations of domination. It offers the possibility of a repetition of the law which is not its consolidation, but its displacement.

(Butler, 1990: 30)

Making 'gender trouble', or displacing its laws of domination, is both to 'call the frame into question' *and* to run the risk of 'losing one's sense of place in gender' (Butler, 2000a: xi). Developing her earlier emphasis on performative acts, Butler elaborates on her ontology in this respect, reiterating that 'performativity is not a singular act, but a repetition and a ritual, which achieves its effects through its naturalization in the context of a body' (Butler, 2000a: xv). Gender norms, as she puts it, 'establish the ontological field in which bodies may be given legitimate expression' (Butler, 2000a: xxiii). At the moment of 'gender trouble' (when one's 'staid and usual cultural perceptions fail' and we are unable to 'read' the bodies we encounter in established, gender bifurcated ways), 'the sedimented and reified field of gender "reality" is understood as one that might be made differently' (Butler, 2000a: xxiii). This is what it means, in Butler's terms, to 'make trouble' with/through gender: to challenge the binary and hierarchical, normative expectations governed by the heterosexual matrix.

But doing so also carries with it, as Butler acknowledges in the Preface to the 10th anniversary edition of *Gender Trouble*, the risk of being 'in trouble', losing one's sense of place within the dominant frame of reference. 'Trouble' also remains perpetually vulnerable to co-optation; as Butler (2000a: xxi) puts it, 'subversive performances always run the risk of becoming deadening clichés through their repetition and, most importantly, through their repetition within commodity culture where "subversion" carries market value'.[9]

As noted above, the heterosexual matrix—'a masculinist sexual economy' (Butler, 2000a: xxx–xxxi)—positions men and women according to a bifurcated and hierarchical configuration of the relationship between sex, gender and desire, establishing 'gender categories that support gender hierarchy and compulsory heterosexuality' (Butler, 2000a: xxviii). According to this schema (what she later describes as 'the heterosexual logic', Butler, 1993: 239), 'if one identifies *as* a given gender, one must desire a different gender' (Butler, 1993: 239, *original emphasis*). Yet, acts and gestures, articulated and enacted desires 'create the illusion of an interior and *organizing* gender core' (Butler, 2000a: 173, *emphasis added*); an illusion that is discursively and symbolically maintained for the purposes of regulation, but which in being so, can be done differently or 'troubled', including in parodic ways. The performance of gender according to the frame of reference established by the heterosexual matrix therefore means that, as she puts it, 'it becomes impossible to separate out "gender" from the political and cultural intersections in which it is invariably produced and maintained' (Butler, 2000a: 6).

Elaborating on her earlier discussion of feminist theory (see Butler, 1988), she develops her critique of the category 'woman' as the subject of feminist theory and politics, and particularly of the conflation of 'the name's multiple significations' (Butler, 2000a: 6). As she puts it, alluding to developments in feminist thinking at the time,

> Although the claim of universal patriarchy no longer enjoys the kind of credibility it once did, the notion of a generally shared conception

of 'women', the corollary to that framework, has been much more difficult to displace.

(Butler, 2000a: 7)

Framing this as a rhetorical reflection, she asks:

Is the construction of the category of women as a coherent and stable subject an unwitting regulation and reification of gender relations? And is not such a reification precisely contrary to feminist aims? To what extent does the category of women *achieve stability and coherence only in the context of the heterosexual matrix*?

(Butler, 2000a: 8–9, *emphasis added*)

Here Butler again hints at a growing concern in her writing, namely with the 'costs' attached to coherence, a theme she develops further in *Undoing Gender* (Butler, 2004b). In *Gender Trouble*, she directs her critique particularly at feminist reliance (at the time she was writing) on the term 'patriarchy', arguing that

The very notion of 'patriarchy' has threatened to become a universalizing concept that overrides or reduces distinct articulations of gender asymmetry in different cultural contexts. As feminism has sought to become integrally related to struggles against racial and colonialist oppression, it has become increasingly important to resist the colonizing epistemological strategy that would subordinate different configurations of domination under the rubric of a transcultural notion of patriarchy.

(Butler, 2000a: 45–46)

This reflects both wider articulations within feminist thinking at the time and Butler's increasingly substantive, contextual concern with the social construction of gender according to normative expectations. As she puts it, 'the ostensibly natural facts of sex' can be thought of as 'discursively produced by various scientific discourses in the service of other political and social interests'. Hence,

Gender ought not to be conceived merely as the cultural inscription of meaning on a pre-given sex; . . . gender must also designate *the very apparatus of production* whereby the sexes themselves are established. As a result, gender is not to culture as sex is to nature; gender is also the discursive/cultural means by which 'sexed nature' or 'a natural sex' is produced and established as 'pre-discursive', prior to culture, a politically neutral surface *on which* culture acts.

(Butler, 2000a: 11, *original emphasis*)

This passage sums up Butler's performative ontology of gender and the relationship of the latter to sex as she sees it. It frames gender in such a way that the internal stability and binary frame for sex—its apparent social coherence, functionality and pre-social immutability is secured 'by casting the duality of sex in a pre-discursive [pre-organizational] domain' (Butler, 2000a: 11) whereas for Butler gender is very much the outcome of an organizing/organizational process.

In her account of this process of becoming gendered, Butler draws her emphasis on cultural compulsion and social constraint directly from De Beauvoir (2011). In her discussion of subversive bodily acts, for instance, she develops De Beauvoir's Hegelian emphasis on alterity to argue that 'those bodily figures who do not fit into either gender fall outside the human, indeed, constitute the domain of the dehumanized and the abject against which the human itself is constituted' (Butler, 2000a: 142).

As already noted, Butler's starting point is De Beauvoir's contention that becoming a man or a woman is a dynamic social process, one that acknowledges both the agentic capacity at work in social construction as well as the weight of compulsion (to 'become' in particular ways). It is precisely this dynamic inter-relationship between agency, social compulsion and structural constraint that De Beauvoir encapsulates in her most oft-cited line from *The Second Sex*, and which characterizes the processual ontology underpinning this text and many of her other works, and arguably feminist theory subsequently. And it is this that Butler takes as the ontological starting point for her performative theory of gender.

As Kruks has put it, in her emphasis on gender attribution as bound up with the perpetual process of 'becoming' a subject, De Beauvoir makes two ontological moves that are particularly important to Butler: first, she acknowledges the full weight of social construction that the subject must bear, and yet at the same time, she refuses to reduce the subject to a free-floating 'effect'. In doing so,

> She can grant a degree of autonomy to the self—as is necessary in order to sustain key notions of political action, responsibility, and the oppression of the self—*while also acknowledging the real constraints on autonomous subjectivity produced by oppressive situations.*
> (Kruks, 1992: 92, *emphasis added*)

In this sense, De Beauvoir is vital to Butler in so far as she approaches subjectivity in a way that is neither removed from, nor caught up in, biological, material or discursive determinism, but instead positions the self as existing 'in situation', simultaneously socially compelled and constrained. From this, Butler takes the idea that 'gender is always acquired' (Butler, 2000a: 142). While critical of what she regards as De Beauvoir's assumption that 'sex is immutably factic' (Butler, 2000a: 142), Butler's primary emphasis in drawing on *The Second Sex* is to tease out what she sees as its radical possibilities for rethinking gender ontology. As she puts it:

> De Beauvoir's theory implied seemingly radical consequences . . . if sex and gender are radically distinct, then it does not follow that to be a given sex is to become a given gender; in other words, 'woman' need not be the cultural construction of the female body, and 'man' need not interpret male bodies.
>
> (Butler, 2000a: 142)

As she goes on (also echoing De Beauvoir), mapping out an important ontological shift in the 'grammar' of gender,

> If gender is something that one becomes—but can never be—then gender is itself a kind of becoming or activity, and . . . ought not to be conceived as a noun or a substantial thing or a static cultural marker, but rather as an incessant and repeated action of some sort.
>
> (Butler, 2000a: 143)

The category of sex, she argues (hinting at the organizational context of this becoming),

> is a specifically political use of the category of nature . . . there is no reason to divide up human bodies into male and female *except that such a division suits the economic needs of heterosexuality and lends a naturalistic gloss to the institution of heterosexuality* . . . 'sex' is . . . naturalized but not natural.
>
> (Butler, 2000a: 143, *emphasis added*)

Drawing further on Monique Wittig, she argues that 'men and women are political categories and not natural facts' (Butler, 2000a: 147). For Wittig, the 'straight mind' is oppressive because it requires that the subject, in order to be (to become something or rather someone credible, recognizable), must participate in the very terms of its own oppression.

Hinting at another important theme in *Gender Trouble*, Butler also draws on Wittig when she describes heterosexuality as 'both a compulsory system and an intrinsic comedy, a constant parody of itself' (Butler, 2000a: 155). Masculine and feminine subject positions, the result of what Butler describes as 'bodily inscriptions', are 'binary reifications of gender' so exaggerated that they are intrinsically comical (Butler, 2000a: 160).

Before turning to a discussion of the politics of parody in *Gender Trouble*, it is important to pick up on the theme of becoming in her writing, a concern that she traces through De Beauvoir, but which ultimately owes its origins to Hegel's (1977) account of the dialectical encounter between the Lord and Bondsman. In Butler's hands, this narrative evolves into a gendered account of the desire for recognition, her interest being in 'the discursively variable construction of each in and through the other' (Butler, 2000a: 181). For Butler, 'the dialectic of master-slave, here fully reformulated within the non-reciprocal terms of gender asymmetry, prefigures . . . the masculine signifying economy that includes both the existential subject and its Other' (Butler, 2000a: 17). She describes the 'tactics' of the masculine signifying economy as a 'dialectical appropriation and suppression of the Other, . . . deployed centrally but not exclusively in the service of expanding and rationalizing the masculine domain' (Butler, 2000a: 19).

This is a theme that Butler returns to slightly later in her work (Butler, 1993) in a point that has important resonance for organizational scholars and activists concerned with the instrumental co-optation of difference (see Ahmed, 2012; Tyler, 2019). Her preoccupations are largely with 'the ideal of transforming all excluded identifications into included features— of appropriating all difference into unity' through an all-consuming imperialism or synthesis (Butler, 1993: 116) which, albeit in slightly cryptic terms, we might take to refer to a process of 'organization', as Ahmed hints (2012) in her account of institutional co-optations of difference premised upon 'non-performative' rhetorical commitments to equality.

Also echoing De Beauvoir's emphasis on gender as a perpetual becoming, and injecting this with insights from Derrida, Butler argues that 'gender is a complexity whose totality is permanently deferred, never fully what it is at any given juncture' (Butler, 2000a: 22). Yet, 'persons only become intelligible through becoming gendered in conformity with recognizable standards of gender intelligibility' (Butler, 2000a: 22). What she describes as 'intelligible genders' are those which 'in some sense institute and maintain relations of coherence and continuity among sex, gender, sexual practice, and desire' (Butler, 2000a: 23). As noted already, the heterosexual matrix 'institutes the production of discrete and asymmetrical oppositions between "feminine" and "masculine" ' (Butler, 2000a: 23). What this means is that, through the terms of the heterosexual matrix, the desire for recognition comes to be organized in such a way as to compel the performance of a relatively narrow range of culturally (organizationally) intelligible subjectivities. What Butler describes as 'disordering practices', those that subvert 'the matrix of intelligibility' (Butler, 2000a: 24), potentially 'bring into relief the utterly constructed status of the so-called heterosexual original' (Butler, 2000a: 41). Such practices therefore have the capacity to serve as 'sites for intervention, exposure, and displacement of these reifications' (Butler, 2000a: 42). As she puts it in this respect, again in one of the most widely quoted lines from *Gender Trouble*,

> Gay is to straight *not* as copy is to original, but, rather, as copy is to copy. The *parodic repetition* of 'the original' . . . *reveals* the original

to be nothing other than a parody of *the idea of the natural and the original.*

(Butler, 2000a: 41, *original emphasis*)

Returning to the evocation, cited above, of a grammatological way of thinking about gender Butler reiterates that

> *Gender is not a noun*, but neither is it a set of free-floating attributes, for we have seen that the substantive effect of gender is performatively produced and compelled by the regulatory practices of gender coherence. . . . In this sense, *gender is always a doing*, though not a doing by a subject who might be said to preexist the deed.
>
> (Butler, 2000a: xx, *emphasis added*)

Because gender is a project that has social survival as its end, 'the term *strategy* better suggests the situation of duress under which gender performance always and variously occurs' (Butler, 2000a: 178, *original emphasis*). 'Discrete genders are part of what "humanizes" individuals within contemporary culture' (Butler, 2000a: 178). Exposing the contingent acts that create the appearance of 'a naturalistic necessity', she acknowledges has been 'a part of cultural critique since Marx' (Butler, 2000a: 44), but in Butler's (1990/2000a) hands, the focus of this critique, at least at this stage in her work, is largely on parody.

The Politics of Parody and Subversion

Much of the critique of Butler's work, particularly the performative ontology outlined earlier, has focused on its alleged reduction of resistance to the performance of a specific style (especially drag) and particularly to an individualized politics of parody. As Lloyd (2007: 49) has put it, her emphasis on parody is one of the many areas of Butler's work 'that has generated controversy and misunderstanding aplenty'. At its heart, a little like the denaturalizing impetus of drag, Butler's engagement with parody is as a politics of subversion that focuses simply on an exploration of the possible ways in which the normative regimes that govern or condition intelligibility and therefore the terms of recognition might be contested. In her early work (Butler, 1988, 1990), these seem to be focused on mechanisms or tactics of subversion enacted largely at an individual level; in her later work, she turns to more collective means, a theme we return to in Chapters 5 and 6. Connecting both approaches is Butler's emphasis on parody as a resignification 'beyond binary'; that is, as a strategy designed to denaturalize bodily categories through practices that disrupt embodied classifications of sex, gender, sexuality and desire, and which in doing so, 'occasion . . . their resignification and proliferation beyond the binary frame' (Butler, 2000a: xxxi).

Connecting individual and more collective parodic endeavours in her work is Butler's faith in the resignificatory potential of humour; as she puts it, 'laughter in the face of serious categories is indispensable for feminism' (Butler, 2000a: xxviii). An interesting and important question for organizational scholars with this in mind is: what form could, or should, this subversion of the norms of cultural intelligibility governing recognition take, and in what circumstances might laughter 'in the face of serious categories' be possible, and meaningful?

One of the areas of politics and activism in which this approach has certainly flourished since the publication of *Gender Trouble* is that of queer theory, with this book often being cited (as noted earlier) as one of its founding texts. This is not simply because of Butler's performative ontology and her critique of the heterosexual matrix but also as a result of the political emphasis that she places on heteronormativity as self-parody. For Butler (2000a: 155), heterosexuality offers 'normative sexual positions that are intrinsically impossible to embody', recognition of which reveals heterosexuality not only as a 'compulsory law, but as an inevitable comedy', a constant parody of itself, so exaggerated and impossible to realize that it continually mocks itself for even trying.

In *Gender Trouble*, and drawing on her discussion of performativity, Butler argues that 'the normative focus for [queer] practice ought to be on the subversive and parodic redeployment of power rather than on the impossible fantasy of its full-scale transcendence' (Butler, 2000a: 158). Emphasizing the parodic potential of drag by way of illustration, she argues that 'in imitating gender, drag implicitly reveals the imitative structure of gender itself—as well as its contingency' (Butler, 2000a: 175), and herein lies its political capacity.

Glick (2000: 32) has emphasized the significance of this theme in Butler's writing, namely that arguing that cultural construction does not preclude agency, she sees a practice like drag as resistant 'in so far as it works to denaturalize: to reveal the fictive status of coherent identities and to subvert: to repeat and displace normative cultural configurations'. However, Glick has argued that a persistent problem with performativity theory is revealed in the detail of Butler's discussion of drag, particularly her notion of 'resignification as agency' (Glick, 2000: 35). Although Butler presents practices such as drag as subversive, they emerge *within* power and are not therefore 'unproblematically subversive'; they could just as easily be driven by instrumental reasons, or result in continual resignification as a co-optation and appropriation, or in on-going, exhausting struggles over the terms of signification.[10]

However, others such as Lloyd (2007: 43) suggest that this rather misses Butler's point, or at least her intention, when she argues that what drag illustrates is the way in which gender is 'put on'. Heteronormativity naturalizes a set of social relations conditioning the liveability of sex, gender and desire which drag has the potential to reflexively denaturalize.

This shows, effectively that gender 'is fabricated'. As Butler has put it, in another oft-cited line in *Gender Trouble*, 'the notion of gender parody defended here does not assume that there is an original which such parodic identities imitate. Indeed, the parody is *of* the very notion of an original' (Butler, 2000a: 175, *original emphasis*). That said, it is important to recognize that even in her earliest writing on gender constitution and subversion, Butler does not put her faith entirely in a 'politics of acts', but emphasizes the importance of transforming the hegemonic conditions of social action:

> The transformation of social relations becomes a matter, then, of transforming hegemonic social conditions rather than the individual acts that are spawned by those conditions. Indeed, one runs the risk of addressing the merely indirect, if not epiphenomenal, reflection of those conditions if one remains restricted to a politics of acts.
>
> (Butler, 1988: 525)

What is significant about parodic practices such as drag, for Butler, is that they reveal the fictive nature of the relationship between the espoused 'original' and its 'imitation'; parody works not because of a simple, carnivalesque inversion, but because of its capacity to unsettle the very contingency on which a bifurcation of gender to sex as 'copy to original' depends. Gender is revealed as self-parodic; lacking a reference point it is a 'copy' without an original, an approximation of a socially (organizationally) constructed ideal that can never be imitated, only 'sent up'. Gender is thereby understood as a 'corporeal style' (Butler, 1988) whose iterations dramatize its contingency and ontology as a constant struggle, in the Hegelian sense, between what is lived and experienced and what is socially recognizable, or culturally intelligible, as Butler puts it, including the organizational conditions and contexts in which that struggle is enacted. Again, this makes an important link between her performative ontology and the political potential Butler attaches to parody, if:

> To understand identity as a *practice*, and as a signifying practice, is to understand culturally intelligible subjects as the resulting effect of a rule-bound discourse that inserts itself in the pervasive and mundane signifying acts of a linguistic life.
>
> (Butler, 1990: 145, *original emphasis*)

Yet Butler's discussion of drag has caused some ontological confusion, as drag suggests (in a Goffmanesque sense), something that is 'put on', as a temporarily enacted performance, whereas performativity invokes an on-going process through which gender is constantly re-signified. What I think Butler intended to emphasize, in citing drag as illustrative of the potential to 'make trouble' with gender, is that the ability to imitate opens up the structure of gender itself, revealing its performative ontology rather than shoring up its pre-social basis (see Kotz, 1992). This is suggested in her focus on how gender is able to displace the norms by which it is compelled or constrained through parodic, repetitive subversion, a theme she developed in later work (Butler, 2004b).

Perhaps more worryingly, however, Butler's discussion of drag also raises (once again) the political implications of her investment in the omnipresence of language. If, as she puts it, 'all signification takes place within the orbit of the compulsion to repeat' (Butler, 1990: 145), what does this mean for the limits of parodic re-signification? Further, as Benhabib (1995b: 110) has asked (in later work), if one is constituted by discourse without being determined by it, what enables the self to 'vary' the discursive reference points and regulatory mechanisms in such a way that their power effects can be challenged and resisted? In other words, 'what psychic, intellectual or other sources of creativity and resistance must we attribute to human subjects for such variation to be possible?' Further, and as noted above, what kind of institutional arrangements or organizational resources would be necessary for parodic re-signification to be both possible, and/or effective? This is particularly important for organizational scholars, given tendencies towards a corporate appropriation of difference, including of parodic inversions as 'novelty acts' (Ahmed, 2012).

In response to these kinds of questions and challenges, Butler emphasizes in the conclusion to *Gender Trouble* her conviction that agency, including parodic capacity, emerges in the interstices of different and often competing, or contradictory constraints or compulsions, and from variations in patterns of repetition. It is within this 'slippage' that subversion becomes possible, in for instance (in a relatively rare and early reference to organizational contexts), the injunction to be a 'fit worker' (Butler, 1990: 145). It is through the tensions, the frictions that result from the incompatibilities and incoherencies produced by those who are unable or unwilling to conform to such injunctions that subversion becomes possible. 'Rescuing agency' at the end of the book, Butler emphasizes her view that to argue that the subject is an effect does not mean that it is 'fatally determined nor fully artificial and arbitrary' (Butler, 1990: 147).

Kirby's (2006) view is that this logic is compromised, however, due to what is arguably the key to Butler's performative ontology—namely her understanding of language as, ultimately and despite her Foucauldian protestations, a repressive force, the primary purpose of which is a normalizing restriction of what it is possible to be/become. In Kirby's view, this is because of Butler's attempts to bring together distinct approaches without addressing their disjunctions, an endeavour that produces particular tensions and contradictions in her theory of performativity. These revolve not least around the question of whether Butler's poststructuralist reference points can be rendered compatible with her Hegelian and phenomenological influences, and with her leanings towards critical theory, a question that manifests itself in some of *Gender Trouble's* subtle but persistent problems with the relationship between agency and subjectivity, materiality and language and the latter as both a repressive and productive force.

Butler's performative ontology has been subject to considerable critique, not least because of its apparent neglect of the 'real', material circumstances of gender relations and politics. She argues for instance that 'gender reality is performative which means, quite simply, that it is real only to the extent that it is performed' (Butler, 1988: 527), a presumption that at first sight seems at odds with her preoccupation with materiality (yet her emphasis—elaborated most notably in *Bodies That Matter* and in *Undoing Gender* is on *materialization*, or 'mattering'), a theme we return to in Chapter 2.

Organizational Performativity

As noted thus far, Butler's writing on performativity has drawn from a wide range of theoretical influences including Derrida, Freud, Lacan, Foucault, Nietzsche and particularly, Hegel. Harding (2007: 1761) notes that what connects these various writers, a link that has been of particular interest to organization theorists, is an understanding of subjectivity as 'always in a process of becoming'. As discussed earlier, this processual ontology takes as its starting point an understanding of subjectivity as a verb rather than a noun, an approach developed in Butler's critique of gender performativity. Within this line of thought, subjectivities come into effect only through re-iterative performance; 'compelled by the regulatory practices' of social *and organizational* coherence (Butler, 1990: 24).

Butler rarely connects her performative ontology to questions of work, organization and the economy; her discussion of performative agency in the *Journal of Cultural Economy* is a notable exception to this. Here she considers what a 'critical upending' of the presumption that a metaphysical substance that precedes its expression means for, as she puts it, 'the basic ontologies with which we operate' (Butler, 2010: 147). Illustrating her argument with reference to the economy, she argues that the latter only becomes 'singular and monolithic' as a result of the 'convergence of certain kinds of processes and practices that produce the "effect" of the knowable and unified economy'. This could be taken to imply a disavowal of the material substance of economic power relations, processes and practices. However, Butler's rhetorical emphasis here is on trying to counter what she calls 'a certain kind of positivism' that delimits our understanding of what might be possible; specifically she seeks to draw attention to the presumption that certain socially constructed categories are given as pre-social or *pre-organizational*, highlighting the mechanisms of their construction, and the imperatives underpinning these. In other words, and in largely Foucauldian terms, her aim is to bring to the fore ways of thinking about categories such as 'the economy' that she feels are retired in more established ontologies, highlighting the processes that produce ontological effects in order to subject them to critique. Rather than a denial of materiality, arguably her aim is to emphasize the labour involved in bringing about these ontological effects; as she puts it, performativity highlights the ways in which these '*work* to bring into being certain kinds of realities . . . that lead to certain kinds of socially binding consequences' (Butler, 2010: 147, *emphasis added*).

Thinking about the implications of this for understanding organizational life, Butler's performative ontology has had a significant and growing impact on work, organization and management studies over the past three decades or so. Much of this growing interest has been in the form of a thematic, analytical concern with gender and/or sexuality (see Rumens, 2018), but her writing has begun to make significant inroads into organizational scholarship more widely, through several performative analyses of management (Parker, 2002; Harding, 2003; Hodgson, 2005), leadership (Learmonth, 2005) and strategy (Laine et al., 2016).

Nancy Harding's (2003) book, *The Social Construction of Management* draws on Butler in its critique of the textual construction of management subjectivities. Analyzing management textbooks published since the 1950s, Harding illustrates how 'strong management', premised upon rationalism and modernity, is presented as the solution to the purportedly chaotic world of organizational life. Harding (2003: 17) shows how management as 'an epistemological performative endeavour' constitutes a discursive space 'into which the manager climbs'.[11] Just as for Butler the being of gender is a discursive effect, a social-material construction mapped out by the parameters of its own ontology, for Harding (2007: 198–199), management 'reveals a world constituted epistemologically through . . . textbooks and management teachings . . . called into being through discourse'. Presuming the status of something 'real' or representational, management is posited as the object of knowledge rather than as an entity constructed through political rhetoric, or hailed into being in Althusserian terms. This leads Harding to conclude that management is a performative epistemology, a discursive space within which managers perform themselves as managers, and management is established normatively, as a performative accomplishment, rendering the Other of management and managers—notably workers or 'non-managerial' members of staff—abject.

Harding's analysis shows how the drama of management, in this sense, is always incomplete, as managers can never fully approximate the epistemic or ontological (including bodily) ideals of what it means to be a manager. Hence (aspiring and actual) managers identify with their organizations in order to constitute themselves in such a way as to be recognized as competent, convincing managerial subjects in a way that involves *enacting* what it means to be a manager in order to be recognized as such, thereby bringing their own managerial subjectivities into being. This means that, while management education proffers a degree of ontological security, managers' primary function is to continually recite themselves as managers. Management is thus performative 'in that it has no ontological status apart from the various acts, undertaken by managers, which constitute its reality. The job of managers is to undertake this performative function and embody the theory of management' (Harding, 2007: 211). In practice, this means that what we think of as 'management' has the power to subject and subjectify all workers, including those hailed as managers, into being. What is crucial to this process is the continual recitation of cultural norms governing 'managers' and 'management' as performative accomplishments, Harding argues.[12]

Research on the gendered norms associated with other professions or workplace settings and sectors further illustrates how particular subjectivities are brought into being through performative citations. While much of the growing body of Butler scholarship within work and organization studies has drawn from Butler's (1988: 519) emphasis on gender as an identity that is 'tenuously constituted in time', through constant acts of recitation and resignification, research has also focused on how gender is instantiated in organizational space, and workplace settings.

A notable example is Gregson and Rose's (2000) study of community arts workers and car-boot sales as alternative spaces of work and consumption. Their analysis connects insights from Butler's theory of performativity, the sociology of work and phenomenological geography in order to explore workplace settings as performative spaces, emphasizing that 'space too needs to be thought of as brought into being through performances and as a performative articulation of power' (Gregson and Rose, 2000: 434).

With reference to their work in particular locales associated with social and cultural deprivation, the community arts workers in their study articulated a reflexive awareness of power as discursive, resting on 'the performative authority with which it can define, repeatedly, certain places and people in particular ways' (Gregson and Rose, 2000: 439). The difficulty for the community arts workers they interviewed is that they had to 'speak a language audible to funding institutions' in order to secure vital grants that enabled them to continue their work, and to gain recognition for their projects and the communities in which they were embedded. Hence, the workers mobilized or re-cited the terms of the discourses used by funding bodies and other authorities, but did so tactically. Drawing on Butler, Gregson and Rose show how these acts suggest that the arts workers' recitations 'are not simple copies' or replications, but are critical recitations used to benefit the communities in which they worked; they were instances of 'making trouble', in Butler's terms, with and through the dominant, authoritative terms of reference. Through a similarly performative lens, they illustrate how the transitory character of car-boot sales means that as work places,

> They can never be thought of as a fixed, pre-existing stage in the way that department stores, restaurants, banks and so on have been represented. . . . Rather, these are events which depend for their very existence, for their bringing into being, on specific performances: promoters, marshals, vendors, and buyers are all critical to the transformation of field-into-car-boot-sale.
>
> (Gregson and Rose, 2000: 442)

Analysing both spheres of work through the lens of Butler's writing on performativity, Gregson and Rose (2000: 441) argue that since performances of subject positions are iterative, 'slippage is always possible', and that it is not only social actors that are produced by/within power relations, 'but the spaces in which they perform'. The 'stages' of community arts projects and car boot sales do not pre-exist their performative iteration, rather specific performances bring them into being, hence organizational/organizing spaces are performative enactments, embedded within discursive-material power relations, that are 'citational . . . iterative, unstable, performative' (Gregson and Rose, 2000: 447).

Tyler and Cohen (2010) develop a similar approach in their study of the gendered, spatial performativities of workspaces. Focusing on the ways in which a group of female university employees inhabited their office spaces in order to elicit recognition of their workplace viability, Tyler and Cohen show how the women simultaneously enact and signify themselves as capable of conforming to the normative expectations of the heterosexual matrix. Their study illustrates how

> We do not simply occupy space, but rather we become ourselves in and through it. Furthermore, this spatial performativity is driven very much by our desire for recognition as viable, intelligible (organizational) subjects and hence is performed largely in accordance with its governing gender (and organizational) norms.
>
> (Tyler and Cohen, 2010: 192)

Jenkins and Finneman (2017: 157) also examine performativity as a theoretical framework for critically assessing gender identities and relations in patriarchal workplace environments, focusing on the institutional rules and norms shaping gendered interactions in news organizations. They argue that, as a challenge to categorical ways of thinking about gender, performativity offers a conceptual lens through which to develop a critique of newsrooms as 'spaces where expectations for gender can significantly shape professional experiences and success'. They consider the issues that women who work in newsrooms face as they performatively enact gender, as well as the details of the kinds of performances that may be required of them in order to 'function and succeed in a male-dominated field' (Jenkins and Finneman, 2017: 158), or to be accorded recognition, in Butler's terms. They show how, while challenging gender norms may attract criticism for the subject in question (a theme returned to in Chapters 5 and 6), these acts may also disrupt the status quo, 'particularly when the subversive figure is in the public eye or a position of power' (Jenkins and Finneman, 2017: 160).

In a similar vein to Gregson and Rose (2000) and Tyler and Cohen (2010), they emphasize how women journalists working in newsrooms not only operate within environments that privilege heteronormative masculinity but, 'through their reporting, they also consistently navigate gender relations in the outside world', hence, they argue, empowering this group could result in opportunities for gender subversion within newsrooms 'while also potentially inspiring and motivating those reached by journalists' reporting' (Jenkins and Finneman, 2017: 169).

To borrow from Gond et al. (2016) the risk here is arguably that of 'domesticating' or taming performativity's critical capacity, reducing it to a tool for improving organizational lives while leaving the regulatory apparatuses and social structures constraining, compelling or co-opting particular performativities intact.[13] As Lloyd (2007: 56–57, *emphasis added*) has argued, for a gender politics to be subversive, in Butler's sense, it needs to orientate itself towards '(re)-signification, denaturalization and the *critical labour* required to identify when and where gender norms might be challenged'. If the ultimate aim, in the spirit of Butler's critique, is to open up a space—including within/through organizational settings and processes—within which non- or anti-normative ways of being might thrive, then we need to begin thinking and acting beyond simply re-navigating or re-doing normativity in a different guise, even if the aim is for the latter to reach beyond the boundaries of organizational settings into the wider social sphere.

Attempting to undertake this, Sayers and Jones (2015: 94) examine a public debate over menstruation in the workplace triggered by a statement from the CEO of New Zealand's largest body of public sector employers that periods make women take more sick leave than men. Sayers and Jones report how this utterance triggered an astonishing outpouring of public (pro-feminist) criticism and writing about working while menstruating, as well as about wider related issues such as gender and productivity, embodied difference, and equal pay. They discuss how a comment about women's periods 'ruptured the status quo of menstrual repression by using online posts rendered as poems'. In their theoretical reflections, they consider how women's online writing, feminist theory and activism, and bodily experiences of menstruation can come together in a re-significatory way in order to 'make trouble' for regimes of power and the ways in which these are articulated.

Considering similar themes of gender power and resistance in her book *Performing Gender at Work*, Elizabeth Kelan (2009: 35) has explored the implications of Butler's performative ontology for understanding how 'gender performances and gender identities are not something fixed but something that needs to be *done* at work'. However, as Kelan (2009: 50 and 51, *emphasis added*) notes, 'Butler's theories are largely elaborated at a very abstract level, which leads to problems concerning *how the process of gender as a doing can be studied empirically*' so that for her, 'the main problem with Butler's work is . . . that it remains unclear how people negotiate subject positions in everyday situations'. This makes drawing on her work a challenge for organizational researchers, a point returned to later.

Engaging with Butler's theory of performativity, and her slightly later writing on gender as a perpetual un/doing (Butler, 2004b), Kelan locates gender performance within processes of biographic construction, arguing that narration, as a social practice, is a form of 'doing gender' in Butler's terms, or 'a way of rendering the individual readable as a human being' (Kelan, 2009: 107).

Kelan describes a woman executive who is treated like a secretary by a customer, and another woman who reports the need to make a conscious effort to act 'ungendered' in order to avoid discrimination in her workplace. Instances such as these demonstrate, she argues, the extent to which performativity cannot simply be turned on and off (like a performance), but continually constitutes identities, including those enacted and experienced in the workplace.

Kelan's (2009) study of ICT professionals sets out to show how different subject positions are evoked when narrating organizational biographies. However, her focus is not on 'undoing' these narratives in a Butlerian (2004b) sense, or on trying to understand what happens to lived experiences in the construction of these narratives, but rather on revealing *how* narratives are performed at work. This opens up important questions not just about the processes through which narratives are produced and sustained, but also *why*, and with what consequences; in other words to what ends, and at what 'cost', in Butler's terms, does the subject attempt to produce and maintain a coherent self-narrative, a question we return to in Chapter 4 in our discussion of Butler's (2005) writing on 'giving an account of oneself'.

Performative Reflexivity in Organizational Research

In recent years, and drawing on the range of insights already outlined, a debate has opened up within organizational research over what the adoption of a 'critical performativity' might mean for management and organization studies. Spicer et al.'s (2009: 545) call for a reappraisal of how we 'do' critical management research, in order to 'take seriously the life-worlds and struggles of those who are engaged with it' urges organizational researchers to mobilize performativity so as to open up more reflexive spaces for research. They make the case for a rethinking of performativity within the field, in which the term 'performative' has generally been taken to refer, following Lyotard (1984), to an optimal relationship between input and output.

Drawing on Austin and Butler, Spicer et al. (2009: 543) set out to reframe performativity in/for critical management studies as 'a kind of active intervention' or series of subversive re-citations (instead of an over-arching concern for efficiency), a semantic shift that leads them to empha-size the need to rethink the characteristically anti-performative stance of critical management and organization studies (Fournier and Grey, 2000; Parker, 2002), and to become more 'critically performative'. They argue that fostering such a critical performativity constitutes an invaluable way in which researchers might cultivate a pragmatic, engaged 'openness and curiosity about the social world' (Spicer et al., 2009: 549) underpinning what they call a micro-emancipatory approach to critique.

A more radical engagement with performativity, one that has closer parallels with Butler's recent concerns to articulate a performative theory of precarity and dispossession (Butler and Athanasiou, 2013—see Chap-ter 6), encourages us to ask 'uncomfortable questions about our own positions' (Ford et al., 2010: 571) as organizational researchers, practi-tioners and activists. This more politically engaged approach emphasizes the need to 'understand the terms within and through which subjects are performatively constituted' in organizational settings (Cabantous et al., 2015: 8). Cabantous et al. (2015: 8) argue that two fundamental ques-tions follow from engaging a Butlerian ontology of performativity within organization studies in this way: 'Who are you? [And] what are the condi-tions of the possibility of your becoming?' This more 'macro' approach, and these kinds of questions, focuses critical attention not simply on micro-emancipatory practices, or on the terms of performativity, but rather on their wider social, political and economic context. It brings to the fore a concern with understanding and challenging the ways in which regulatory norms continually strive to organize the pluralities and com-plexities of being into a fictional—instrumental—coherence, a coherence which then assumes a pre-organizational status and which, in doing so, conceals its own performativity, including the terms of that performative becoming. Critical performativity as Cabantous et al. (2015) advocate it develops the specifically organizational implications of Butler's work, opening up future avenues for theoretical analysis and activism in seek-ing to uncover and undo the organizational process which she subjects to critique, attesting to its exploitative consequences for those involved. It draws attention, in particular, to the materialities of this process, notable through the ways in which organizations distinguish between bodies that 'matter' and those that don't, the theme in Butler's writing and in organi-zation studies that we turn to next.

Notes

1. Butler herself compares the phrasing of this oft-quoted line in *The Second Sex* to Aretha Franklin's sentiment, written by Carole King, 'you make me feel like a natural woman', in its intimation that 'natural womanhood' is a perpetually elusive but nevertheless continually pursued ideal central to gender identities and relations (see Butler, 2000a: 199, n.34).

2. This is further confused by some of Butler's own conceptual slippage, when she refers, for instance, to gender as 'a kind of persistent impersonation that passes for the real' (Butler, 2000a: xxviii), implying a theatrical meaning.

3. Benhabib misquotes Butler when she attributes to her the idea that 'we must bid farewell to the "doer *beyond* the deed"' (Benhabib, 1995a: 21, *emphasis added*), a position that in her view, undermines the very possibility of feminism as 'the theoretical articulation of the emancipatory aspirations of women' (Benhabib, 1995a: 29). In her direct response, Butler maintains that her critique of the subject is not the same as the latter's 'negation or repudiation' but is rather an interrogation of its normative construction on 'a pre-given or foundationalist premise' (Butler, 1995a: 42; see also Butler, 1993). To argue (or misconstrue) that there is no doer 'beyond, or rather or *behind* the deed' is not the same, she argues, as 'bidding farewell to the doer' altogether (Butler, 1995b: 135). What Butler actually argues is that 'the "doer" is variably constructed *in and through the deed*' and that each one of us is variably constructed 'in and through the other' (Butler, 2000a: 181).

4. The Danish fashion model, Hanne Gaby Odiele, describes how the standard medical procedure 'to force the body into one sex or the other' continues to be the norm, recalling, 'Most people I've met have had surgery. To normalize the body, they just cut things out. . . . It's a human rights violation, an age-old impulse to correct things that don't conform to the binary ways in which men seek to shape the world' ('her' is Odiele's preferred pronoun), in Hicklin (2017).

5. See Kelan (2010: 46) for a notable example. Kelan fully acknowledges the difficulty of attaching labels to Butler's work, arguing that any that are assigned should be treated as 'shorthand for the sake of simplicity'. Nevertheless, Kelan goes on to position Butler primarily as a 'discursive/poststructuralist' thinker in her analysis of gender performativity at work, focusing largely on performativity and discourse as analytical categories. See also Hirst and Schwabenland (2018), whose analysis of gendered experiences of office space begins from the premise that Butler's emphasis on gender performativity situates her as a poststructuralist.

6. Butler (2016: 17, *emphasis added*) notes both criticisms in later work when she acknowledges that her formulation of gender as performative 'became the basis for two quite contrary interpretations: the first . . . that we radically *choose* our genders; the second . . . that we are utterly *determined* by gender norms'.

7. Butler returns to this idea in later writing (see Butler, 2016: 17), arguing that gender is an 'assignment' in so far as it is both an allocation/attribution and a project/task.

8. Here Butler draws directly from Foucault's (1980: 155, *emphasis added*) conviction that 'we must not make the mistake of thinking that sex is an autonomous agency. . . . On the contrary, sex is the most speculative, most ideal, and most internal element in a deployment of sexuality *organized* by power in its grip on bodies and their materiality, their forces, energies, sensations and pleasures', an argument that ostensibly makes no concession to an 'outside' of this organizing process.

9. As an example, Duffy et al. (2017) show how Virgin Atlantic's 25-year anniversary advertising campaign, 'Still Red Hot', while (self)purportedly parodying sexualized and ageist iconography associated with the airline industry, can also be read as an illustration of the ways in which organizations appropriate feminist ideas about gender, sexuality and subjectivity. Their analysis emphasizes how the 'scenography of gender construction' to borrow Butler's phrase, in this particular instance, is dependent upon 'the commodification of a knowing, ironic and playful subjectivity preoccupied with the self as a performative project', one that characterizes neo-liberal post-feminism and is at odds with a critique of the discrimination perpetuated within and by the industry.

10. Benhabib, in particular, has raised concerns about Butler's discussion of drag in *Gender Trouble*, refuting her own alleged misinterpretation by arguing that the distinction made between a linguistic and a theatrical understanding of performativity 'was not sharply drawn' because in the sections of the text on drag, cross-dressing and so on, 'the theatrical and Goffmanesque metaphors of gender constitution, as opposed to the linguistic ones, become prominent' (Benhabib, 1995b: 120, n.4).

11. Harding (2007: 25) emphasizes that her use of the term 'performative' differs from the Lyotardian sense on which Fournier and Grey (2000) draw in their espousal of an 'anti-performative' stance for critical management studies (CMS). Rather, Harding draws explicitly on Butler's reading of Althusser's notion of interpellation that sees performative acts as 'forms of authoritative speech . . . statements that, in the uttering, also perform a certain action and [in doing so] exercise a binding power' (Butler, 1993: 225, cited in Harding, 2007: 25).

12. Ahmed (2012: 202–203, n.7) cites the significance of reiteration being embedded within institutional power relations in her critique of discursive commitments to equality. Speech acts such as 'we are diverse' are citations that depend, for their performative success, on being re-cited across institutions and embedded within organizational power relations and formal modes of recognition such as accreditations and other endorsements, for instance.

13. See for further discussion, Nentwich et al.'s (2014) study of the duality of agency in maintaining the organizational status quo and in generating change in which organizational change agency is discussed as an embedded performativity. See also Fine's (2016: 69) analysis of intelligibility, organizational change and leadership discourse which draws on Butler to reimagine critical, reflexive leadership practices in order to render a broader range of subjects intelligible as leaders and to 'catalyze social change'.

2 The Organizational 'Matter' of Bodies at Work

Butler's (1988, 1990, 1993, 2000a) performative analysis of gender considered in Chapter 1 draws critical attention to the body as the medium through which gendered subjectivity is brought into being, or made to 'matter'. Here Butler characteristically plays on the term 'matter' as simultaneously a process of materialization through which something is given a substantive form,[1] and its successful performance, taking 'successful' to mean performed in such a way as to be accorded recognition, resulting in 'the acquisition of being' (Butler, 1993: 15) or becoming of significance. This duality emphasizes Butler's understanding of mattering as both 'having a material form' and 'possessing the capacity to signify meaning' whereby 'to signify [is] to be known, to acquire value' (Butler, 1993: 5). Set against the wider backdrop of Butler's performative theory discussed in Chapter 1, this suggests that, to borrow from Orwell, all bodies 'matter', but some bodies matter more than others; that is, have the capacity to signify what is deemed to be intelligible and viable in any given context.

Considering this process of mattering as an organizational one through which certain ways of being come to be attributed more value than others is the focus of this chapter, which examines both the conditions of this mattering as well as the consequences for those whose bodies can't or don't matter. As Butler herself emphasizes, drawing on Joan Scott's (1988) writing on gender and the politics of history, once we come to understand subjects as 'formed through exclusionary operations, it becomes politically necessary to trace the operations of that construction and erasure' (Butler, 1995a: 48), a critical, reflexive practice that underpins much of the work undertaken within organization theory.

When Butler (1993: x) asks,

> How are we to understand the constitutive and compelling status of gender norms without falling into the trap of cultural determinism? How precisely are we to understand the *ritualized repetition* by which such norms *produce and stabilize* not only the effects of gender but the materiality of sex?

it strikes me that these are profoundly organizational questions; they are questions about what organizations are, about what they do, and about how and why they do it through 'ritualized repetitions' that produce and stabilize normative subjectivities that are simultaneously cultural and material in form. These questions also bring to the fore Butler's (1993: xi) notion of construction as a 'constitutive constraint', as simultaneously bringing something into being at the same time as placing unfeasibly narrow limitations around what form that being takes within the context of hierarchical, regulatory schemas.[2] Not only do these constraints and compulsions produce an organizationally legible domain of intelligible subjectivities and bodies, they also depend upon the designation of 'a domain of unthinkable, abject, unliveable bodies' (Butler, 1993: xi). Butler's *Bodies That Matter* shows how the latter is not the opposite of the former, but rather is integral to its organizing impetus and structure; as she puts it, 'the latter is the excluded and illegible domain that haunts the former domain as the spectre of its own impossibility . . . *its constitutive outside*' (Butler, 1993: xi, *emphasis added*). In *Bodies That Matter*, Butler connects her performative ontology of gender to the materiality of the body, and hence her critique of the organization of the desire for recognition to the question of 'mattering', by asking, simply: 'which bodies come to matter—and why?' (Butler, 1993: xii).

Although, as noted above, Butler's analysis of gender performativity focuses primarily on the recitation of cultural norms over time, it is her reference to the materialization of gender in space, and her passing comments on gender as 'instituted in an exterior space' (Butler, 2000a: 141) that is also of importance to understanding mattering as a simultaneously organizational and organizing process. With this in mind, the discussion in this chapter derives insight from a wealth of organizational research on gendered aesthetics, embodiment and spatiality that draws on and develops insights from Butler's writing, examining some of the ways in which gender, and particularly women's perpetual Otherness, is played out in and through organizational settings and processes.

As considered in the previous chapter, in their study of community arts projects and car boot sales as alternative spaces of consumption, Gregson and Rose (2000) noted some time ago now that more work needs to be done to tease out the performative qualities of organizational spaces and to understand the organizational practices that bring particular spaces into being. With this in mind, one of the aims of this chapter is to explore this theme through Butler's writing on 'mattering' considering the latter as an organizational process, or rather (much like performativity) as a process of *organizing*, exploring how subjectivity is performed in and through organizational materiality and 'mattering'.

In her earlier writing (see Chapter 1), Butler emphasizes that the effect of gender 'is produced through the stylization of the body', so that gender is an embodied 'performative accomplishment' (Butler, 2000a: 179). This leads her to focus, particular in *Bodies That Matter* (Butler, 1993) and in *Undoing Gender* (Butler, 2004b—see Chapter 3), on the bodily configurations compelled by the matrices of cultural intelligibility that govern social life—those that 'matter'. Gender, she argues, 'is the repeated stylization of the body, a set of repeated acts within a highly rigid regulatory frame that congeal over time to produce the appearance of substance' (Butler, 2000a: 43–44). Hegemonic discourse restricts, places limits on, the range of subject positions that are available thereby constraining what can be performed and materialized. As Butler puts it, her concern is largely with 'the limits to bodily intelligibility' (Butler, 1993: 82) and ultimately, with broadening these limits to make way a wider range of liveable lives.

In exploring these themes, as Lloyd (2007) highlights, Butler responds to critics of the presumed voluntarism in *Gender Trouble* by emphasizing right from the outset how the recitation of gender norms is imperative for a person 'to count and persist as a credible . . . subject' (Butler, 1993: 7–8). In this sense, she replaces what some critics take to be an ontological, cultural free for all with a greater emphasis on 'the constraints and limitations underpinning gender performativity' (Lloyd, 2007: 64). In Lloyd's (2007: 64) summation, Butler maps out two possible results of performing gender against the norm: either a subversive de-naturalization through which gender norms might be contested and reconfigured *or* 'the person who performs them is punished for behaving unnaturally'. Thinking about mattering as an organizational process highlights a third response to non-normative performativity that Butler herself hints at in her discussion of appropriative encounters with difference, namely those through which potentially subversive attempts at re-signification become construed as organizational resources, the potentially denaturalizing or critical tendencies of which are mobilized in the service of corporate rather than emancipatory ends. This raises a challenge that Butler frames as follows:

> What is called for is the difficult work of cultural translation in which difference is honoured without (a) assimilating difference to identity or (b) making difference an unthinkable fetish of alterity.
>
> (Butler, 1995b: 140)

If subversion 'calls into question the abjecting power that it sustains' opening up the possibility of re-signification (Butler, 1993: 67), an important question for organizational scholars is how might this be brought about, in a way that differentiates between subversion and abjection, and at the same time, staves off the constant threat of appropriation, the 'fetish of alterity'. Further, how might organizational resources, network and capacities be mobilized subversively, when these very same resources and so on are those that organize some bodies into 'mattering' more than others. Butler poses a simple question but one that has important implications for organizational politics that is pertinent to these kinds of challenges, namely what are the conditions necessary 'to establish and sustain bodies that matter' (Butler, 1993: 240)?

Butler's own response to this question begins to emerge in *Gender Trouble* if not earlier, when she argues that the body is always, already 'a cultural sign' (Butler, 1990: 90); in other words, as the medium of recognition, the body carries the weight of social expectation. As Lloyd (2007: 70) picks up, the idea of a pre-social, natural body, free of the fetters of signification, 'falsely ontologizes what is actually a culturally fabricated physicality'. As she reminds us, critics such as Martha Nussbaum (1999) and Lynne Segal (1994) all draw attention to what, in their view, amounts to a de-materialization of the body in Butler's performative account of gender, giving insufficient attention to, or misrepresenting, the corporeal realities of women's lives. Responding to these concerns, Butler sets out to refute this interpretation of her work, emphasizing that her concern is with developing a theory of the way in which bodily materiality constitutes 'a scenography and topography of construction' (Butler, 1993: 28), her primary purpose being to open up 'new possibilities, new ways for bodies to matter' (Butler, 1993: 30). It is precisely with the process of materialization that she is concerned, as Lloyd (2007) brings to the fore in her discussion of *Bodies That Matter*. As she puts it,

> When Butler talks of materialization, she is talking about how particular ideas about the body come to have life, how they begin to order reality, and hence how they gather ontological force.
> (Lloyd, 2007: 73)

The principle of this ostensibly organizing process is that what materializes or 'matters' is what has both substance and significatory capacity.[3] In other words, 'bodies that matter' are those that can both carry meaning at the same time as elicit recognition of themselves as culturally intelligible forms. In this sense, as Lloyd (2007: 73, *emphasis added*) neatly sums it up, 'matter and meaning are inextricably linked. *To materialize is to become meaningful*', just as to 'mean' is to be sustainable, intelligible and therefore viable, in one's materiality. Responding to her critics, Butler wrests material corporeality from its implicitly retired position[4] and emphasizes its significance—its significatory capacity—as the materiality on and through which the struggle for recognition is played out.[5]

In this sense, Butler's analysis in *Bodies That Matter* is not a simple 'reversal of order' (Kirby, 2006: 48) of the insistence that natural, pre-social foundations generate cultural processes and identities, but a characteristically dialectical reading of this relationship, one that emphasizes the material limits of construction and in turn, the constructive limits of materiality. As noted above, this ontological move underpins a political project for Butler in so far as her work rests on a critical interrogation of the apparent coherence of bodies that matter; as Kirby (2006: 66, *emphasis added*) puts it, 'the need to reconfigure materiality becomes the *pivot* of Butler's argument'.

Butler on the Matter of Bodies

As noted thus far, in *Bodies That Matter* Butler (1993) developed her discussion of performativity into a theory of the relationship between sex and the materiality of the body. Like gender, sex is not a possession of the individual—a thing one has or is; rather, with strong echoes of De Beauvoir (2011 [1948]), it is the means by which one becomes viable as a social subject, or comes to 'matter'. In other words, performing one's sex, gender and sexuality in such a way as to conform to the normative terms of the heterosexual matrix[6] 'qualifies a body for life within the domain of cultural intelligibility' (Butler, 1993: 2). Again, playing on multiple meanings of the term, by 'for life' Butler suggests both that bodies will be recognized as culturally viable for as long as they continue to uphold performative coherence, and for those who have the capacity to do so, their viability will continue to be recognized, thereby accumulating value, through continual re-vivification of their designation as 'fully human', with all the rights and responsibilities associated with being recognized as such. This latter emphasis reminds us of Butler's reading of Hegelian dialectics as always 'unfinished', and as instantiating a reflexive relationship between subjectivity and substance.

To reiterate, the embodied subject of Hegel's (1977) *Phenomenology of Spirit* requires others for its own constitution, and the subject's encounters with otherness are experienced and mediated through substantive, bodily forms. Drawing on this notion of the body as the medium through which the struggle for recognition is played out, as Butler puts it in *Subjects of Desire*, 'mutual recognition only becomes possible in the context of a shared orientation toward the material world' (Butler, 1987: 57, original emphasis). Borrowing from Hegel, she explains what this means for the relationship between recognition and bodily inhabitation of the social contexts in which we encounter—and work on—one another and the social world:

> Self-consciousness is mediated not only through another self-consciousness, but each recognizes the other in virtue of the form each gives to the world. Hence, we are recognized not merely for the form we inhabit in the world (our various embodiments), but for the forms we create of the world (our works).
>
> (Butler, 1987: 57–58)

The lives and experiences of trans people who break with the terms of the 'conditional' recognition on which self-conscious subjectivity depends are a notable illustration of what happens when bodies don't or can't 'matter' in Butler's terms, that is, become unwilling or unable to sustain a coherent, linear presentation of their sex, gender and sexuality as specified by the terms of the heterosexual matrix, or of compelled heteronormativity. Trans people, a little like the drag artists discussed in *Gender Trouble* show us—materialize—the power of sex categories to 'demarcate, circulate, differentiate' the bodies they instantiate, but they also reveal this 'mattering' as a performative approximation, an 'imitation' of an ideal that can never be fully embodied. That such categorization constitutes a discursive ordering through which bodies are produced 'in accord with the category of sex is *itself a material violence*' (Butler, 1995a: 52, *emphasis added*).

An example of the latter, of the organizational designation and treatment of trans people as bodies that don't 'matter', and of what Butler means when she describes 'the injurious action of names' (Butler, 1997a: 28), is illustrated in the case of Primark's recent treatment of a trans employee. The employment tribunal of Miss A. de Souza E Souza v. Primark Stores Ltd, reached a unanimous decision in December 2017 that De Souza had been subjected to harassment related to gender reassignment. De Souza is a trans woman who had been dressing and living as a woman for approximately sixteen years when she started working at Primark in 2016. When she was recruited to a sales assistant job at the Oxford Street (West) branch, she presented as a woman, using only the name 'Alexandra' on her application and during the interview. She explained that she was a trans woman and asked for reassurance that her preferred name would be used. The night shift manager who interviewed her confirmed that the company would have to use her legal name (the name on her passport) for payroll purposes, but that she could use her chosen name on her name badge, and be known to colleagues only as Alexandra, although there is no record of this agreement and when she arrived for her first day of work, De Souza was given a badge with the name 'Alexander' on, in an illustration of what Butler means when she emphasizes the way in which language constitutes the subject, or particular kinds of subjects, through acts of disavowal and foreclosure (Butler, 1997a); revealed here is the power of 'name-calling' as a speech act (Butler, 2016: 16), one that *organizes* identity not according to terms of our own making.[7]

The Tribunal reported that the bullying to which De Souza was subject at Primark included 'outing' her in front of co-workers and customers, calling her 'Alexander/Alexander' while laughing at her, and continuing to refer to her using male pronouns and as 'Alexander', even when she asked them not to do so. Also reported to the Tribunal was an incident that involved a co-worker spraying scent near her, claiming that she smelt of urine, 'like a man's toilet', and discussing her voice as manly and as 'too deep' for a woman. Another staff member said that she would pray for her, as 'she's got evil inside her'.

In her evidence to the Tribunal, De Souza also reported that she had overheard co-workers and a supervisor laughing about her, saying 'She's a joke', and 'She has become the joke of the shop'. Referring to De Souza, a male security guard had also been overheard telling a customer, 'She is evil'. When Miss De Souza tried to seek recourse through the company's grievance procedure, she reported being laughed at by co-workers and supervisors as she sat outside HR waiting for her meeting. After taking time off work due to the stress all of this caused, De Souza then resigned from her job.

The Tribunal found that, under the terms of the UK Equality Act 2010, Alexandra De Souza had been directly discriminated against on the basis of gender reassignment. She was awarded £47,433.03, including lost past and future earnings and pension contributions, and injury to feelings (plus interest). In addition to this financial compensation, the Tribunal ordered Primark to adopt and publicize a written policy to support trans employees (or prospective trans employees), and to amend recruitment, induction and training materials. They were also ordered to raise awareness of trans rights amongst existing employees.

The Tribunal found that the discrimination had, again not surprisingly, made De Souza 'insecure about her gender identity *and her very self*' (*emphasis added*). She described to the Tribunal her experience of 'looking in a mirror and not seeing herself anymore'. The Tribunal summed up the impact of this on De Souza's sense of self, concluding that although she had dressed as a woman for over sixteen years prior to working at Primark, she had now become self-conscious about it, so much so that:

> When she walks into a room, the first thing she wonders is how people will see her. She feels they will just see a man dressed as a woman. All her confidence has gone. She feels she has to constantly explain herself to people. [She] has been unable to work, and will be unable to work for some time because of the impact of the discrimination on her. She has lost all confidence in how she will be viewed and treated in a new job. . . . The injury to [her] feelings is very severe indeed, going to her very identity and ability to function in society.
> (De Souza E. Souza v. Primark Stores Ltd., 2017: 26)

The findings of De Souza's Tribunal illustrate an organizational environment and set of experiences that responds to encounters with difference, and claims to recognition, through negation and exclusion. De Souza's experiences show how sex materializes gender and power; it is a poignant example of what Butler means when she says that 'gender is *an assignment*', one that can never quite be carried out according to expectations, 'whose addressee never quite inhabits the ideals s/he is compelled to approximate' (Butler, 1993: 231, *emphasis added*).

But (again, in Hegelian terms) gender is a materialization that is never complete, as bodies never fully comply or conform to rules, regulations and idealistic expectations; as organic, living matter inhabited or embodied by social subjects, they can never approximate the terms of reference by which they are governed. Hence, while bodies have the capacity to call into question the regulatory norms by which they are made to mean, or to 'matter' their subjects, they do so at considerable risk. In *Bodies That Matter* Butler seems to deal with this at a largely individual level (reflecting her emphasis on performativity in *Gender Trouble*). In her later work, however, she begins to consider what 'mattering', and hence embodied performativity, might mean at a more collective, political level, and to consider the potential but also the risks attached to bodily exposure and vulnerability—a theme to which we return in Chapter 6.

For now, it is important to note the extent to which, for Butler, herein lies the embodied, combined power of performativity and materiality as a set of practices that might not always be consistent or coherent, and which in this sense have the potential to reconceptualise which bodies matter, and which do not, and on what basis. In this respect, thinking about embodied subjectivity as a combined process of materialization and value attribution (or recognition) dialectically has the potential to open up questions of individual or collective re-signification, bringing the issue of how bodies might be made to matter to the fore.

In this respect, *Bodies That Matter* provided an important basis for Butler to revisit and develop her earlier discussions on the bifurcation of agency and subjectivity, and also on discourse. With regard to the latter, she shows how materialization occurs through effects, or 'vectors of power' (Butler, 1993: 187), that constitute the domain of cultural intelligibility. Her critical emphasis in understanding this is on the conditions of possibility according to which the subject is able to act and to be accorded recognition. To reiterate, underpinning this interest for Butler is a political commitment to broadening the range of subjectivities that are deemed recognizable, or which come to 'matter', including those (for example) of trans people. By way of further illustration, Butler suggests that practices associated with 'queering' might be understood as a political reworking of abjection, suggesting what she calls the 'political promise' of resignification.[8] In an oft-quoted line she argues in this sense that queer constitutes a strategic 'reversal', one that both 'retains and reiterates the abjected history of the term' (Butler, 1993: 223).

Bodies that exist somehow beyond the realm of cultural intelligibility constitute the domain of the dehumanized; 'the abject against which the human itself is constituted' (Butler, 2000a: 142), and a concern to understand how and why this is the case recurs as a thread throughout *Bodies That Matter*. The experiences of those caring for people who died from AIDS-related illnesses in the 1980s are a poignant example of this erasure, that is, of the fate of bodies deemed not to matter. Butler discusses the film *Paris is Burning* to illustrate her argument that just as gender is the site on which normative subjectivity is articulated, so it can be the means through which gender is rearticulated and annihilating norms can be 'mimed, reworked [and] resignified' (Butler, 1993: 125). With reference to the trans people whose lives are depicted in *Paris is Burning*, Butler argues that through practices of imitation, performing gender is not only shown to be like drag, but *as* drag: imitative and 'beset by an anxiety that it can never fully overcome' (Butler, 1993: 125); it is also shown to be a defiant, affirmative 'creation of kinship and of glory'. In this sense, drag constitutes a reflexive critique of the naturalization of gender as a pre-social, or pre-discursive given and the materialization of bodily normativity.[9] As Butler puts it,

> Drag is subversive to the extent that it reflects on the imitative structure by which hegemonic gender is itself produced and disputes heterosexuality's claim on naturalness and originality.
>
> (Butler, 1993: 125)

It is in *Bodies That Matter* that Butler reaffirms her view that the formation of the subject is *per*formative 'precisely because it initiates the individual into the subjected status of the subject' (Butler, 1993: 121). Here she reminds us of the political importance of her distinction between agency and subjectivity, and of her concern to understand the latter as an outcome of the conditional recognition, or *organization*, of the former.

In this respect, and to reiterate insights from *Gender Trouble* noted in Chapter 1, the category of sex, she argues,

> is a specifically political use of the category of nature . . . there is no reason to divide up human bodies into male and female except that *such a division suits the economic needs of heterosexuality* and lends a naturalistic gloss to the institution of heterosexuality . . . 'sex' is . . . naturalized but not natural.
>
> (Butler, 2000a: 143, *emphasis added*)

Masculine and feminine subject positions, the result of what Butler describes as 'bodily inscriptions', are therefore 'binary reifications of gender' (Butler, 2000a: 160). This discrete, hierarchical organization of gender, as 'part of what "humanizes" individuals within contemporary culture', is produced through the stylization of the body as 'a performative accomplishment' (Butler, 2000a: 178–179). This conviction leads Butler to her critical, analytical emphasis in *Bodies That Matter* and in *Undoing Gender* (see Chapter 3) on those bodily configurations that are compelled by the matrices of cultural intelligibility that govern social (and we might add, organizational) life. If, as noted earlier, gender subjectivity is the outcome of a 'repeated stylization of the body, a set of repeated acts within a highly rigid regulatory frame that congeal over time to produce the appearance of substance' (Butler, 2000a: 43–44), exposure of the ways in which this repetition creates the appearance of 'a naturalistic necessity', an imperative that has been 'a part of cultural critique since Marx' (Butler, 2000a: 44), is the critical endeavour that underpins *Bodies That Matter*.

Bodily Categorization and Signification

For Butler, the body is not merely 'a ready surface awaiting signification, but . . . a set of boundaries, individual and social, politically signified and maintained' (Butler, 2000a: 44). Methodologically in this respect, 'the strange, the incoherent, that which falls "outside", gives us a way of understanding the taken-for-granted world of . . . categorization as a constructed one, indeed, as one that might well be constructed differently' (Butler, 2000a: 140). This dialectical understanding of mattering, as the material site or substance of recognition, is the ontological starting point, the analytical focus and the political imperative that underpins *Bodies That Matter*.

Amongst many theoretical threads and influences, Butler develops her earlier discussions about the categorisation of culturally intelligible (recognizable) bodies drawing directly on Mary Douglas's (1966) argument that the contours of the body are established through 'markings' that seek to ascertain certain specific codes of cultural coherence that serve to organize bodies by reifying difference:

> Ideas about separating, purifying, demarcating, and punishing transgressions have as their main function *to impose system on an inherently untidy experience. It is only by exaggerating the difference* between within and without, above and below, male and female, with and against, *that a semblance of order is created.*
>   (Douglas, 1966: 4, cited in Butler, 2000a: 167, *emphasis added*)

Douglas, of course, argues that 'the body is a model that can stand for any bounded system. Its boundaries can represent any boundaries which are threatened or precarious' (Douglas, 1966: 155, cited in Butler, 2000a: 168). As Butler notes, this 'suggests that all social systems are vulnerable at their margins, and that all margins are accordingly considered dangerous' (Butler, 2000a: 168). Kristeva's (1982) account of abjection develops this structuralist analysis, exploring the role of boundaries in the social constitution of a discrete subject through exclusion. Drawing from this in her discussion of bodily categorization, Butler argues that abject bodies are the 'constitutive outside' of intelligible ones (Butler, 1993: xi); that is, they are the bodies that *don't* matter.[10] As she reminds us,

> Abjection (in Latin, *ab-jicere*) literally means to cast off, away, or out and, hence, presupposes and produces a domain of agency from

which it is differentiated . . . implying a foreclosure which founds the subject and which, accordingly, establishes that foundation as tenuous. . . . The notion of *abjection* designates a degraded or cast out status within the terms of sociality.

(Butler, 1993: 243, n.2, *original emphasis*)

What interests Butler most about Kristeva's account of abjection is her concern with the 'problematic of exclusion, abjection and the creation of "the human"' (Butler, 1993: 244, n.4). In this sense it is an important source of conceptual insight for Butler in her discussion of the *organizing* processes through which some bodies come to materialize and signify value, while others do not, and on what grounds. As 'the sedimenting effect of a regulated iterability' (Butler, 1993: 252), abjection is the process through which the cultural viability, or significatory capacity of some bodies comes to be realized at the expense of others. Butler sees this very much as a process of organization, the perpetual, dialectical nature of which appeals to her Hegelian awareness that 'identity always requires precisely that which it cannot abide' (Butler, 1993: 188). Reminding us that her reading of abjection is one undertaken through this philosophical lens, she emphasizes how

That which is not included—exteriorized by boundary—as a phenomenal constituent of the sedimented effect called 'construction' *will be as crucial to its definition as that which is included.*

(Butler, 1993: 245, n.8, *emphasis added*)

Connecting her discussion of abjection as the organizing process through which the materiality of the body, or rather the materiality of certain bodies, comes to 'mean' (that is, signify value) to the performativity of gender, Butler argues that

The regulatory norms of 'sex' work in a performative fashion to constitute the materiality of bodies and, more specifically . . . to materialize sexual difference in the service of the consolidation of the heterosexual imperative.

(Butler, 1993: 2)

The heterosexual matrix (Butler, 1990/2000a) therefore enables certain identifications and forecloses or disavows others. Again developing themes introduced in *Gender Trouble*, Butler reminds us that regimes of intelligibility such as the heterosexual matrix, through which subjects are formed, require

The simultaneous production of a domain of abject beings . . . who form the constitutive outside to the domain of the subject. The abject designates here precisely those 'unliveable' and 'uninhabitable' zones of social life which are nevertheless densely populated by those who do not enjoy the status of the subject.

(Butler, 1993: 3)

In Butler's (Hegelian) reading of subject formation as an embodied process of constant struggle, the abject remains as 'a threatening spectre' (Butler, 1993: 3); a disavowal which constantly risks 'exposing' the subject, 'grounded as that subject is in a repudiation whose consequences it cannot fully control' (Butler, 1993: 3). Her concern then is firmly with the *materialization* of gender rather than merely its construction, and in this sense she acknowledges '*the repetitive labour*' involved in the recitation of gender norms (Butler, 1993: 10). Performativity is reaffirmed as a process of material repetition and recitation, so that viable, intelligible bodily forms are those that cohere around patterns of sedimentation and congealment established by the heterosexual matrix and the wider social, economic and organizational imperatives compelling or constraining particular (normative) embodied performances.

In this sense, Butler sets the groundwork for considering how the constitution of the subject is situated within power relations that do not cease to operate, or somehow stabilize, at the point that the subject emerges so that the self is never fully formed, 'but is subjected and produced time and again' (Butler, 1995a: 47). Through this perpetual, organizing process viable subjectivity is 'orchestrated through regulatory schemas [including, but not limited to the heterosexual matrix] that produce intelligible morphological possibilities'.

Yet, as noted above, and again reiterating the philosophical and political bases of *Gender Trouble*, Butler emphasizes how 'these regulatory schemas are not timeless structures, but historically revisable criteria of intelligibility which produce and vanquish bodies that matter' (Butler, 1993: 14). What Butler highlights in particular in her discussion of abjection is that through a binary, hierarchical classification through which some bodies come to matter more than others, bodily differences come to be perceived not simply as deviations from a norm, but as pathological or morphological deficiencies. Because this process connects the denigration of matter (as materiality) with a pre-social, natural 'fault' (lacking the capacity to 'matter' in a significatory sense), the organizing process through which some bodies become abject is tautological. As Kirby (2006: 67) has put it, 'the inherent failure of these bodies to "make proper sense" renders them unintelligible', and a social process of differentiation posits this as pre-social. As she goes on,

Refused entry into the domain of the fully human, these outcasts are then aligned with the unruly dangers of the natural, the brutish and the animal, in other words, with the threat that is perceived to emanate from matter itself. *Butler's goal is to disrupt the economy of this logic* by asking 'What challenges does that excluded and abjected realm produce to a symbolic hegemony that might force a radical re-articulation of what qualifies as bodies that matter?' (Butler, 1993: 16).

(Kirby, 2006: 67–68, *emphasis added*)

This is an important question for organizational scholars, practitioners and activists, one that once again brings Butler's implied separation of agency and subjectivity to the fore. Responding to her critics, and re-affirming her Hegelian and De Beauvoirian understanding of subjectivity, Butler's account of the materialization of the subject ('the acquisition of being', as she puts it—1993: 15) does not, she argues, 'foreclose the possibility of agency' but rather locates or *situates* agency 'as a reiterative and re-articulatory practice, immanent to power, and not a relation of external opposition to power' (Butler, 1993: 15).

Taking some time in *Bodies That Matter* to revisit her (in this respect also Foucauldian) thinking on the relationship between agency and subjectivity leads Butler to argue that social constraint marks 'at once the *limits* of agency and its most *enabling conditions*' (Butler, 1993: 228, *original emphasis*). In this sense, she maintains that 'gender performativity cannot be theorized apart from the forcible and reiterative practice of regulatory . . . regimes' that enable the formation of a subject (Butler, 1993: 15). Abject bodies, as already noted, are those which 'fail to materialize' and which 'provide the necessary "outside", if not the necessary support, for the bodies which, in materializing the norm, qualify as bodies that matter' (Butler, 1993: 16), where 'to matter' means at once 'to materialize' and 'to mean' (Butler, 1993: 32). The formation of the subject through the materialization of the body (through, for instance, giving form to gender) is 'a morphogenesis that takes place through a set of identificatory projections' (Butler, 1993: 17).

It is in this context that Butler clarifies an ontological point that is central to her approach to subjectivity, namely that 'the discursive condition of social recognition *precedes and conditions* the formation of the subject: recognition is not conferred on a subject, but forms that subject' (Butler, 1993: 226, *original emphasis*). Her analysis of what she calls the 'the scenography . . . of construction' (Butler, 1993: 28) attempts to think through the relationship between gender performativity, materiality and signification in this respect.

Again, evoking her analytical and political concern with the organization of bodies that matter, she argues that 'the very *formulation of matter takes place in the service of an organization and denial of . . . difference* as that which defines, instrumentalizes, and allocates matter in its own service' (Butler, 1993: 52, *emphasis added*). Further echoing Douglas she argues that 'the boundaries of the body are the lived experience of differentiation' (Butler, 1993: 65). This leads her to ask: if 'normative subject positions . . . depend on and are articulated through a region of abjected identifications', what does this mean for those for whom strategies of abjection, as organizing imperatives, wielded through and by hegemonic subject-positions, come to 'structure and contain the articulatory struggles of those in subordinate or erased positionalities' (Butler, 1993: 112)?

It is in responding to this question throughout *Bodies That Matter* that Butler posits bodies as the 'matter of signification' (Butler, 1993: 67). Yet as per Butler's dialectical understanding of subjectivity as a performative evocation, this materialization is 'far from fully stable' (Butler, 1993: 187), as already noted. Considering the politics of this, Butler introduces, in *Bodies That Matter*, a central theme of her later work, *Undoing Gender* (Butler, 2004b—see Chapter 3) arguing that the 'subject produces its coherence at the cost of its own complexity' (Butler, 1993: 115). She goes on, 'if identity is constructed through opposition, it is also constructed through rejection' (Butler, 1993: 115). As she puts it, once again reaffirming her Hegelian starting point and reading this through Douglas and Kristeva, and hinting at another theme to come in her later discussion of 'accounting' for oneself as a narrative process (Butler, 2005):

> The normative force of performativity—its power to establish what qualifies as 'being'—works not only through reiteration, but through exclusion as well. And in the case of bodies, those exclusions haunt signification as its abject borders or as that which is strictly foreclosed: *the unliveable, the non-narrativizable.*
>
> (Butler, 1993: 188, *emphasis added*)

It is in this sense that Butler evocatively describes the experience of misrecognition as the 'uneasy sense of standing under a sign to which one does and does not belong' (Butler, 1993: 219), connecting subject formation to the capacity to signify, a theme that is crucial to her critique of 'mattering'. It is one that highlights Butler's understanding of the process of becoming differentiated as a necessary condition in the formation of the self, and the degree to which, to put it simply, 'there are better and worse forms of differentiation, and that the worse kinds tend to abject and degrade those from whom the "I" is distinguished' (Butler, 1995b: 140). It is with thinking about this problem of abjection as a political one that Butler is particularly concerned in her discussion of mattering. Alluding to Adorno's (2005) influence on this aspect of her thinking, she frames her critique of abjection as both ontological and ethical, and she is worth quoting at length on this:

> If the 'I' that I am requires the abjection of others, then this 'I' is fundamentally dependent on that abjection; indeed that abjection is installed as the condition of this 'I' and constitutes that posture of autonomy as internally weakened by its own founding disavowals.

My objection to this form of disavowal is that it weakens the sense of self, establishes its ostensible autonomy on fragile grounds, and requires a repeated and systematic repudiation of others in order to acquire and maintain the appearance of autonomy.

(Butler, 1995b: 140)

As Lloyd (2007) emphasizes, what Butler's body politics means is that she needs to be able to show, or at least to suggest, how culturally unintelligible bodies—those that don't matter—might contest the normative violence to which they are subject. Her creative and critical adoption of Kristeva's writing on abjection helps her to think through abject people as those with 'unliveable lives' because they 'circumscribe the domain of the subject' (Butler, 1993: 3). Denied recognition and thereby excluded from viable subjectivity, abject bodies, those that fail to materialize or signify according to normative expectations, 'provide the necessary "outside" . . . for bodies which, in materializing the norm, qualify as bodies that matter' (Butler, 1993: 16). The suggestion here is that abjection is both a process of organization, and an organizational imperative within which some potential for challenging, and perhaps radically reconfiguring, hegemonic bodily norms can be found.

As Lloyd notes, in saying that abject bodies don't matter, Butler is not disavowing their physical existence (although this is, of course, an eminent risk for those denied recognition as subjectively viable); rather, she is emphasizing that abjection means that some bodies come to matter more than others, with the latter denied the legitimacy accorded to subjects whose bodies mean (value) more. Just like performativity, the regulatory regimes governing this organizing process require constant reiteration. As Lloyd (2007) also stresses however, this reiteration remains open to the possibilities of resignification, which in turn has the potential to lead to a reconfiguration of those same governmental norms and organizing imperatives[11]—a theme to which we return in Chapter 6. For now, it is important to note that in Butler's account of materialization the emphasis that she places on 'having significance' (mattering) is not more important than substance or materiality (matter); the two are inexorably, *dialectically* intertwined. To put it simply, 'mattering' is how matter comes to be organized. The precise phrasing of Lloyd's (2007: 76) summation of this provides important clarity, when she notes that 'in aligning matter with value, Butler makes clear that what concerns her is not matter *as such*; it is the mechanisms of denigration that lead certain bodies to become devalued'.

Butler's concern throughout *Bodies That Matter* is with understanding, challenging and ultimately expanding, 'the very meaning of what counts as a valued and valuable body in the world' (Butler, 1993: 22). She no more denies the possibility of agency than she does the significance of materiality; what is of concern to her is how materiality comes to be organized in such a way as to bestow recognition on some, while/as denigrating others, thereby bringing to the fore the dialectics of mattering as an organizational 'problem', to which we now turn.

Organizational Mattering

Developing alongside and evolving from her performative ontology of gender, Butler's concern to understand why some bodies come to matter more than others has been a significant strand of her thinking that has been woven into work and organization studies. Of central concern has been the ways in which organizations accentuate the compulsion to present and perform our bodies in order to conform to the normative expectations of the labour market and of particular workplace sectors and settings, or to embody a specific corporate or brand identity.

One of the earliest critiques of corporate 'mattering' can be found in McDowell and Court's (1994: 727) discussion of embodied subjectivities in merchant banks, in a study that begins by acknowledging that 'not only is the workplace a significant site of the social construction of feminine and masculine identities but in an increasing range of service sector occupations, a gendered bodily performance is a significant part of selling a product'. McDowell and Court draw on both *Gender Trouble* and *Bodies That Matter* to consider the relationship between gender performativity and embodiment. With reference to the City of London, they show how the necessity of selling oneself as part of the product or service challenges idealisations of male workers 'as disembodied rational subjects, while not necessarily disrupting the inferior position of embodied women'. Their analysis focuses on cultural representations of bankers in mainstream media and in corporate materials produced by banks and other financial institutions, and bankers' self-images constructed through their everyday sense-making processes and relations between colleagues and clients.

Their account shows how women are 'literally out of place at work', especially so in an environment in which, at least at first sight, 'disembodied pinstripe suits are the major actors' (McDowell and Court, 1994: 729 and 727). Their analysis of gendered 'mattering' in the City emphasizes Butler's point (discussed earlier) that to argue that gender performativity is temporally and spatially specific does not mean that there is no substance or material form to the body; on the contrary, it highlights how and why that materiality takes the form that it does, and what this means in specific contexts, in this case, a very distinctive organizational sector and setting. As they summarize it, their study shows how 'materiality, representations of appropriate workplace gendered performances, and everyday social practices in combination differentially position men and women at work' (McDowell and Court, 1994: 732).

As Borgerson (2005) has also emphasized, Butler's work on performativity and materiality provides an important linkage between semiotics and phenomenology in thinking through the process of 'mattering' within/through organizational life. Butler's emphasis on what she calls 'the scenography . . . of construction' (Butler, 1993: 28), noted above, could be a direct reference to organization, connecting to systems of thought such as the heterosexual matrix as signifying economies that wield power, to paraphrase Butler, in the demarcation of the conditions of possibility framing cultural intelligibility. Seen in this way, that is as a largely organizational process, mattering becomes 'a morphogenesis that takes place through a set of identificatory projections' (Butler, 1993: 17), producing bodies as the 'matter of signification' on organizational terms and through organizational processes, within/through organizational settings. Bodies, understood in this way, therefore constitute an 'intentionally *organized materiality*' (Butler, 1988: 521, *emphasis added*), compelled, constrained and ordered according to terms and imperatives that produce a sedimentation of the norms of cultural (organizational) legibility through which particular, organizationally valuable, performances (materializations) are either accorded or denied recognition.

Echoing Adorno's (1973 [1966]) critique of identity thinking—the social effort that continually works to maintain congruity between the conceptual and experiential—Butler's (2004b) understanding of this fundamentally organizational process as one of a perpetual un/doing (see Chapter 3) captures her sense of how we are simultaneously acted upon and act in the social (organizational) life world. This is important to understanding her sense of how identity thinking perpetuates a binary, hierarchical organization of the desire for recognition, and of how this is mediated and materialized in social life and relations—arguably the central theme of *Bodies That Matter*.

Emphasizing her (again, Hegelian) view of the subject as 'a structure in formation', and alluding only in passing to her account of this as 'a theory . . . of organization' (Butler, 1987: 10 and 11), Butler brings to the fore the fundamental role of signification in compelling a particular model, or materialization, of subject formation. In doing so, she highlights the importance of signification to the relationship between performativity, materiality and the organization of the desire for recognition as this is mediated in, and materialized through, for instance, the landscaping of corporate artefacts that shape organizationally compelled ways of being. Seen in this way, corporate imagery can be understood as cultural configurations that organize, for example, particular versions of gender in order to produce organizationally legible and therefore viable subjects. This production can be read as a form of organizational performativity, with the significatory effects that are produced evoking what Butler (1993: 219) describes, alluding to the ek-static status of the signified self as a situation of being always outside of or beside oneself (see

Introduction and Chapter 1), as the 'uneasy sense of standing under a sign to which one does and does not belong', as noted earlier. As

> strategic interventions into the perpetual process of becoming a . . . subject at work, mediations that seek to integrate human being and human doing on organizational terms, [corporate] images can be construed as attempts to manage and materialize limited levels of mutual recognition.
>
> (Hancock and Tyler, 2007: 528)

This means that they rely on a contrived process of misrecognition, designed to ensure that the emergence of the subject is configured on corporate terms and in the form of a 'corporate body':

> So as to result in a particular sense of self-consciousness, the attainment of which appears to be possible only through an institutionally mediated relationship that entices the individual to act upon and enter into inter-subjective relations in a particular, embodied way.
>
> (Hancock and Tyler, 2007: 528)

Phenomenologically, this highlights the working body as a medium through which viable, intelligible subjectivity is constituted as congruent with organizational imperatives, in and through a process of organization, enacted within and through organizational settings (including virtual ones), echoing Hegel's concern with the body as a mechanism through which the Self encounters its Other. The body is encoded with compelled meanings through which organizations develop and sustain a *modus vivendi* and hence, 'elicit recognition and identification, albeit in a reified state of ontological anthropomorphism' (Hancock and Tyler, 2007: 529).

Bodies that materialize employability are therefore those that come to 'matter' in this sense, yet the idea of a final, full 'mattering', or being able to embody a resolution to the difference between a corporate bodily ideal and the complexities and imperfections of the lived body, remains (as Butler contends, of course) perpetually elusive. As Cremin (2010) has emphasized, the deliberate ambiguity of the conditions governing the possibility of attaining mutual, inter-corporeal identification both with, and within, an employing organization are *strategically* elusive, tactically signifying the negatively dialectical relationship between ontological desire and the performative demands of organizational life. To put it simply, we can never be or become 'enough' as organizations value, for instance, gender and other bodily ideals that can never be fully, corporeally realized, or espouse a deliberately unattainable, open-ended ideal such as 'excellence'. In affective, embodied terms, this results in organizations perpetuating 'a predominantly aestheticized regime of meaning that repeatedly constructs gender in accordance with organizational imperatives that continue to co-opt its binary, hierarchical configuration' (Hancock and Tyler, 2007: 529).

The way in which these aestheticized regimes of meaning shape inter-sections between gender and other aspects of identity such as social class has been an on-going concern for organizational scholars and activists. In professions such as the law, for instance, research shows that women have to negotiate a binary, hierarchal gender divide in/through their bodies along other fault lines such as those shaping age, social class, disability, race, culture and ethnicity. As one partner in a law firm (cited in Haynes, 2012: 10) described it, women have to tread 'a very fine line between assertive and shrill and you can't go over the shrill line'. This meant that, for the lawyers and accountants in Haynes' study, 'they were aware of the need to be assertive but not to be perceived as overly aggressive even though the nature of the job requires a degree of physical presence, performativity and authority'. The implication of this is that the range of 'corporeal signs and other discursive means' (Butler, 1990: 185) available to women as they performatively enact embodied, subjective credibility in a courtroom for instance, is relatively limited.

In a similar vein, in their recent discussion of the organization of the menopausal body, Jack et al. (2019) highlight concerns with how time 'matters' for women's embodied and subjective experiences of menopause at work, suggesting that time is significant/significatory for two interrelated reasons. First, 'temporal modalities matter because they present distinct conditions of possibility for gendered agency in organizational settings'. Second, time matters to accounts of organizational embodiment and subjectivity because of 'the political and ethical implications of the disruptive temporality associated with generative forms of gendered agency', a point demonstrated in their discussion of the immediacy, locality and contextual specificity of what they call 'a body politics of surprise'. The latter emphasizes feminist inter-corporeality as distinct from a programmatic and normative containment of embodied lived experience as a way of potentially recognizing the complexity of lived experience that becomes conflated in the coherence of an organizationally intelligible embodied self, as the possible basis for a feminist workplace politics and ethics that draws from and develops insights from Butler's (1993) writing, notably her play on the dialectics of 'mattering'.

A similar case is made in Lee's (2018) discussion of breastfeeding bodies which, although drawing primarily on Diprose's (2012) writing on corporeal generosity (see Hancock, 2008), shares much in common with Butler's concern with the fate of bodies that don't matter, as in, those that materialize difference in such a way as to render them subject to constant misrecognition or negation. For Lee, difficulties accommodating breastfeeding in contemporary workplaces (not just practically, we might argue, but ontologically as well, due to the liminal nature of the bodily processes involved) reflect wider problems with how bodies and intimacies are understood when they are encountered organizationally. Lee argues that, while the concept of corporeal generosity is useful in theorizing the intimate relationship involved in breastfeeding, 'it is also essential to recognise that the labour involved in this embodied, relational practice goes largely unvalued' (Lee, 2018: 77), so that women's association with giving has led to the devaluing of reproductive labour and care work.

Van Amsterdam and van Eck (2018) make similar points in their critique of how bodies deemed to be 'fat' are stigmatized as 'not mattering' within work organizations and the labour market more widely. Their study brings to the fore how those whose bodies are deemed to be overweight within social and organizational contexts that mark 'fatness' as offensive, shameful and abject are attributed only a limited worth in a labour market that thrives on a thin ideal, partly as a result of being denied the capacity to signify anything of value.

What analyses such as Lee's, and van Amsterdam and van Eck's highlight is how, through the relationship between performativity and signification, women's bodies (e.g. when breastfeeding or when labelled as 'fat') come to be misrecognized and rendered abject, so that while their materiality in terms of their physical substance is accentuated, the meaning of this materiality (the 'matter' of its value and in turn, the 'value' of its matter) gets negated. The latter includes a devaluation of breastfeeding *as work*, even though (perhaps especially though) that work may involve the formation and nurturance of a close emotional bond between mother and child as well as the vital provision of physical sustenance and nourishment (Lee, 2018).

A similar process of misrecognition is depicted in Rajan-Rankin's (2018) account of the identity work undertaken by service workers in a transnational context. By 'identity work', Rajan-Rankin refers specifically to the labour involved in masking national identity to imply geographical proximity to a western client by those employed in outsourced call centre operations in India. Also drawing on Butler, she shows how a 'West-Rest' critical dichotomy over-simplifies complex processes of identity construction involving a dynamic set of embodied practices that, in a similar way to breastfeeding, accentuate the materiality of bodily substance yet at the same time, de-value the (unmanaged) body's significatory potential; like breastfeeding mothers, Indian call centre workers' bodies matter in a material sense, but not in a meaningful way, and hence are subject to managerial modification. This takes various forms, including:

> *Voice and accent training* (removal of mother tongue influence and developing a generic Americanized accent), *locational masking* (to keep up appearances that the service is provided in the same location as the client base), *deceptive mimicry* (ability to hold short conversations that include references to the customers' cultural context), and

visualization techniques used to imagine the western client and their context.

(Rajan-Rankin, 2018: 11)

As Rajan-Rankin (2018: 13) emphasizes, such techniques have their origins in colonial power relations that continue to frame hierarchical relations between outsourced workers and western clients, perpetuating 'the process of othering and potential for rejection if the presumed identity performance falters'.

Highlighting the very situated nature of 'mattering', Jack et al. (2019), Lee (2018) and Rajan-Rankin (2018) remind us that as well as organizational bodies, workspaces and settings are important sites on which the power dynamics shaping the relationship between performativity, signification and materiality are played out. This means that gender, for instance, is materialized in and through work 'spaces that matter' in accordance with the dominant norms that condition recognition (Tyler and Cohen, 2010). This illustrates how gender performativity and its materialization in the form of bodies that matter in Butler's account, is driven largely by the desire for recognition of the gendered self as a viable, intelligible, *organizational* subject. In other words, underpinning our performance of gender is the desire to project a coherent and compelling self, one that is likely to be recognized and valorised by those who 'matter' to us in our workplaces and settings, and in the labour market more generally (e.g. actual or potential employers, managers and supervisors, colleagues and other co-workers, and customers/clients or service users/consumers). But this self is one which, in Butler's (2004b) terms, produces its coherence at the cost of its own complexity—see Chapter 3, as the recitation of a relatively, instrumentally narrow range of norms shapes the terms on which subjectivity will be deemed viable, or worthy of recognition.

As a reminder, Butler's (2000a: xxiii) view is that gender norms 'establish the ontological field in which bodies may be given legitimate expression'. Drawing on insights from *Gender Trouble*, this means that intelligible performances are those that conform to the binary and hierarchical terms of heteronormativity, and to the norms governing social and organizational life more widely. Although Butler's analysis of this process focuses primarily on the citation of cultural norms over time, it is her references to the materialization of subjectivity *in situ*, and her passing comments on gender as 'instituted in an exterior space' (Butler, 2000a: 141) that have also been of interest to organizational scholars (McDowell and Court, 1994; Gregson and Rose, 2000), as noted earlier. Such approaches emphasize how 'spaces that matter' are those that 'represent a materialization of the cultural forms according to which particular . . . performances are enacted, and through which adherence to those norms is signified, successfully evoking recognition of viable . . . subjectivity' (Tyler and Cohen, 2010: 193).

Hirst and Schwabenland (2018: 174) reiterate this in their study of how gender is performed in the context of an office setting designed to encourage intensive, fluid networking. Analysing how gender norms are materialized, experienced and resisted in this setting, their analysis shows how gender is constantly in contestation, as 'different elements are reproduced, discarded and recombined in many different ways' within the context of physical spaces which shape the ways in which gender is enacted within and through organizational settings.

Despite her criticisms of Žižek's psychoanalytic influences, in particular his insistence on a clear boundary around the Real, Butler draws on his discussion of political signifiers in a way that has important repercussions for organizational scholars concerned to understand—and address—the ways in which organizational spaces materialize who and what 'matters', and on whose terms. Noting how signifiers such as 'woman' should not be thought of as descriptive designations of actual subject positions (because they do not correspond to the complexities of lived experience), Butler aligns herself with Žižek's interest in political signifiers as sites of mobilization and contestation; as Kirby (2006: 73) notes, both see potential in their capacity to act as 'identificatory anchors whose constitutive force is transformational'. Kirby feels that Butler is, again, worth quoting at some length on this when she aruges that:

> Every signifier is the site of a perpetual *méconnaisance;* it produces the expectation of a unity, a full and final recognition that can never be achieved. Paradoxically, the failure of such signifiers. . . . fully to describe the constituency they name is precisely what constitutes these signifiers as sites of phantasmatic investment and discursive re-articulation. It is what opens the signifier to new meanings and new possibilities for political re-signification.
>
> (Butler, 1993: 191; cited in Kirby, 2006: 73)

Following Žižek, the crux of Butler's intervention, opening up a line of thinking that has yet to be fully explored by organizational scholars concerned with 'mattering', lies in her dialectical insistence on signification as a process of demarcation that is perpetually unfinished, the relevance of which becomes clear when we connect it to her emphasis on signification as an organizing rather than a descriptive, representational process. As Kirby (2006: 79) notes, there is 'a permanent recalcitrance, or failure of fit, between the referent and symbolization'; a gap remains that implicitly 'contains' difference as well as the political possibility of its re-signification. Signification or mattering, seen in this way, becomes simply the cultural product of a hegemonic process that is revealed, through semiotic critique, as being open to contestation.

In *Bodies That Matter*, Butler explains this point with reference to the signifier 'woman' as a sign of this discrepancy between language and its referent, when she notes that the extent to which the category 'woman' 'can never be descriptive is the very condition of its political [as opposed to semiotic, or representational] efficacy' (Butler, 1993: 221; cited in Kirby, 2006: 79). Laying out the groundwork for her later discussion in *Undoing Gender* (Butler, 2004b), she emphasizes here that because signification is a process that is always incomplete, any appeal to the integrity of identity is illusive, but more than this, it elides the political potential of this lack of integrity, or coherence.

To refute Lacanian interpretations of this 'lack', Butler (1993) turns to Laclau and Mouffe (1985) to emphasize the open-ended possibilities attached to the constitutive antagonisms and contingencies associated with subject formation as a significatory process, one that, to recap, she frames as profoundly organizational. The latter's faith in the political possibility of re-signification derives from their conviction that ideological structures are unable to fix or foreclose themselves because of the constant presence of ways of being that are 'outside' of posited identity but which remain part of the social. Butler takes this as an endorsement of the political possibility attached to contingency, or negativity in dialectical terms, a strand of her argument in *Bodies That Matter* that Kirby discusses largely with reference to Butler's reading of Derrida, Žižek, Laclau and Mouffe, but which is largely Hegelian in its origins in her thinking here and in other texts. It is to the political potential—and we might surmise—its reorganizing/organizational capacity—that she turns in subsequent work, to which we turn next.

Notes

1. See Butler's (1993: 9, *original emphasis*) explanation for shifting from a focus on gender construction to materialization where she argues that she does so in order to emphasize 'matter' 'not as site or surface, but as *a process of materialization that stabilizes over time to produce the effect of boundary, fixity and surface we call matter*'. In this sense, it is as the 'very principle of the body's cultural formation' that materialization 'can be described as *the sedimenting effect of a regulated iterability*' (Butler, 1993: 252, n.12).

2. Butler explains that she draws specifically on the Aristotelian notion of the 'schema' as a culturally variable set of principles governing 'formativity and intelligibility'. However, she also goes on to note that her understanding of how bodily schemas come to materialize normativity within specific historical contexts is similar to that described by Foucault (1991) in *Discipline and Punish* (Butler, 1993: 33) in relation to the materialization of the prisoner's body. In her analysis of the regimes governing bodies that come to 'matter', she argues that it is 'cultural configurations of power' that organize the 'normative and productive operations of subject-constitution' (Butler, 1993: 106), but (in contrast to Foucault), she remains quite vague on the empirical detail of who or what modes of organization lie behind these cultural configurations.

3. Kirby (2006: 82) notes that Butler deliberately uses the term 'matter' rather than 'substance' when referring to the materiality of the body because 'the

former is a synonym for significance/signification'. In Kirby's reading, Butler avoids bodily substance—the 'very meat of carnality that is born and buried, the stuff of decay that seems indifferent to semiosis' as she puts it—focusing her attention instead on the surface of the body and its constant subjection to 'a process of on-going signification, contestation and re-inscription' (Kirby, 2006: 83).

4. Butler refers in later work to her sense that, between *Gender Trouble* (Butler, 1990) and *Bodies That Matter* (Butler, 1993), she was accused of having made the body 'less, rather than more relevant' (Butler, 2015b: 17).

5. For her, taking this process as a political problematic is not the same as 'doing away with the subject'; on the contrary, as she puts it, 'to deconstruct the concept of matter or that of bodies is not to negate or refuse either term. To deconstruct these terms means . . . to displace them from the contexts in which they have been deployed as instruments of oppressive power' (Butler, 1995a: 49 and 51).

6. In *Bodies That Matter* Butler replaces the term 'heterosexual matrix' with 'heterosexual hegemony' as the framework responsible for 'the crafting of matters sexual and political' (Butler, 1993: xii).

7. When Butler makes this latter point, she draws on Eve Sedgwick's (2002) critique of the marriage vow, arguing that through this particular speech act, 'marriage organizes sexuality'; just as in the case of Alexandra de Souza, persistent dead naming organizes her gender subjectivity according to terms not of her own choosing, reminding us of the disorientating experience of 'standing under a sign to which one does and does not belong', as Butler (1993: 129) puts it.

8. Elsewhere, Butler also refers to the 'possibility' of resignification 'as an alternative reading of performativity and politics' (Butler, 1997a: 69).

9. Butler makes a similar point about transgendering. Speaking in an interview in 1999 (and mindful of a 'globalization' of trans experiences as being a possible interpretation of her words), she suggests that while she did not adequately engage with transgendering in *Gender Trouble*, the arguments were 'theoretically very sympathetic' to trans lives and experiences. In particular, she emphasizes what she describes (alluding to Freud's writing on the uncanny) as the spectral presence of transgendering in 'mundane heterosexuality'. As she puts it, 'there is a kind of spectre of transgendering that heterosexuals work with all the time . . . that . . . haunts any stable gender identity' (More, 2016: 286 and 294).

10. In an interesting example of what this means that might be familiar to many readers, Sara Ahmed (2012) describes her own experience of being in a departmental meeting in which she was the only female professor. The colleague who was chairing the meeting introduced people in turn using everyone's academic titles, except for her: 'This is Sara', announced the chair. Ahmed recalls, 'In taking up the space that had been given to me, I feel like a girl, and I giggle'. Hers is a 'girling' moment in Butler's (1993: 7) terms, one that marks her off, separates her, as different from the bodies that materialize gendered perceptions of what it means to be, and to appear in the designated physical and conceptual space in question, as a professor. For Butler, it is a process that reiterates the 'founding interpellation' of gender attribution (Butler, 1993: 8). As Ahmed puts it, 'when you look like what they expect a professor to be, you are treated like a professor. A sombre and serious mood follows those who have the right kind of body, the body that allows them to pass seamlessly into the category, when the category has a certain affective value' (Ahmed, 2012: 176). I had a similar experience when attending a graduation event once. A PhD student who was with her family asked if her

son could have a photograph taken with me as he had never met a professor before. She said he was shocked as he had expected me to look more like Dumbledore, headmaster of Hogwarts school in the Harry Potter stories. All in good humour, I found myself apologizing for not being a man with a long grey beard (or having any magical powers). For a similar discussion, see Mair and Frew's (2018) account of gender performativity at academic conferences, which emphasizes how the performance pressures associated with being an academic connect to those governing gender credibility within knowledge intensive environments.

11. Others are more critical however, notably Fraser (1995a: 68), who in extending her critique of what she describes as Butler's esoteric and self-distancing idiom, is sceptical about the political capacity of her use of the term 'resignification'. Replacing critique with signification is a move that Fraser describes as 'puzzling' because Butler does not have a clear response to the problem 'why is resignification good?'. In opting to valorize such as epistemologically neutral term, Butler seems to disempower normative critique—a point that has significant implications for organization theorists concerned with developing critical accounts of workplace settings and/or corporate practices that are often replete with reificatory resignifications of discourses and idioms that circulate within social movements and struggles—the ubiquity of corporate commitments to equality and inclusion is but one widespread example (Ahmed, 2012). Since it 'surrenders the normative moment', Fraser argues (1995a: 69), resignification is no substitute for critique.

3 Un/Doing Organization— Coherence at the Cost of Complexity

As an important link between *Excitable Speech* and *Undoing Gender*, Butler's (1997b: 14–15) book, *The Psychic Life of Power* takes time to think through a question that vexes her work, or at least her critics' views on her work, namely the relationship between agency and subjectivity. As she frames it in this text, her concern is largely that the subject is a site of some ambivalence, emerging 'both as the *effect* of a prior power and as the *condition of possibility* for a radically conditioned form of agency'. For Butler, any credible theory of subjectivity must take account of this ambivalence as both the basis of subjection and as the locus of resistance to that subjection; subjectivity is simultaneously 'acted on' and 'acted by', a dynamic captured in her notion that gender is what is 'put on'.

In her exploration of how the subject is formed in subordination, Butler draws variously from Hegel, Althusser, Nietzsche and Foucault to emphasize the dialectical nature of the relationship between the subject's inauguration in relations of subordination and the extent to which that very subordination provides the subject's 'continuing condition of possibility' (Butler, 1997b: 8). Her concern is with the ways in which subjection exploits the desire for recognition, circumscribing the domain of liveable sociality, effectively by 'forgetting' the basis of that sociality as our embodied mutual vulnerability.

Returning once again to *The Phenomenology of Spirit* (Hegel, 1977), Butler reminds us of the transition that Hegel makes from his narration of 'Lordship and Bondage', a section of text that has provided an important philosophical reference point for subsequent emancipatory political theories and movements, to 'The Freedom of Self-Consciousness'. In the latter, Hegel emphasizes that the freedom of self-consciousness remains 'enmeshed in servitude' (cited in Butler, 1997b: 31), amounting to what Butler calls a dystopic resolution that has gained a timely resonance, particularly when applied to theoretical analyses of work, organization and society.

The complex question of how power can be both oppressive and enabling, crudely equating to moral categories of 'bad' and 'good', and signifying respectively, 'a power that breaks' and a 'power that makes' as

Kirby (2006: 109) neatly sums it up is a preoccupation that Butler once again, 'fleshes out' in *Undoing Gender* (Butler, 2004b). The underlying concern of this text is with the preconditions attached to 'the production and maintenance of legible humanity' (Butler, 2004b: 11), and with the work that goes into sustaining subjective coherence, and securing recognition for that coherence.

It is here, in what is perhaps the second most influential of Butler's books in work and organization studies, that Butler explains how, just as gender is always a process of doing, so too is it simultaneously an undoing. Here, as with the case of 'mattering' considered in Chapter 2, Butler plays on the term 'undoing' as referring both to an unravelling of the subject as well as to the subject's capacity to challenge and resist this unravelling. She builds on her earlier explorations of how the subject becomes 'passionately attached to his or her own subordination' (Butler, 1997b: 6), re-engaging this concern with her performative reading of Hegel's master-slave dialectic and Althusser's (2001) scenography of the subject's interpellation[1] (see Chapter 4) to consider the relationship between subjectivity, vulnerability and agency. If, as she puts it, we are made up at least in part by virtue of our embodied, mutual vulnerability, then 'we are constituted as fields of desire and physical vulnerability, at once publicly assertive and vulnerable' (Butler, 2004b: 18).

In *Undoing Gender* Butler gives more explicit methodological treatment to these 'signature themes in her work',[2] considering *how* the subject comes to be simultaneously, perpetually 'undone' (Kirby, 2006: 123). She also introduces themes developed in more depth in later works, notably her view that gender and sexuality are not 'possessions' but rather *'modes of being disposed*, ways of being for another or, indeed, by virtue of another' (Butler, 2004b: 19, *emphasis added*). In this sense, the challenge becomes how to think through what kinds of communities might be composed of those who live perpetually beside themselves as we open up the possibilities attached to a politics of inter-corporeal vulnerability, considering what this might mean in and for social and organizational life, a theme we return to in later chapters (see Chapters 5 and 6, and Postscript).

As noted above, as well as the normative violence enacted by the subject's 'undoing', Butler also emphasizes both the agentic capacity of the subject, or to be more precise, the subjective potential of human agency, at the same time as recognizing the constraints that compel particular performances through which that capacity may or may not be realized. Her view is that normativity is what binds us to who we are, and who we might be, in so far as it both creates unity only through exclusion, and in doing so both constrains and enables life; this is what Butler (2004b: 206) describes as 'the doubleness of the norm'. This 'doubleness' or paradoxical nature of social norms means that while we cannot accept them as they are, equally 'we cannot do without them' (Butler, 2004b: 207); this is what she alludes to when she argues that governmental norms make our lives 'unliveable', particularly for those rendered abject by their negating effects and by the material consequences of that negation.

Butler's understanding of subject formation as a perpetual un/doing, normatively enabled and constrained, bound through 'sameness' and 'difference', has clear Hegelian origins in her thinking, highlighting as it does the continual presence of the Other as both necessary and potentially counter to the premise of the Self. It has significant implications for work and organization studies: as the basis of critique, this ontology opens up important connections between the processes and power relations involved in becoming an organizational subject at an individual level, as well at a more corporate, collective level and within the wider context of labour markets shaped by normative expectations governing subjective viability.[3]

With this as her starting premise in *Undoing Gender*, Butler (2004b) develops themes introduced in *Bodies That Matter* arguing that subjectivity is always a process of un/doing through which, as she puts it (and as noted earlier), 'the subject produces its coherence at the cost of its own complexity' (Butler, 1993: 115). She also, as Lloyd (2007) notes, draws from the conceptual framework established in *Gender Trouble* (and earlier—see Butler, 1987, 1988) in her critique of the norms governing cultural intelligibility and the question of who or what will be accorded recognition, and on what basis. In essence, it is to the question of liveability or 'a politics of human life' that Butler (2004b: 225) turns. The aim, as she puts it, is 'not to celebrate difference as such but to establish . . . conditions for sheltering and maintaining life that resists models of assimilation' (Butler, 2004b: 4). A critical question for her, and for organizational scholars, is how might the world be *reorganized* so as not to impose a model of life that demeans the complex ways in which lives are crafted and lived, through assimilatory encounters with difference, at the same time as resisting the on-going threat of negation, a theme that also draws from her concern in *Bodies That Matter* with the violent foreclosure of lives deemed abject.

Turning its focus quite specifically to questions of liveability, what *Undoing Gender* emphasizes is Butler's view that viable subjectivity requires sustaining a performance that conforms to normative expectations and the terms of recognition. For organizational scholars, this raises significant questions about the role that is played by organizations in compelling or constraining convincing performances, and about the impact of organizing schemas such as the heterosexual matrix on shaping lived experiences of organizational life. In Butler's terms, working lives are a constant struggle for recognition through which a person's sense of self has to be continually put 'at risk' (Butler, 2004b: 149); as she puts it, 'becoming' is 'no simple or continuous affair, but *an uneasy practice of repetition and its risks*' (Butler, 1997b: 30, *emphasis added*). This process, and its connection to the organization of the desire for recognition, is the focus of this chapter.

Butler's concerns beg the question of what needs to be done by organizational scholars, practitioners and activists in order to maximize 'the possibilities for a liveable life', and to minimize the likelihood of living 'an unbearable life, or indeed, [of] social or literal death' (Butler, 2004b: 8). For Butler, the starting point for answers to these questions lies in recognition as the connection between politics and ethics, a theme to which we return in Chapters 4, 5 and 6 with reference to Butler's discussions of relationality and corporeal vulnerability. In *Undoing Gender* Butler already introduces these latter themes, however, through a return to her focus on the ek-static character of existence which, she argues, 'is essential to the possibility of persisting as human' (Butler, 2004b: 33), reminding us of the ontological, political and ethical significance of living beside oneself.

Un/Doing (as) Recognition

Butler's understanding of 'undoing' is particularly influenced by what is arguably one of the most radical propositions in her writing, namely her insistence that if becoming a subject is a process of doing then, as noted earlier, it is always also a process of undoing. Here undoing is linked to the desire for recognition of oneself as a viable, culturally intelligible subject. For Butler (2005) all subjectivities are precarious in so far as our need for mutual recognition renders us vulnerable; at best, we open ourselves up to being overlooked, snubbed or ridiculed, at worst subject to physical or physic harm. However, some subjectivities are more precarious than others, such as those who appear to challenge, resist or simply elide gender norms, for instance (O'Shea, 2018; Schilt and Connell, 2007; Thanem and Wallenberg, 2016).

It is in this respect that Butler connects her more ontological concerns with performativity (Butler, 1988, 1990/2000a) to her growing interest in bringing more explicitly political issues into focus in her later work, from *Undoing Gender* (Butler, 2004b) onwards. It is in making this link that she builds on her earlier suggestion that subjectivity can be 'undone', at least in part, by revealing its constructed and performative qualities (Butler, 1990/2000a), including those which are oppressive and exploitative. In other words, in the very performativity of being a subject lies the potential capacity to reflexively undo its constraining effects, opening up the possibility of reinstating alternative performances that potentially challenge subjective normativity, or at least open to question the terms of recognition upon which it depends, and through which it comes to be organized.

Research on lived experiences of 'organizational undoing' considered here indicate the ways in which attributing recognition to certain forms of subjectivity while disavowing others constitutes a significant, but often overlooked, process of organization. How this is woven into performative practices enacted within and through organizational settings is important to consider. Foregrounding not only 'the fluidity and uncertainty of gender categories' (De Souza et al., 2016: 600), but the *organization* of gender, Butler's critique of performativity as a process of un/doing has significant implications for our understanding of subjectivity, and particularly (but not limited to) gender subjectivity, in work and organization studies.

Butler on Gendered Un/Doing

Butler introduces the idea of gender as a perpetual un/doing in earlier writing on performativity and phenomenology, when she emphasizes that

> gender is not a radical choice or project . . . but neither is it imposed or inscribed upon the individual. . . . The body is not passively scripted with cultural codes, as if it were a lifeless recipient of wholly pre-given cultural relations.
>
> (Butler, 1988: 526)

Here she sets out her understanding of gender as enacted not within a performative vacuum, but as compelled and constrained within specific social—and organizational—contexts.

Butler is well aware of the political challenges associated with a performative critique of gendered undoing, also addressing this concern in some of her earliest writing (see Butler, 1988). Citing Benjamin's (1988: 37, *emphasis added*) observation that the critique of gender complementarity results in a paradox that at once challenges gender as an oppositional category while at the same time, 'recognizing that these positions inescapably *organize* experience', she highlights that non-identity thinking poses an ontological and political quandary for feminism's emancipatory impetus, and by implication, for critical accounts of work and organizational life.

In *Undoing Gender*, as noted earlier, Butler develops themes introduced in her earlier writing (particularly in her discussion of 'critically queer' in *Bodies That Matter*) and focuses explicitly on 'what it might mean to undo restrictively normative conceptions of sexual and gendered life' (Butler, 2004b: 1). Equally, she emphasizes that the essays contained in *Undoing Gender* are about the lived experience of '*becoming undone*' (Butler, 2004b: 1). This builds on her earlier account of the process of becoming as one of misrecognition shaped by the logic of the heterosexual matrix, and also her discussion of abjection as central to the production of viable subjectivities. Gender, she argues here, is a kind of doing but not one that is automatic or mechanical, but rather 'a practice of improvisation *within a scene of constraint*' (Butler, 2004b: 1, *emphasis added*).

In this latter statement, she emphasizes how those who come to 'matter' are simultaneously those whose bodies and performances conform to the semiotic reference points shaping viable ways of being, and at the same time, are recognized as having the capacity to signify who and what is of value within any given context. Again, this has important implications for how we think about subject formation in relation to work identities and labour market opportunities. As Butler argues, emphasizing the dialectics of un/doing as she sees it:

> One does not 'do' one's gender alone. One is always 'doing' *with or for another,* even if the other is only imaginary. What I call my 'own' gender appears perhaps at times as something that I author or, indeed, own. But *the terms that make up one's gender are, from the start, outside oneself, beyond oneself* in a sociality that has no single author.
>
> (Butler, 2004b: 1, *emphasis added*)

Here, Butler articulates several important aspects of her theory of gender performativity that are significant for her approach to 'un/doing' and for organization studies; first, she reaffirms her largely phenomenological commitment to a processual ontology that frames becoming gendered as an inter-subjective process but also (in a departure from De Beauvoir) one that does not precede but rather enables subject formation. In this sense, she reaffirms her commitment to an effective or performative ontology of gender. Second, she also emphasizes (echoing her concern with the heterosexual matrix) the significance of citationality to this process (the 'terms') implying both a cultural reference point and a boundary (as in a contractual agreement). Further, she *situates* Hegel's account of the desire for recognition within social relations and contexts, arguing that:

> The terms by which we are recognized as human are socially articulated and changeable. And sometimes the very terms that confer 'humanness' on some individuals are those that deprive certain other individuals of the possibility of achieving that status.
>
> (Butler, 2004b: 2)

If the domain of intelligibility is 'that which is produced as a consequence of recognition according to prevailing social norms' (Butler, 2004b: 3), the politics of un/doing gender in part lie in recognizing that

> if my doing is dependent on what is done to me or, rather, the ways in which I am done by norms, then the possibility of my persistence as an 'I' depends upon my *being able to do something with what is done with me.*
>
> (Butler, 2004b: 3, *emphasis added*)

This latter point, in particular, has important implications for how we think about resistance to organizational power relations and modes of subjectification. As noted earlier, Butler's approach is more discernibly critical here than in earlier writing in so far as she highlights the importance of critique as a politically engaged endeavour, whereby

> Critique is understood as an interrogation of the terms by which life is constrained in order to open up the possibility of different modes of living [and working]; in other words, not to celebrate difference as such but to establish more inclusive conditions for sheltering and maintaining life that resists modes of assimilation.
>
> (Butler, 2004b: 4)

By way of illustration, she goes on to emphasize that the gendered organization of the desire for recognition, manifest in strategic interventions into the process of un/doing gender (such as attempts to diagnose gender dysphoria, for instance) 'imposes a model of coherent gendered life that *demeans the complex ways in which gendered lives are crafted and lived*' (Butler, 2004b: 5, *emphasis added*). The dialectics of desire/recognition, and of un/doing gender imply however that strategic or tactical cooperation may be the route through which oppressive ways of being can be undone, if for example,

> The diagnostic means by which trans-sexuality is attributed implies a pathologization, but undergoing that pathologization process constitutes one of the important ways in which the desire to change one's sex might be satisfied. *The critical question thus becomes, how might the world be reorganized so that this conflict can be ameliorated?*
>
> (Butler, 2004b: 5, *emphasis added*)

This question, one that revisits some of Butler's earlier quandaries revolving around the implications of her performative ontology for feminist emancipatory politics, has important implications for a range of political movements—her primary concern being with 'the production of the parameters of personhood' (Butler, 2004b: 56). In this respect, she focuses on, as she puts it, 'the critical . . . condition of the human as it speaks itself at the limits of what we think we know' (Butler, 2004b: 74). Moving beyond individual acts of undoing, she highlights that 'changing the institutions by which humanly viable choice is established and maintained is a prerequisite for the exercise of self-determination' (Butler, 2004b: 7). Framed in this way, 'organization' is positioned simultaneously as the problem and as part of the possible solution.

In her first essay in *Undoing Gender*, 'Beside Oneself: On the Limits of Sexual Autonomy', evoking/echoing (but not explicitly engaging with) contributions to the debate on feminist ethics by Benhabib (1992) and

Diprose (2012 [2002]), Butler articulates her concern with a politics of corporeal vulnerability, arguing that 'we are constituted politically in part by virtue of the social vulnerability of our bodies; we are constituted as fields of desire and physical vulnerability, at once publicly assertive and vulnerable' (Butler, 2004b: 18). Neither sexuality or gender 'is precisely a possession, but both are to be understood as *modes of being dispossessed*, ways of being for another or, indeed, by virtue of another' (Butler, 2004b: 19, *original emphasis*). Yet, her concern is with 'what kind of community is composed of those who are beside themselves' (Butler, 2004b: 20). Echoing Levinas (1961), she reminds us that we are

> by virtue of our embodiment, given over to an other: this makes us vulnerable to violence, but also to another range of touch, a range that includes the eradication of our being at one end, and the physical support for our lives, at the other.
>
> (Butler, 2004b: 23)

Crucially, we cannot (should not?) endeavour to ' "rectify" this situation' (Butler, 2004b: 23); on the contrary, we should recognize (remember) it. Resonating particularly with Diprose (who also draws on Levinas), Butler emphasizes that

> The value of being beside oneself, of being a porous boundary, given over to others, is finding oneself in a trajectory of desire in which one is not the presumptive centre. The particular sociality that belongs to bodily life, to sexual life, and to becoming gendered (which is always, to a certain extent, becoming gendered *for others*) *establishes a field of ethical enmeshment with others*. . . . As bodies we are always something more than, and other than, ourselves.
>
> (Butler, 2004b: 25, *original emphasis*)

Also echoing Hegel's (1977) account of the body as the medium through which the Self encounters the Other, and hinting at this field of ethical enmeshment as an organizational/organizing one, Butler argues that 'it is through the body that gender and sexuality become exposed to others, implicated in social processes, inscribed by cultural norms, and apprehended in their social meanings' (Butler, 2004b: 20). In other words, the body is 'the site where "doing" and "being done to" become equivocal' (Butler, 2004b: 21). In this sense, 'embodiment denotes a contested set of norms governing who will count as a viable subject' (Butler, 2004b: 28). The body is thus 'a mode of becoming' (Butler, 2004b: 29), but one that is contextually compelled and constrained in and through its becoming.

Twisting the Hegelian narrative in a more Foucauldian direction, as she puts it, leads Butler to argue that 'norms of recognition function to produce and to reproduce the notion of the human' (Butler, 2004b: 31–32).

Her analysis however, remains fundamentally Hegelian, concerned as it is with the ways in which

> our very sense of personhood is linked to the desire for recognition, and that desire places us outside ourselves, in a realm of social norms that we do not fully choose, but that provides the horizon and the resource for any sense of choice that we have.
>
> (Butler, 2004b: 33)

Her second essay, on 'Gender Regulations', emphasizes that 'gender is the mechanism by which notions of masculine and feminine are produced and naturalized, but gender might very well be the apparatus by which such terms are deconstructed and denaturalized' (Butler, 2004b: 42). Again evoking a concern with the semiotics of gender, she argues that 'the field of reality produced by gender norms constitutes the background for the surface appearance of gender in its idealized dimensions' (Butler, 2004b: 52). With reference to the routine surgical 'correction' of intersexed bodies she argues that, for some, being recognized as viably human involves submission to 'the knife of the norm' (Butler, 2004b: 53); 'here the ideality of gendered morphology is quite literally incised in the flesh'. As is characteristic in her writing, here she plays on dual meanings of the term 'regulation', using it as a reference to both 'that which makes regular' and also, following Foucault, a mode of discipline and surveillance.

This is a theme Butler explores particularly in relation to sex reassignment, in her (third) essay in *Undoing Gender* on 'Doing Justice to Someone'. Here (again following Foucault and also drawing on De Beauvoir and Kate Bornstein) she argues that 'the . . . criterion by which we judge a person to be a gendered being . . . posits coherent gender as a presupposition of humanness' (Butler, 2004b: 58). Through sex reassignment, Butler argues, the ideality of gendered morphology marks out 'the parameters of personhood' (Butler, 2004b: 56) heteronormatively. At the end of this essay, she notes that at the time *Undoing Gender* was going to press in 2004, she learnt that David Reimer, about whom she writes in this essay, had ended his own life at the age of 38. As she puts it:

> The norms governing what it is to be a worthy, recognizable, and sustainable human life clearly did not support his life in any continuous or solid way. Life for him was always a wager and a risk, *a courageous and fragile accomplishment*.
>
> (Butler, 2004b: 74, *emphasis added*)

In 'Undiagnosing Gender' she focuses on the paradox of being on the receiving end of a 'gender identity disorder (GID)' diagnosis; desiring recognition, needing support and access to insurance benefits at the same time as resisting pathologization and being reduced to the status of being a passive object of the medical gaze. Her analysis questions why we accept some choices and not others—why is a woman who has breast implants or a man who enlarges his penis not questioned, but a transsexual who seeks surgical adjustment or confirmation is? Why is 'nature' evoked in some such instances but not others? The social meanings of choice and constraint are her main focus here, particularly in terms of the power effects of regulatory discourses and modes of gender organization.

Her Hegelian concern with the desire for recognition is developed particularly in the sixth essay in the book, 'Longing for Recognition'. Here she reminds us that

> It is not the simple presentation of a subject for another that facilitates the recognition of that self-presenting subject by the Other. It is, rather, a process that is engaged when subject and Other understand themselves to be reflected in one another.
>
> (Butler, 2004b: 131)

This dialectical understanding of recognition underpins Butler's conception of subjective un/doing, perhaps most apparent when she argues that 'recognition is motivated by the desire to find oneself reflected [in the Other] where the reflection is not a final expropriation' (Butler, 2004b: 241). Thus, as in Hegel's 'Lordship and Bondage',

> recognition is itself a cultivated form of desire, no longer simply the consumption or negation of alterity, but the uneasy dynamic in which one seeks to find oneself in the Other only to find that that reflection is the sign of one's expropriation and self-loss.
>
> (Butler, 2004b: 241)

In this sense, she reminds us of the philosophical basis of her political critique of the 'tactical' subjection to pathologization discussed earlier, and perhaps to other forms of co-optation. When she explains, for instance, with reference to Jessica Benjamin's (1988) Hegelian discussion of recognition,[4] that recognition takes places within communication, in which subjects are transformed through the communicative action within which they are engaged, Butler notes the theoretical or therapeutic model that this provides. But she is aware that it also provides the possibility of a more assimilatory template (for managerial action, for instance), through mechanisms within organizational life that co-opt not simply the communicative modes of action and engagement on which recognition depends but also the concept of recognition itself (see Ahmed, 2012). What this suggests, and what Butler hints at is that in managerial hands, recognition itself becomes a pathology albeit one that is often (much like the sex reassignment that she writes about more explicitly) tactically acquiesced to. As Butler is very aware, just as exclusionary discourses and imperatives have been appropriated for progressive uses, emancipatory ideals and movements are all too easily co-opted for instrumental ends; the problem within organizational contexts, in this sense (one that again raises Fraser's critique of Butler's faith in the political possibilities attached to resignification[5]) is how we might distinguish between the two, discerning between reified forms of recognition, and those that might be more meaningful. It may well be that 'the lines we draw are invitations to cross over' (Butler, 2004b: 203), but in organizational life, those lines can be disconcertingly blurred and for those living and working on the margins of viability, they can be (literally) lifelines.

This discussion serves as both a point of departure for Butler's concern with the primary bonds of humanity that (following Hegel) she asks us to 're-cognize', as well as a metaphor for her reflections on the conditions required by current social relations for one to be considered a viable human subject. These two issues have important implications for thinking about how oppressive structures and relations might be undone.

In Butler's analysis, the Self in Hegel is marked by 'a primary enthrallment with the Other', one in which that self is put at risk. Thus, it is at the moment of fundamental vulnerability that recognition becomes possible: 'what recognition does at such a moment is, to be sure, to hold destruction in check. . . . And the ethical content of its relationship to the Other is to be found in this fundamental and reciprocal state of being "given over"' (Butler, 2004b: 149). Butler's main concern in this sense is, as she puts it, to think about 'what it might mean to recognize one another when it is a question of so much more than the two of us' (Butler, 2004b: 151); again, this is a theme that has profound implications for the study of organizational life, and to which we return in due course.

Towards the end of *Undoing Gender* Butler explores the state of contemporary feminism in an essay that questions its future as an emancipatory project. Here, she quite bluntly argues that

> Feminism is in a mess, unable to stabilize the terms that facilitate a meaningful agenda. Criticisms of feminism as inattentive to questions of race and to the conditions of global inequalities that condition its Euro-American articulation continue to put into doubt the broad coalitional power of the movement.
>
> (Butler, 2004b: 175)

Noting again how 'progressive terms can be appropriated for regressive aims' (Butler, 2004b: 179), she is particularly critical of the tempered, liberal forms of moderate feminism that have a strong presence in business schools, notably those 'that focus on actualizing women's entrepreneurial potential, hijacking models of self-expression from an earlier, progressive period in the movement' (Butler, 2004b: 175). In the final essay (on 'The Question of Social Transformation'), she reminds us that the norm that binds us creates unity only through a strategy of exclusion; this 'double-ness of the norm' as she puts it (Butler, 2004b: 206) and as noted earlier, both constrains and enables our existence.

In place of Rich's 'compulsory heterosexuality' as her earlier reference point (Butler, 1988, 1990/2000, 1993), Butler offers 'presumptive hetero-sexuality' arguing that 'sexual difference is neither fully given nor fully constructed, but partially both' (Butler, 2004b: 186). What we mean by gender she argues is 'that part of sexual difference that *does* appear as the social . . . as the negotiable, as the constructed' (Butler, 2004b: 186, *original emphasis*).[6] This reiterates her conviction that construction is not only an interpretive or hermeneutic activity that attributes meaning to pre-existent matter such as sex but is instead an active process of mate-rialization. It also reminds us that the category of 'matter' is not simply an ossified product of the activity of the subject but an interminable process articulating a largely Foucauldian notion of productive power, positioning the body as 'a crucial link in the circuit of social production and reproduction, both constituted by and also constituting a given social order' (Cheah, 1996: 112).

Un/Doing Gender in Organization Studies

In one of the few texts to engage with Butler as a phenomenological thinker in work and organization studies, Borgerson (2005) argues that largely Derridean and Lacanian or Foucauldian readings of her work tend to dominate discussions of her ideas, resulting in a relative neglect of the Hegelian aspects of her thinking and particularly her commitment to phenomenology and critical theory.

In her own reading, Borgerson teases out Butler's concern with the desire for recognition, noting how engaging with Hegelian insights and avenues in her work 'can be inspiring and productive—whether one ulti-mately agrees with her or not' (Borgerson, 2005: 66). Borgerson empha-sizes that Butler's performative ontology (see Chapter 1) has important implications for understanding organizations, particularly since 'ste-reotyped, foreclosed and, often, damaging representations of iterations derived from essentialist standpoints remain a crucial concern for organi-zation theory, as well as for understanding and changing organizational environments' (Borgerson, 2005: 71). As she puts it,

> Certain tableaux—repeated representations, imposed codes of behav-iour, or organizational cultures—endlessly re-create normative values and identities which are made available to, constitute and exist in tandem with the subject in contemporary culture. In this way, the iterative normativity of an environment contributes to the subject's constitution.
>
> (Borgerson, 2005: 71)

While her references to organization, certainly in her earlier writing, are relatively passing, it is from *Undoing Gender* (Butler, 2004b) onwards that Butler begins to make more direct, sustained connections between her critique of subject formation and, as she sees it, the gendered organization of the desire for recognition. As Butler (2004b: 215, *emphasis added*) herself puts it, 'we are compelled to ask how the *organization* of gender comes to function as a presumption about how the world is structured' and this opens up important avenues for thinking not simply about performativity within/through organizational life but about organization itself as a performative endeavour that is perpetually un/done.

Un/Doing as an Organizational Process

To recap, Butler's thesis rests on the idea that in the very performativity of subjectivity lies our capacity to reflexively undo its constraining effects, opening up the possibility of reinstating alternative performances that potentially challenge subjective normativity, or at least open to question the terms of recognition upon which it depends, and through which it comes to be organized.

Understanding lived experiences of this 'organizational undoing' is therefore important, not just methodologically but politically, in order to reveal the ways in which attributing recognition to certain forms of subjectivity while disavowing others constitutes a significant, but often overlooked, process of organization, as well as a series of practices enacted within organizational settings.

In her discussion of performing gender in ICT work, Elisabeth Kelan (2010: 5) shows how doing gender at work is a way of rendering individuals readable not simply as social beings, but as 'ideal workers'. Kelan (2010: 183) argues that undoing gender can be accomplished in two ways: by 'ignoring the gender binary . . . [or] the binary itself can be destabilized and thereby come undone'. How individuals, particularly in the workplace, might be able to ignore the gender binary merits further consideration given the persistence of normative regimes of binary, hierarchical classification, and the extent to which these are embedded even within legislative and/or policy measures which are themselves designed to address gender and other inequalities. The multiple and persistent ways in which the latter continue to hail gendered subjects into being through binary, hierarchical modes of recognition also merits further critical consideration.

A related set of concerns revolve around the organizational mechanisms and modes of communication through which what Butler calls 'assaultive speech' rely upon bringing into being or materializing derogated subject positions, precisely in order for them to be 'undone'. Connecting with the themes of *Undoing Gender*, Butler (1997a: 1) explores this most notably in *Excitable Speech* which she begins with the following question: 'When we claim to have been injured by language, what kind of claim do we make?' She returns here to questions posed of the term 'queer' in *Bodies That Matter* (Butler, 1993), in which she asked how a linguistic practice whose purpose was to 'shame the subject it names' (Butler, 1993: 226) might be re-signified. Her starting point, in thinking this through, is to consider not simply *how* language instantiates an undoing, but rather why it does so, and again, this raises important questions and concerns for organizational scholars.

While *Excitable Speech* might be read simply as a liberal defence of free speech (see Lloyd, 2007), Butler's concern is ultimately with how this principle recites norms of intelligibility that serve to disavow the subjective viability of some lives, by allowing only certain subject positions to be accorded linguistic recognition. Organizational discourses, practices and modes of relating that reinforce this, often while purporting to do the opposite, are a notable example.

Ahmed (2012) develops this line of critique in her account of 'making difference' in/through organizational discourse. Her work picks up on an important point made by Butler (reflecting Kirby's acknowledgement of the more social scientific tone of *Undoing Gender*), namely that, as Butler puts it,

> What is most important is to cease legislating for all lives what is liveable only for some, and similarly, to refrain from proscribing for all lives what is unliveable for some.
>
> (Butler, 2004b: 8)

In Butler's hands, queer becomes a form of citational politics that constitutes an important un/doing, or as she puts it, 'a specific reworking of abjection into political agency' (Butler, 1993: 21) that proceeds from this premise. This means that being 'critically queer' implies 'a reversal that retains and reiterates the abjected history of the term' (Butler, 1993: 223), and a re-projection of a coherent subject position, a theme that underpins her theoretical and political preoccupations in *Undoing Gender*. As Kirby (2006: 126) notes, this is also reminiscent of the Hegelian origins of Butler's thinking, and it has significant resonance for organizational scholars and activists seeking to expose, challenge and resist organizational power relations.

Organizing/Disorganizing Gender

Taking theoretical and conceptual cues from Butler (2004b), exploring un/doing gender as a series of social and discursive practices has been a sustained interest of organizational research in recent years. Pullen and Simpson's (2009: 561) study of men who do traditionally female-dominated and feminized work (in nursing and primary school teaching) is a notable example that thinks through not only how men constitute a minority, often marginal group of workers in these contexts, but also their Otherness. As they put it, their study highlights the necessity to manage difference, and the 'processual, emergent, dynamic, partial and fragmented nature of gendered identities' apparent in these circumstances'. They show how men reinstate their masculine subjectivities by appropriating femininity, effectively 'redoing' gender through difference in ways that partially disrupt but ultimately reaffirm gender norms and hegemonic practices in work organizations.

In a similar vein, Mavin and Grandy (2016: 1095) draw on Butler's (2004b) writing to develop a critique of the bodily norms governing abject appearance, a concept they cite to explain how women leaders' embodied identity work is enacted within workplace settings. They argue that thinking about women's appearance in abject terms illuminates 'dynamic and dialectical processes whereby women elite leaders "manage" the ambiguities of their "in-between" and "abject" status'. This is because, they explain, while women leaders may occupy powerful subject positions through their formal organizational roles, they remain marginalized within workplace social relations and labour market hierarchies 'because their feminine bodies are out of place in organizations'. Their study shows how women leaders' accounts of their embodied experiences of organizational life depict a dialectical, abject process of simultaneous disgust and attraction whereby female bodies are both repulsive and seductive corporate resources, both done and undone. Hence, while women who secure organizational positions historically held by men might 'have achieved a particular parity with the One', in De Beauvoir's (2011) terms, at the same time they continue to embody what it means to be Other; 'out of place in elite leadership . . . women's bodies may trigger simultaneous disgust-attraction' (Mavin and Grandy, 2016: 1111).

A special issue of *Gender, Work and Organization* in 2007 gave sustained consideration to the implications of Butler's writing on un/doing for the study of work and organizations. This issue starts from the premise that gender is 'done' in and through organizations 'routinely and repeatedly', and hence with a degree of automaticity that 'conceals its precariousness and performativity' (Pullen and Knights, 2007: 505). The focus of papers in the issue, and of Pullen and Knights' editorial overview, is on how gender is un/done in organizations and through organizing, and with what consequences for those subject to its regulatory imperatives. As the inspiration for the special issue, *Undoing Gender* (Butler, 2004b) is seen as connecting gender performativity to interwoven processes of organization and disorganization, whereby the former is framed as a doing of gender, the latter as its (and simultaneously 'our') undoing. As co-editors, Pullen and Knights' (2007: 506) starting point is Butler's emphasis on how, in the search for recognition, we can all too easily become undone by governmental norms, leaving us to live a (working) life that is not worth living, or which is unworkable, giving the example of women who, in order to secure workplace identities, 'have to endorse the very masculine norms and values that they might otherwise wish to discredit'. But their discussion captures the dynamism of this dialectical process, emphasizing Butler's contention that:

> Sometimes a normative conception of gender can undo one's person-hood, undermining the capacity to persevere in a liveable life. Other times, the experience of a normative restriction becoming undone can undo a prior conception of who one is only to inaugurate a relatively newer one that has greater liveability as its aim.
>
> (Butler, 2004b: 1, cited in Pullen and Knights, 2007: 506)

Among the many challenges for organizational scholars that is posed by this claim is to understand what happens when the organization itself intervenes into this inauguration of 'greater liveability', seeing and seiz-ing on an opportunity for corporate revivification, instantiating a reified form of undoing, that accentuates subjective 'unravelling', rather than opening up the possibility for a genuine, recognition-based undoing, as Butler might understand, it to emerge. Other contributors to the issue develop this theme, showing how gender is both done and undone within the context of organizational scenes of compulsion and constraint.

Hall et al. (2007), for instance, examine the embodied experiences of men in occupational contexts, namely hairdressing, estate agency and fire-fighting, that are commonly perceived as 'masculine' or 'feminine', showing how men and women simultaneously draw upon and resist the gendered norms shaping their workplace personas and performances. Drawing on Butler's (2004b) focus on the scenes of constraint that shape gendered un/doing, they conclude that 'gendered subjectivities are gener-ated . . . through men's embodied engagement with prevailing body-based masculine stereotypes and sometimes highly local processes of inter-subjective negotiation and resistance' (Hall et al., 2007: 550).

In an empirically informed account of workplace credibility, Jeanes (2007) reflects on an employment tribunal in which she participated, developing a reflexive analysis of how a woman who was subject to sexual harassment at work was unable to convince the tribunal of the credibility of her case. Jeanes understands this as an instance of gendered un/doing because the question of the woman's credibility was steeped in normative expectations that framed a credible victim of sexual harass-ment as passive and subordinate, whereas the woman in question was confident and assertive in giving her evidence. Jeanes (2007: 557) argues that the woman in question was caught in a double bind that positioned her as not feminine enough to be a victim, hence her status as both a woman and as a woman who had been subject to sexual harassment was undone through a legal process that effectively amounted to 'redoing the binary' and in doing so, undoing both her and her testimony.

A recent legal case in Italy brings similar issues to the fore. It emerged after a Court of Appeal ordered a retrial of a case that in 2017, in a court in Ancona, Italy, had cleared two men of raping a woman after the judge declared her to be 'too masculine and unattractive'. Not finding her claim to be believable, the widely reported case revealed that the judges involved surmised that the accused men 'did not even like the woman', with one of them storing her phone number in his contacts list under the name, 'Viking'. The latter was an apparent reference to her masculine frame, with one of the judges commenting that 'the photograph in her file would appear to confirm this'.

Schilt and Connell's (2007) study of trans men and women's 'post-transition' workplace experiences highlights similar issues, emphasizing how as individuals work hard to craft identities designed to secure social and organizational acceptance, co-workers often reinstate gender rituals that serve to repatriate them into a rigid gender binary. These include, for instance, changes in interactional styles (including 'back slapping' trans men) and 'gender apprenticing' (activities such as helping with make-up and clothes shopping for trans women). Taken together, these practices had the effect of limiting the political possibilities associated with trans identities and experiences for making 'gender trouble' (Butler, 1990/2000a). However, since job security and workplace friendships are central concerns for trans people seeking recognition (see Rumens, 2018), options to resist this collegial 'reintegration' are restricted.

In this same issue, Hancock and Tyler (2007) draw on Butler's explicit focus on the dialectical interplay between 'what it might mean to undo restrictively normative conceptions of sexual and gendered life' and the performative citation and materialization of gender normativity as a process of '*becoming undone*' (Butler, 2004b: 1, *original emphasis*). Their main concern is with how this process, which they consider as an organizational one, 'imposes a coherent model of gendered life that demeans the complex ways in which gendered lives are crafted and lived' (Butler, 2004b: 5). Picking up on the idea, also explored by Hall et al. (2007), that gender is enacted within 'a scene of constraint' (Butler, 2004b: 1), their analysis draws from two important points (noted earlier) that Butler argues Hegel's narration of the dialectic of recognition misses:

> The terms by which we are recognized as human are socially articulated and [thereby] changeable. And sometimes the very terms that confer 'humanness' on some individuals are those that deprive certain other individuals of the possibility of achieving that status.
>
> (Butler, 2004b: 2)

Hancock and Tyler emphasize how Butler's concept of un/doing originates from her reading of Hegel's narration of the process of self-loss whereby recognition is motivated by the desire to find oneself reflected in the Other, 'whereby reflection is not a final expropriation' (Butler, 2004b: 241).

Taking issue with the ways in which organizations appropriate this vulnerability through the aesthetic management of recruitment and selection practices, Hancock and Tyler (2007: 521) argue that corporate imagery and gendered discourses framing perceptions of ideal employees illustrate how the gendered organization of the desire for recognition is mediated and materialized within/through organizational life through 'the landscaping of corporate artefacts and organizationally compelled ways of doing gender'.

Linking Hegel's (1977) account of the desire for recognition and its development in *Undoing Gender* to a critical analysis of the organization of aesthetics, they consider how gender is un/done through its materialization and mediation in processes of landscaping. Their semiotic analysis considers a series of images in corporate recruitment brochures and advertisements that, they argue, function as cultural configurations that 'organize and compel particular versions of gender . . . concerned with the production of organizationally legible and therefore (to borrow from Butler), viable subjects' (Hancock and Tyler, 2007: 521). This production can be read, they suggest, as a form of organizational performativity, and the images as sites of gender articulation. In particular, their analysis highlights the conditions and costs attached to doing gender in accordance with the aesthetic norms governing organizational recognition.

This latter theme is developed further in Mavin and Grandy's (2013: 232) account of the work undertaken by erotic dancers, highlighting in particular how the latter manage the various stigmas attached to their work and identities. Considering the experiences of twenty-one dancers employed in a UK chain of lap dancing clubs, they conclude that in order to be perceived as good at their job by managers, customers and co-workers, dancers 'are expected to do gender well, that is, perform exaggerated expressions of femininity'. Performance in this sense is taken to refer not simply to a surface or interaction-orientated gestural stylistics but also to the embodied materialization of specific gender norms and expectations, such as having large breasts, being attentive, being overtly sexual, and presenting themselves as 'needing to be rescued'.

Echoing the normative compulsions and constraints of the heterosexual matrix, their account emphasizes how dancers must do gender according to industry-specific terms of recognition. In sum, what their study highlights is the extent to which, as they put it, doing gender well 'is a complex process of identity construction with different consequences for different workers' (Mavin and Grandy, 2013: 236). Reinstating this complexity and understanding what happens to it when it becomes 'undone' by the normative expectations governing employment in different settings is an important task for organizational research.

Undoing Organizational Research

Relatively underdeveloped within work and organization studies thus far is a sustained consideration of how insights from Butler's writing might inform this research, including the methodological ways in which we might, in practical ways, develop our understanding of organizational life. This raises the question of what it might mean to develop a Butlerian performative methodology, designed to reflexively 'undo' organizational/ organizing processes and the ways in which these are often replicated in research design.

Taking up this challenge, Riach et al. (2016) seek to counter some of the criticisms levelled at Butler's performative ontology and political concern with un/doing as overly abstract and difficult to apply empirically (Fraser, 1997; Morison and Macleod, 2013). They also strive to address the very practical question of how we might actually 'do' organizational research inspired by theoretical insights from Butler's writing considered thus far by mapping and evaluating a practice-based methodological application of her theoretical analysis of the dynamic relationship between organizational subjectivity and the norms by which it is both compelled and constrained.

This builds on earlier research on un/doing chrononormativity (Riach et al., 2014), based on a series of 'anti-narrative' interviews designed to explore the ways in which lived experiences of age, gender and sexuality are negotiated and narrated within organizations in later life. It draws on Butler's (1988, 1990/2000a) performative ontology of gender, particularly her account of the ways in which the desire for recognition is shaped by heteronormativity, considering its implications for how we understand ageing and organizations. Their research develops a critique of the impact of heteronormative life course expectations on the negotiation of viable subjectivity within organizational settings.

Focusing on the ways in which 'chrononormativity' shapes lived experiences of ageing within organizations, at the same time as constituting an organizing process in itself, Riach et al.'s (2014, 2016) analysis draws on Butler's (2004b) writing on un/doing in its account of the simultaneously affirming and negating organizational experiences of older self-identifying LGBTQ people. Their study concludes by emphasizing the theoretical potential of a performative ontology of ageing, gender and sexuality for organization studies, as well as the methodological insights to be derived from an 'anti-narrative' approach to organizational research, arguing for the need to develop a more inclusive politics of ageing within both organizational practice and research, an issue to which we return in Chapter 4.

In particular, Riach et al.'s (2014) research highlights, as one of their participants Chris, put it, the sheer effort that goes into securing recognition within/through organizational life for those who live outside of a heteronormative understanding of the life course. As he put it,

> If some part of you already realizes you're an outcast . . . you're always busy negotiating a line. . . . You're always busy. You want to belong, you want to be yourself . . . and of course you want affection and intimacy.

Riach et al. (2014) argue that a critique of chrononormativity presents a fruitful means of exploring the temporal orders inscribed in organizational life which produce assumed and expected heteronormative trajectories that may include (but are not exclusive to) ideas about the 'right' time for particular life stages surrounding partnering, parenting and caring vis-à-vis career progression, promotions and flexible working. To explore further how chrononormative conditions affect organizational lives, they turn to conceptual and theoretical insights from Butler's performative ontology of gender and her account of the heteronormative organization of the desire for recognition as a process of un/doing to ask a number of questions: how are age, gender and sexuality simultaneously experienced, understood and 'managed' within and through organizations; what are the conditions and limits of cultural intelligibility, and employability, in this respect, and how are these understood and interpellated? Second, what are the organizational implications of individuals violating chrononormative life course expectations, and in what ways do such violations constitute an un/doing in Butler's terms? Finally, where might a performative ontology of age(ing) within organizations and a recognition-based critique of chrononormativity lead us, and what might such an approach imply for our theoretical and methodological understanding of lived experiences of sexuality, ageing and gender at work?

In responding to these questions, Riach et al. (2014: 1679) connect Butler's concept of the heterosexual matrix—replaced in *Undoing Gender* with 'presumptive heterosexuality' (Butler, 2004b: 186)—to Freeman's (2010) notion of chrononormativity, arguing that 'the latter constitutes the temporal corollary of the former'. They argue that, in practice, this means that complying with the life course expectations associated with the heterosexual matrix constitutes the condition of viable subjectivity upon which the conferral of recognition within organizational settings depends. They emphasize that, in practice, 'this means that chrononormativity as the normative assumptions associated with a heterosexual life course serves to effectively "undo" older LGBTQ workers in Butler's terms, negating their complex lived experiences, requiring them to constantly negotiate carefully narrated identities' (Riach et al., 2014: 1679), as Chris explains above.

Methodologically, they develop an approach described as 'anti-narrative' interviewing (Riach et al., 2016) designed to provide a reflexive space through which the narration of organizational selves might be 'undone', therefore developing the methodological implications of Butler's performative ontology and opening up its potential for organizational research.

The theoretical premise underpinning this approach draws from a number of strands in Butler's writing, notably her emphasis on subject formation as a perpetual process of un/doing through which 'the subject produces its coherence at the cost of its own complexity' (Butler, 1993: 115), a point she makes in *Bodies That Matter* and spends much of *Undoing Gender* elaborating upon, as noted earlier. What this suggests for LGBTQ people, Riach et al. argue, is that (i) viable subjectivity requires conforming to normative expectations associated with the heterosexual life course as they grow older; and (ii) that organizations play a significant role in compelling or constraining convincing performances of intersections of gender, ageing and sexuality within organizational settings.

With reference to LGBTQ people's experiences of growing older as workers, they show how the terms of cultural intelligibility therefore enable certain subjectivities to emerge and be accorded recognition, at the same time as foreclosing and disavowing others. In other words, they configure viable subjects, those that are produced 'as a consequence of recognition according to prevailing social norms' (Butler, 2004b: 3) that comply with chrononormative assumptions shaping the working life course.

Drawing on older LGBTQ people's accounts of their working lives, Riach et al.'s (2014) discussion emphasizes the complex and dynamic interplay between affirmation and negation this brings about, revealing how chrononormativity is experienced within organizations, and also acts as an organizing process in itself. On the one hand, the relative freedom from chrononormativity that many of their participants attached to growing older as LGBTQ people meant not being restricted by what they saw as the constraints and associated life course expectations of a conventional, heterosexual existence. On the other hand, many participants also recounted experiences of marginalization and exclusion, emphasizing the negating effects of violating chrononormativity as the temporal corollary of the heterosexual matrix.

In practice this dynamic meant, as Chris describes, that older LGBTQ people felt a need to maintain a constant vigilance; they were always 'busy negotiating a line' and conscious in and of their performance in the workplace. Chris also summed this up when he reflected on the ambivalences attached to LGBTQ life courses and the dynamics of freedom and negation, emphasizing what in Butler's terms might be understood as a very performative sense of self; as he put it, 'life story, biography, can change. There's a freedom in that. But it also means that there's a lot of remorse' ('Chris', in Riach et al., 2014: 1692). Understood in this way, chrononormativity both enables and constrains the precarious, fragile narrations of LGBTQ people as viable organizational subjects as they grow older. As Riach et al. (2014: 1692–1693) put it, 'this emphasizes that the fundamental vulnerability of being "given over" to the Other that allows for the possibility of both recognition and negation discussed by Butler . . ., can and must be understood in relation to chrononormativity'. Hence, the normative expectations associated with the heterosexual life course serve to constrain LGBTQ people's working lives, 'undermining their complex lived experiences and denying or mis-recognizing their attempts to narrate themselves as coherent subjects within organizational settings'. As a result, many of the men and women they interviewed recounted experiences of conditional acceptance at best, reflecting on their working lives as a constant struggle for recognition through which their sense of self has to be perpetually 'put at risk' (Butler, 2004b: 149) articulated, for instance, in references to their ever-present fear of being 'outed' in circumstances not of their choosing.

What Riach et al.'s (2014) study suggests, in this respect, is the importance of working towards an appreciation of the ways in which multiple yet marginal performativities require constant negotiation and narration within/through organizational settings and processes. Doing so demands that we begin to think more about how organizations are lived and managed, and how they *might* be experienced and understood in order to make a wider range of possible ways of being, and of living and working together viable. As Butler (2004b: 17, *emphasis added*, cited in Riach et al., 2014: 1693–1694) puts it:

> It becomes a question for ethics . . . not only when we ask the personal question, what makes my own life bearable, but when we ask, from a position of power, and from the point of view of distributive justice, *what makes, or ought to make, the lives of others bearable?* Somewhere in the answer we find ourselves not only committed to a certain view of what life [and organization] is, and what it should be, but also of what constitutes the human, the distinctively human life, and what does not.

Riach et al. (2014, 2016) show how and why these are fundamental questions for organizational scholars, practitioners and activists. In doing so, they emphasize how finding ways to disrupt the apparent linearity of workplace narratives, and what Butler (2004b) describes as the illusory coherence of performativity, in order to provide a critical, reflexive space in which to 'unravel' apparent organizational coherence, calling it 'to account' as it were, becomes of vital importance.

In practice, this means devising methods that facilitate an un/doing, in Butler's (2004b) terms, finding spaces in which to reflect on the performative processes at stake in sustaining socially recognizable, seemingly coherent narratives, and considering what these do to those who are able to conform to their normative expectations, and crucially, to those who are not, or will not. Drawing on Butler we can understand these experiences in terms of the dynamics of desire and recognition. Articulated through their participants' accounts of 'undoing chrononormativity', Riach et al. (2014) consider, on the one hand, the sense of relative freedom from constraint that undoing can foster, whilst at the same time, recognizing how we can be 'undone' by the negating effects of organizational life, on the other. As such, their study adds an important diachronic dimension to Butler's discussion of the conditions of viable subjectivity, and of the dynamics of recognition, effectively calling organizations to account for themselves, a theme explored by Butler (2005) in a book in which she makes more explicit than in previous work, the ethical and political concerns that underpin her critique of un/doing, and to which we turn in Chapter 4.

Notes

1. In *The Psychic Life of Power*, Butler (1997: 3) draws on Althusser's account of hailing or what she refers to as 'turning' to emphasize responding to being interpellated into being as a situated, embodied process in order to develop an analysis of what she calls the 'tropological inauguration of the subject'.
2. In this sense, as Kirby (2006: 123) argues, *Undoing Gender* takes on a more sociological feel than Butler's earlier works, with more attention being paid to empirical illustrations, institutional practices 'and the historical contexts that inform contemporary political struggles'. In this respect, it is perhaps not surprising that the book has had relatively widespread appeal amongst organizational scholars. As Kirby puts it, the book is notably 'more grounded and alive to the broader anthropological questions that haunt the human condition' than many of Butler's other texts.
3. South Korea's 'Escape the Corset' movement is a notable example of what Butler (2004b) means by the dynamics of un/doing. Within this movement, South Korea's exacting beauty standards (resulting in an estimated one-third of women undergoing aesthetic surgery, and a cosmetics industry worth about $12.5 billion) mean that a growing number of women are using social media, notably YouTube channels (more commonly used for make-up tuition) to raise awareness of the inequalities perpetuated by the cosmetics industry, and the gendered bodily ideals that it depends upon. A recurring theme in their discourse is the idea that beauty regimes are a form of unpaid labour, one that only, or predominantly, women are expected to perform. In one video, two women shatter cosmetics products such as foundation, eye shadow, blusher, and nail varnish over a blank canvas, producing a Jackson Pollock style image, declaring 'They can't have any power over me when it's so easy to break them' (see Haas, 2018).
4. Not surprisingly, Butler suggests that Benjamin's (1988) understanding of recognition as embedded within communication is a very Habermasian reading of Hegel.
5. To be fair, Butler (2004b: 223) is quite explicit about her view that resignification 'alone is not a politics, is not sufficient for a politics, is not enough'. She is fully aware that some forms of resignification (racist, Far Right) 'we might abhor', others (queer, feminist) 'we might embrace'. Her interest is in

exploring what *might* work in the service of a radical, democratic politics. See her social media posts and blogs on feminist activists' tactical use of humour during the anti-Trump marches in January 2017 and since.

6. Trans activists and artists often allude to un/doing gender as a 'negotiation'. As an example, artist Grayson Perry referred to the 'sweet spot' between glamour and passing, the dilemma for him—as a transvestite man—being 'to look more glamorous but less passable; or to go for the dowdier end and be unnoticed (Perry, 2018).

4 Accounting for/in Organization

Giving and Working an Account of One's Self

Judith Butler's writing can be understood at least in part as an active, evolving response to her critics, as well as to changing social, political and economic circumstances. While her later work (see Chapters 5 and 6) best illustrates the latter, *Bodies That Matter* is perhaps the clearest example of the former, responding to what some took to be an implied sense that different subjectivities could be simply 'put on' on the basis of individual whim.[1] In *Bodies That Matter* Butler tries to put paid to this 'free-wheeling sense of performance' (Kirby, 2006: 86) in a way that sets the tenor for her later discussions of language in *Excitable Speech* (Butler, 1997a, *emphasis added*), importantly subtitled 'a *politics* of the performative'. This latter text marks two notable shifts in Butler's writing, signalling both the emergence of a perspective on language that 'retains a felt, corporeal dimension' through its focus on the wounding power of words, and a more sustained interest in performativity as a collective, political endeavour. With regard to the power of language, Butler's concern with the efficacy of assaultive speech lies in the latter's capacity 'to bring into being or *materialize* derogated subject positions' (McNay, 1999: 179, *emphasis added*). To understand the significance of this, and its connections to Butler's concern with collective performativity, Lloyd (2007) argues that we need to turn once again to Butler's recognition-based account of the dialectics of subject formation.

In *Giving an Account of Oneself* (Butler, 2005), Butler continues with her titular motif of playing on the multiple meanings of the term 'account', using the term to refer both to the self's struggle to come into being as a narrative endeavour, at the same time as acknowledging the nature and meaning of that struggle as a response to being 'hailed' into a particular subject position, one that is enacted in accordance with the need to 'count', a compulsion that is both ontological and normatively compelled and constrained.

Developing what Morison and MacLeod (2013: 57) call a 'politics of narration', in *Giving an Account of Oneself* Butler (2005) considers the self as a narrative composition in a way that links her theory of subject formation to a framework for understanding ethical responsibility through the idea that ethical subjectivity is assumed by means of the process of providing an intelligible (recognizable) 'response' to being hailed in Althusserian terms, or called to account for oneself as she puts it. This 'accounting' for oneself involves not simply telling a story about oneself, but providing a convincing ethical defence of one's claim to recognition, particularly when that claim involves accounting for one's difference. As with so many of the ideas explored in this book, these themes have particular resonance for management, work and organizational scholars. For Butler (2005: 17, *emphasis added*), accounting for oneself is simultaneously an ontological and ethical process, establishing the normative parameters around who or what counts as fully 'human', and hence might be accorded the capacity—the recognition, and associated rights and responsibilities—of an ethical subject. As Butler puts it:

> It becomes a question for ethics . . . not only when we ask the personal question, what makes my own life bearable, but when we ask, from a position of power, and from the point of view of distributive justice, *what makes, or ought to make, the lives of others bearable?* Somewhere in the answer we find ourselves not only committed to a certain view of what life is, and what it should be, but also of what constitutes the human, the distinctively human life, and what does not.

Butler's (2005) understanding of narrative, developed most fully in *Giving an Account of Oneself*, provides a performative lens through which to understand how narratives operate in the process of becoming an ethical subject. In particular, Butler's largely phenomenological understanding locates narrative, as an attempt to cohere and convey a liveable life, within the context of the desire for recognition of oneself as a viable subject; as she puts it: 'I come into being as a reflexive subject only in the context of establishing a narrative account of myself' (Butler, 2005: 15). Framed in this way, narrative is not simply telling one's life story, as noted above, but is rather the response we are compelled to provide when being 'held to account' for ourselves (Butler, 2005: 12). This applies particularly to one's difference within the context of social (organizational) power relations:

> Giving an account thus takes a narrative form, which not only depends upon the ability to relay a set of sequential events with plausible transitions but also draws upon narrative voice and authority, *being directed toward an audience with the aim of persuasion.*
> (Butler, 2005: 12, *emphasis added*)

Here, (much like performativity and mattering) narrative is framed as a process of organization through which the desire for recognition of oneself as a viable, coherent self is both compelled and constrained; it necessitates a self-questioning, premised upon 'putting oneself at risk' (Butler, 2005: 23), in so far as the narrative account that one gives of oneself always, already carries with it the risk of 'unrecognizability as a subject'. Drawing together insights from Hegel (1977) and Levinas (1961), Butler maintains that subjectivity, or rather the risky business of becoming a subject, is dependent not simply upon the other's recognition, but also on the 'social dimension of normativity that governs the scene of recognition' (Butler, 2005: 23).

Returning to concerns explored initially in *Subjects of Desire* (Butler, 1987), Butler emphasizes here that recognition can never be 'a pure offering' (Butler, 2005: 27) in the philosophical sense in which Hegel narrates it in his phenomenological account of the struggle for recognition; that is, wrenched from its social setting. As well as emphasizing how this struggle is always socially situated, embedded within power relations, Butler also reminds us that she refutes assimilationist readings of Hegelian dialectics as gestures of appropriation in the style of imperialism, preferring an ek-static reading that emphasizes the self as always in social and self servitude:

> That the 'I' repeatedly finds itself outside itself, and that nothing can put an end to the repeated upsurge of this exteriority that is, paradoxically, my own. *I am, as it were, always other to myself.*
> (Butler, 2005: 27, *emphasis added*)

The scenographic recognition-based understanding of the Hegelian struggle as a narrative process, and the latter's connection to subjective performativity that Butler outlines in *Giving an Account of Oneself* offers important insights into how subjectivities come into being organizationally in two distinct but related ways. First, Butler's *social* theory of recognition, one infused with a phenomenological emphasis on perception as socially situated, highlights that we constantly come into contact with the norms governing subjective intelligibility '*mainly through proximate and living exchanges*, in the modes by which we are addressed and asked to take up the question of who we are and what our relation to the other *ought to be*' (Butler, 2005: 30, *emphasis added*), including, we might surmise, those situated within organizational settings and encountered through organizational processes. Second, she emphasizes that it is only through narrating ourselves in a way that conforms to the normative conditions governing viable subjectivity that we are able to stake a credible claim to recognition. This continually reaffirms that there is simply 'no wishing away our fundamental sociality' (Butler, 2005: 33). Within organizational settings, and through organizational relations and practices, the ability to provide a coherent narrative and the capacity to give a convincing account of one's ethical capability becomes conflated with the constitution of the self as a performative narration, or organizational phenomenon. This conflation and its associated costs constitutes what in Butler's terms, we might think of as an 'organizational undoing' whereby the complexities of our lives become conflated in the service of an over-riding organizational identification and set of imperatives.

This more sociological reading of reified forms of recognition also high-lights that 'not everything counts as recognition in the same way' (Butler, 2005: 33). A challenge for organizational scholars is, therefore, how to differentiate between different forms of recognition, and the credibility or rather viability of the subjectivities they bring into being. If, as Butler (2005: 33) puts it, 'it still matters that we feel more properly recognized by some people than we do by others', it presumably also matters that we feel more genuinely, relationally recognized in some ways, and by some processes, than we do by or through others. Her discussion also brings to the fore, in this respect, the costs attached to securing recognition through particular accounts. As she reminds us, 'the account of myself that I give in discourse never fully expresses or carries [my] living self' (Butler, 2005: 36). Not only does this have significant consequences for organizational research that seeks to understand working lives through interview-based methods, themselves 'accounts' of working lives and selves, it also opens up the need to critically, reflexively interrogate the costs attached to the performance of our 'organizational selves' as these are premised upon an expectation of narrative coherence, and to bring to the fore the normative, psychic and even physical violence that these engender. Again, Butler is worth quoting in full on this for the specifics of her thinking here provide an important link between themes considered in her other works (and in other chapters), yet it is only in *Giving an Account of Oneself* that she examines the costs attached to narrative coherence explicitly through the lens of accountability in a way that has particular resonance for understanding the process of 'giving an account' as one through which the desire for recognition comes to be organized:

> My account of myself is partial, haunted by that for which I can devise no definitive story. I cannot explain exactly why I have emerged in this way, and my efforts at narrative reconstruction are always under-going revision. There is that in me and of me for which I can give no account. But does this mean that I am not, in the moral sense, accountable for who I am and for what I do? If I find that, despite my best efforts, a certain opacity persists and that I cannot make myself fully accountable to you, is this ethical failure? Or is . . . there in this affirmation of partial transparency a possibility for acknowledging a relationality that binds me more deeply . . . to you than I previously knew? And is this relationality . . . not, precisely, an indispensable source for ethics?
>
> (Butler, 2005: 40)

In posing this question by thinking through the connections between that which elides narrative coherence and relationality, Butler sets the groundwork for her explication of a recognition-based, non-violent ethics. The basic premise of this is that the reflexive awareness that an ability to recognize that which is contingent and incoherent, or spectral, in oneself opens up the possibility of affirming the same in others 'who may or may not "mirror" one's own constitution'. In practical terms, what this suggests is that it is not an awareness of sameness, or an overcoming or, in the case of corporate diversity discourse, a celebratory reification of difference that constitutes the basis of recognition, but a mutual awareness and recognition of narrative *incoherence* as a sign of our basic relationality.

This shift, from what Butler describes as the 'tacit operation of the mirror in Hegel's concept of reciprocal recognition', replaces the latter with an emphasis on reflexive recognition as the basis for a potentially more radical form of relating to one another. Such a move is more than semantic; it suggests that no longer does recognition depend upon the identification of an other that is 'like me', and who makes the same acknowledgement of our likeness, but rather upon a reciprocal relationality premised upon a more 'muddled' sense of similarity based on the idea that we are simply doing the best we can to be coherent. In doing so, it strives to move beyond the depressing prospect of 'a bad infinity of recursive mimesis' (Butler, 2005: 41), a category that we might place many forms of corporate or organizational recognition, including those that profess to 'champion' equality, into.

For Butler, this revisionist move is ethically and politically important for the recognition that we are not quite the same as how we present ourselves using the only means available to us; it is one that implies, 'in turn, a certain patience with others', extending the possibility that others might suspend the demand that they be 'self-same at every moment', or fully accountable (Butler, 2005: 42). This, for Butler, is a potential counter to the constant threat of ethical, normative violence, constituting instead 'a disposition of humility and generosity alike' (Butler, 2005: 42), one that, Butler reminds us, is premised upon an understanding of recognition as 'in principle, unsatisfiable' (Butler, 2005: 45), or to be more precise, of the struggle for recognition as perpetual, and of recognition itself as always partial and provisional.

'You There!'—Being Called Into Being

It is not simply Hegel (1977) that Butler grounds her situated understanding of recognition in, however. As with all of her work, her analysis of being called to account takes its theoretical cues from a wide range of sources, perhaps most notably Marxist philosopher and social theorist, Louis Althusser. In her own words, Althusser provides Butler with a '"*scene*", as it were, on which to set the question: what does it mean to appropriate the terms by which one is hailed or the discourse in which one is constituted?' (Butler and Bell, 1999: 164, *emphasis added*). In responding to this question, Butler examines Althusser's discussion of hailing, itself grounded in a concern with recognition, and considers it through the ontological lens of performativity. She does so in order to develop what is effectively a scenography of subject formation understood as an inter-subjective moment through which coming into being is enacted as a process of giving an account of oneself. When one is beckoned into being, even fleetingly, a subject position is taken up which is outside of oneself, ek-static as it were, and which gives the language of hailing a material, embodied form.

For Althusser, an individual is hailed or interpellated through an inter-subjective act of recognition and a corresponding response to the call of another. The basic premise of his account is that '*all ideology hails or interpellates concrete individuals as concrete subjects*' (Althusser, 2001: 117, *original emphasis*). It is through this process that ideology 'acts' or functions in such a way that it 'recruits subjects . . . or "transforms" individuals into subjects' (Althusser, 2001: 118). At the risk of oversimplification, interpellation is the mechanism through which the social order speaks to us, or 'calls us by name' (Jameson, 2001: xiv). The example Althusser gives is that of a police officer who calls out 'Hey, you there!' dramatizing the implicit authority of the officer and the act of calling out through the same action, setting the 'scene' for interpellation, in Butler's interpretation.

As Althusser describes it, assuming that the act of hailing takes place in the street, in the physical process of turning around—recognizing the officer's authority and its implications—the individual becomes a particular subject, in this case a 'suspect', acknowledging a simultaneously linguistic and social (discursive) positioning as the person the call was intended for. It is through this collision of this linguistic, social and physical conversion that the individual becomes a subject, *recognizing* to whom the hail was addressed. That this process of recognition is enacted in and through language, sociality and the 'matter' of bodies is important to Butler's reading and development of Althusser in her own theory of subject formation (Butler, 1990/2000a, 1993, 2004b), particularly in *Giving an Account of Oneself* (Butler, 2005).

For Althusser, this moment of interpellation is what brings the subject into being, even fleetingly, as a result of acknowledging and responding to the call. In other words, it is through recognizing the mode of address that the subject is formed, a process that implies responsibility, that of being called to account for oneself *as one emerges*. This means that being called to account does not succeed subject formation; it is the very process through which the subject comes into being. Althusser is at pains to emphasize this and it is likely that this is what appeals to Butler so much in his narration of subject formation in this way. As Althusser puts it,

For the convenience and clarity of my little theoretical theatre I have had to present things in the form of a sequence, with a before and after, and thus in the form of a temporal succession. . . . *But in reality these things happen without any succession.* The existence of ideology and the hailing or interpellation of individuals as subjects are one and the same thing.

(Althusser, 2001: 118, emphasis added)

Equally, just as what seems to take place outside of ideology (e.g. in the street) 'in reality takes place in ideology' (Althusser, 2001: 118), and vice versa; hailing is at one and the same time an ideological and material act through which (literally, in Althusser's own example), the subject's head is turned. Thus, ideology hails or interpellates individuals and subjects who, in turn, come to embody and enact the ideological positions into which they are beckoned. In a way that Butler's discussions of the relationship between agency and subjectivity echo, and in what he argues might appear to be a paradoxical assertion, Althusser then goes on to explain that subjects are 'always-already interpellated', as even before birth, ideology has already hailed individuals into particular subject positions.[2]

In Butler's hands, 'turning' in response to the hail is not necessary however, as the subject can be constituted without being aware of it. Further, interpellation can take place even, perhaps especially, when the subject resists it, or rejects its terms, by recognizing but consciously not responding to the naming process to which Jameson (2001) refers. Butler also hints at organizational interpellations, hailing the subject into being in an embodied way, but without requiring the presence of an actual speaker, through 'bureaucratic forms, the census, adoption papers, employment applications' and so forth (Butler, 1997a: 33).

This is important to Butler's own political interpretation of the significance of interpellation, as a process of naming what it instantiates. For, if naming is what enables the subject to come into effect, being called by a demeaning name or hailed into an unliveable life has the same effect. As she puts it, being 'called by an injurious name, I come into social being' (Butler, 1997b: 104). In her discussion of being called to account, one that builds on her 'ambivalent' theory of power in *Undoing Gender*, Butler highlights how all interpellations, even those that are not ostensibly harmful, are injurious in some way as they conflate the complexity of lived experience through their compulsion to provide semblances of narrative coherence. In doing so, and as what are effectively narrative forms of categorical thinking, they foreclose ways of being that do not conform to the proscribed templates of subjectivity. This is especially the case for those utterances of derogatory or otherwise negating terms that serve to continually re-inaugurate subordinated subject positions; the so-called dead naming of trans people being perhaps one of the more poignant examples.

In this respect, Butler's *Giving an Account of Oneself* is to her *Excitable Speech* what *Bodies That Matter* was to *Gender Trouble*; it literally 'fleshes out' her theory of subject formation, showing how the latter is materialized and situated, socially and politically as it becomes organized into being in a particular way. Being called to account, in Althusser's description of it, cannot be explained simply in terms of feelings of guilt; rather it is driven by the desire for recognition of oneself as a viable, social subject, one capable of 'giving an account'. In Althusser's narrative, the passer-by turns both to acquire and bestow recognition, acknowledging both the authority of the police officer's act of hailing, and the ethical capacity to respond (to 'clear' one's name from the weight of accusation). From this, Butler (1997a: 25) draws the idea that 'the act of recognition becomes an act of constitution'; it is precisely this address that 'animates' the subject—as the coalescence of a linguistic, social and embodied positioning.

In her insightful commentary on this, Kirby notes that the 'temporal condensation' of interpellation has several important implications for the way in which Butler understands the relationship between power and subjectivity. At a simple level, the police officer appears to be invested with the power of the state, embodying 'the anonymous instrument of authority who enacts power *over* the subject' (Kirby, 2006: 89, *original emphasis*). However, the subject's response is evidence of something more significant which Kirby describes as a social conscience, but which we might take to refer to the desire for recognition; for Butler it is the passer-by's need for belonging that underpins the articulation of power's 'calling to account'. Kirby rightly argues that in order to understand why Althusser's account of interpellation is so significant to Butler's writing on being called to account, we need to place it in the context of her preoccupation with the Hegelian struggle, or more precisely, 'the dynamic of inter-subjectivity' (Kirby, 2006: 89) in which all of her work is grounded, as discussed earlier.

For Levinas (1961), whose thinking has also had a significant impact on Butler's writing on accountability, the moment at which a subject is summoned into existence marks the establishment of an ethical relationship. For him, ethical responsibility arises, as Butler sums it up, 'as a consequence of being a subject to the unwilled address of the other' (Butler, 2005: 85). Although Butler reads the nature of this address in a different way to Levinas (he seems to frame it as largely accusatory, whereas for Butler it is more constitutive), Butler acknowledges that the subject's vulnerability to the other is the basis of its exposure to the risk of harm, *at the same time* as being the basis of its ethical relation to the other.

In Butler's own words, *Giving an Account* is a text that tries to address the question of whether a non-unitary subject that is always 'partially opaque to itself can nevertheless take responsibility and give an account of its actions' (Butler, interview with Kirby, 2006: 154) within the context of this ethical relationship. Here Butler explains that her concern is with understanding subject formation as an ethical process; it is, as she puts it, 'her foray into moral philosophy' (Butler, interview with Kirby, 2006: 154). While she *appears* to frame this as a largely individual process, it is anything but.

Rather, efforts to give an account of oneself insist that in doing so, we take account of the social and discursive, not to mention material conditions of our emergence. To put it simply, this means that self-narration always also involves social critique, a theme that Butler takes up with reference to Adorno's (2005) problematic, 'of what it is to live a good life in a bad one' (Butler, interview with Kirby, 2006: 154). The basic premise of *Giving an Account of Oneself* as a simultaneously ontological, political and ethical endeavour is outlined in Butler's exchange with Kirby, when she says:

> Our narratives fail to be seamless and unified. . . . One cannot always relate one's life in narrative form. . . . We all need to be able to give some accounts of ourselves in order to live and survive . . . it is equally implausible though to demand that a life always conform to the criterion of a story.
>
> (Butler, interview with Kirby, 2006: 154)

In practice, this means that 'there are gaps or fissures in the accounts that we give' (Butler, interview with Kirby, 2006: 155). We are held to account in order to instil subjective responsibility for our actions as the basis of recognition, but this process is based, Butler argues, on a juridical notion of responsibility rather than on an ethics of relationality.

Accounting for Oneself as a Political and Ethical Process

Drawing on Adorno, Foucault, Levinas and also Jean Laplanche, Butler develops her concern with the normative constitution of the subject into a consideration of what it means to lead an ethical life for a subject who struggles against the social norms and relations through which s/he emerges. In this sense, *Giving an Account of Oneself* is a text that is preoccupied with ethics and methodology; to put it simply, it is a methodological commentary on subject formation as an ethical endeavour. Butler's account is of an ethics of responsibility, one that is responsive to the need for critical autonomy, yet which is also grounded in what she calls the opacity of the subject. She situates much of her argument in Adorno's claim that violence consists in part, in our indifference to the social conditions under which living appropriations become possible, at the same time as emphasizing that while there is no morality without an 'I', there is no 'I' that can fully stand apart from the social conditions of its emergence, including those self-same conditions that are indifferent to the suffering of others. As she puts it,

> The 'I' does not stand apart from the prevailing matrix of ethical norms and conflicting moral frameworks. In an important sense, this matrix is also the condition for the emergence of the 'I'.
>
> (Butler, 2005: 7)

She goes on,

> We must ask, however, whether the 'I' who must appropriate moral norms in a living way is not itself conditioned by norms, norms that establish the viability of the subject.
>
> (Butler, 2005: 9)

Echoing the political concerns of *Undoing Gender*, and drawing on the problems posed by Adorno (2005) in *Minima Moralia*, her argument is that giving an account of oneself means 'to risk unrecognizability as a subject' (Butler, 2005: 23). This raises two important rhetorical questions:

> First, what are these norms, to which my very being is given over, which have the power to install me, or indeed, to de-install me as a recognizable subject? Second, where and who is this other, and can the notion of the other comprise the frame of reference and normative horizon that hold and confer my potential for becoming a recognizable subject?
>
> (Butler, 2005: 23)

Butler's response to these questions draws particularly on Levinas (1961) and reminds us of the scenography of subject formation she derives from Althusser, when she emphasizes (as noted earlier) that 'the very being of the self is dependent, not just of the existence of the other in its singularity . . . but also on the social dimension of normativity that governs the scene of recognition' (Butler, 2005: 23). Also reminding us that this scene is the site on which Hegel's narration of inter-subjectivity is played out, her concern is with the normative expectations governing recognition, so that 'whether or not the other is singular, the other is recognized and confers recognition through a set of norms that govern recognizability' (Butler, 2005: 25). This means that 'I can never offer recognition in the Hegelian sense as a pure offering, since I am receiving it, at least potentially and structurally, in the moment and in the act of giving' (Butler, 2005: 27). The opacity of the subject means that (in Hegelian terms—and in contrast to assimilationist readings of Hegel—see Butler, 2005: 27 and previous discussion), 'nothing can put an end to the repeated upsurge of this exteriority that is, paradoxically, my own. I am, as it were, always other to myself' (Butler, 2005: 27).

Taking this opacity of the subject as her starting point, and working it into a relational politics grounded in a social theory of recognition, Butler argues that the exposure and vulnerability of the other makes a primary ethical claim upon the self, as does the other's imposition; the substantive ethical claim that is made is through the simultaneous exposure and imposition of the other. Our political and ethical situation consists in part in learning how to best handle this—and to honour it—acknowledging the necessarily mutual vulnerability that this encounter engenders.

The notion of giving an account of oneself, and of enacting a non-violent ethics of reflexive reciprocity, is therefore grounded for Butler in the onto-logical premise that 'we are, from the start, ethically implicated in the lives of others' (Butler, 2005: 64). This is very much an ethical rather than an empirical observation, although it of course has important implications for the latter, especially in understanding how organizational life precludes this relationality as the basis of ethics and politics. As Butler puts it,

> The purpose here is not to celebrate a certain notion of incoherence, but only to point out that our 'incoherence' establishes the way in which *we are constituted in relationality.*
>
> (Butler, 2005: 64, *emphasis added*)

Butler traces this relationality back to her Hegelian preoccupations in *Subjects of Desire* (Butler, 1987), noting its ontological origins in inter-subjectivity, or more precisely, the reflexive recognition that 'I am . . . given over to a "you" without whom I cannot be and upon whom I depend to survive' (Butler, 2005: 81). This recognition throws into relief the idea that the ethically ideal 'I' is free of 'humility about one's constitu-tive limitations' and generosity, where the latter is taken to denote 'a dis-position toward the limits of others' (Butler, 2005: 80). While in no sense dispensing with the need to give an account of oneself, this necessitates a rethinking of the conceit of a self that is fully transparent to itself and oth-ers. Indeed, to take responsibility for oneself is to establish the limits of self-understanding, 'and to establish these limits not only as a condition for the subject but as the predicament of the human community' (Butler, 2005 83). As a primary 'ethical interpellation' (Butler, 2005: 89), rela-tionality is the means by which we are both dispossessed and constituted within the sphere of recognition.

At its simplest level, 'giving an account' is the self-narration of this process, 'a kind of showing of oneself' (Butler, 2005: 131). But this 'show and tell' is by no means arbitrary; it is driven by the norms governing intelligibility shaping the desire for recognition as socially situated. Giv-ing an account is therefore

> A showing *for the purpose of testing whether the account seems right*, whether it is understandable by the other, who 'receives' the account through one set of norms or another. [Hence] I have a rela-tion to myself, but I have it in the context of an address to an other.
>
> (Butler, 2005: 131, *emphasis added*)

And as Butler goes on to emphasize in subsequent work (see Chapter 5), it is through the telling that we, paradoxically, are both constituted and dispossessed. Yet, as already discussed, the account that we give can never tell the full story because it 'relies upon *a formative history, a sociality, and a corporeality* that cannot easily, if at all, be reconstructed in narrative' (Butler, 2005: 132, *emphasis added*). Returning to her (often rather implicit) discussion of the relationship between subjectivity and agency, and its siting in what she calls the 'scenography' of construction, Butler reminds us, towards the end of *Giving an Account of Oneself* that when we act, we act in a world whose structure is in large part not of our making. But this is not the same as saying, as some of her critics have asserted, that 'there is no making and no acting that is mine'; rather it means that, as she puts it, the subject's 'suffering and acting, telling and showing, take place within a *crucible of social relations*' (Butler 2005: 132, *emphasis added*). These social relations condition and set limits on our intelligibility yet at the same time, 'when we do act and speak, we not only disclose ourselves but act on the schemes of intelligibility that govern who will be a speaking being, *subjecting them to rupture or revision, consolidating their norms, or contesting their hegemony*' (Butler, 2005: 132, *emphasis added*). Precisely how this happens, in what circumstances, and to what effect, is arguably an underdeveloped aspect of Butler's work at this stage in her writing, but these are issues that she sets out to attend to in her later work that we return to in Chapters 5 and 6.

For now, and once again drawing from Adorno (2005), she reminds us that the self is clearly 'formed' within a set of social conventions that raise the question of whether a good life can be lived within a bad or damaged one, and whether we might, in re-crafting ourselves with and for others, be able to participate in a reworking of these social conditions. Emphasizing that performativity is both a political (Butler, 1997a, 1997b) and ethical endeavour (Butler, 2005), and that ethical relations are, in turn, thereby performative she hints at the more collective explication of performativity that comes in her later work (see Chapter 6 especially) when she reminds us of the risks that are attached to responding to a demand to account for oneself as a process of simultaneous subject formation and as a presumption of ethical responsibility. As noted earlier, this is because:

> Giving an account of oneself comes at a price not only because the 'I' that I present cannot present many of the conditions of its own formation but because the 'I' that yields to narration cannot comprise many dimensions of itself.
>
> (Butler, 2005: 135)

In the last two pages of *Giving an Account of Oneself* Butler begins to develop a more socially situated analysis of this predicament that has further implications for thinking about 'giving an account' within and through organizational settings. As certain versions of the self are preoccupied with socially compelled modes of individualism that lead to ethical violence, it is important to ask the question, she reminds us: 'How are we formed within social life, and at what cost?' (Butler, 2005: 136). To borrow from this: How are we formed within organizational life, and at what/whose cost, if giving an account of oneself is an organizational process, or rather a process of organization, in itself?

Accounting for One's Organizational Self: 'Showing and telling' at work

For organizational scholars what is particularly insightful in Butler's engagement with Althusser and in posing these kinds of questions on the basis of this engagement is her view that the police officer's call constitutes, as Kirby (2006: 95, *emphasis added*) puts it, a '*presumptive* recognition'; in other words, it is one that is already loaded with a particular set of expectations shaping the scenography of subject formation and its normative parameters. In organizational terms, this presumption is situated not simply in a scenography of subject formation shaped by social norms governing cultural intelligibility, but within power hierarchies and relations of exclusion and/or appropriation premised upon positioning subject formation as an organizational process and resource. Two examples considered here illustrate what this means in organizational terms, drawing first, on the accounts of LGBTQ people's experiences of feeling compelled to present coherent narratives within the organizational settings in which they work and second, on research on indigenous people being called to account by governmental processes that serve to reinstate rather than 'undo' past injustices.

Emphasizing the need to 'understand the terms within and through which subjects are performatively constituted' in organizational settings, Cabantous et al. (2015: 8) argue that two fundamental questions follow from engaging with Butler within work and organization studies: 'Who are you? [And] what are the conditions of the possibility of your becoming?' Taking up the challenge posed by these two, related questions, Riach et al. (2016) illustrate, with reference to the work and organizational experiences of self-identified older lesbian, gay, bisexual and trans- (LGBTQ) adults in the United Kingdom, the methodological opportunities they open up. Responding to questions such as these, drawing on Butler's (2005) writing on giving an account as a critical and reflexive process, enables organizational scholars to understand more about the labour involved in performing and maintaining the semblances of subjective coherence upon which organizations depend. In particular, they enable us to appreciate the importance of analyzing the stories that people tell about the identity work they undertake within—and on behalf of—organizations in order to comprehend the complexities, contradictions and especially the struggles contained within their accounts.

In their discussion of the ethical implications of 'undoing' as a methodological approach, of unravelling these struggles in order to bring the labour on which they depend to the fore, Riach et al. distinguish between what they call an *organizational undoing* through which, in Butler's (1993: 115) terms, 'the subject produces its coherence at the cost of its own complexity', and a more analytical, *reflexive undoing*. While the former requires that constraining and conflating the complexity of lived experience is a condition upon which viable organizational subjectivity depends, the latter is designed to bring this complexity to the fore, revealing rather than concealing the labour required to produce and maintain semblances of subjective coherence within and through organizations.

Riach et al. introduce the term 'organizational undoing' to refer to what Dale and Latham (2015: 168) describe as 'organizational processes which fix and stabilize differences and categories, and apply rules and procedures to maintain these', arguing that subjective viability and organizational recognition depends upon the capacity to maintain a performatively credible conformity to these processes, rules and procedures. In contrast, Riach et al. argue that a 'reflexive undoing', one designed to reveal the organizational processes through which subjects are 'undone' and to emphasize the sheer effort involved in staking a claim to recognition, allows us to examine not only the conditions of organizational recognition but also the consequences of mis-recognition for those whose subjectivity is negated, or who are, in Butler's terms, deemed to be 'non-narratable'.[3]

Considering the methodological possibilities opened up by a reflexive undoing, as well as evaluating its ethical implications, Riach et al. (2016) first consider the methodological potential of Butler's writing for the study of organizational subjectivity, specifically the latter's normative constitution and conditioning within organizational settings and through organizational processes. Second, they outline and evaluate the practical application of this potential through their consideration of what they call 'anti-narrative' research premised upon a reflexive undoing and an ethic of openness throughout the research process.

In particular, they ask: first, how might a methodology underpinned by a performative ontology reflexively 'undo' organizational subjectivities, revealing the normative conditions, and identity work, on which they depend? Second, how might we develop methodologies and methods that do not simply 'fix' the subjects of inquiry, replicating identity thinking in and through organizational research, and thereby reproducing patterns of narrative coherence and processes of organizational undoing? Third, what methodological possibilities might be opened up if we adopt an anti-narrative approach to organizational research? Finally, what are the practical and ethical considerations associated with a methodological, reflexive undoing and with an anti-narrative research practice premised upon Butler's (1988, 1990/2000a) performative ontology and critique of the compulsions and constraints shaping giving an (organized/organizational) account of ourselves (Butler, 2005)?

Riach et al.'s (2016) starting point is that while empirically and theoretically rich, what remains relatively underdeveloped within organizational scholarship that engages with Butler, thus far at least (Borgerson, 2005; Cabantous et al., 2015; Ford and Harding, 2011; Harding et al., 2011, 2013, 2014; Hodgson, 2005; Kenny, 2009, 2010, 2018, 2019; Parker, 2002; Thanem and Wallenberg, 2016; Wickert and Schaefer, 2014), is the methodological integration of insights from her writing into debates about how we might, in practical ways, develop our understanding of organizational subjectivity as the outcome of a process of being called to account. Taking up this challenge, Riach et al.'s (2016) aim is to counter some of the criticisms levelled at Butler's thinking as overly abstract and difficult to apply empirically within the field (Fraser, 1997; Morison and Macleod, 2013). In this sense, they seek to address the very practical question of how we might actually 'do' organizational research inspired by theoretical insights from Butler's writing on giving an account of oneself, in particular drawing from her analysis of the relationship between subjectivity and the norms by which it is both compelled and constrained, framing this relationship as a process of organization.

Considering the hitherto under-explored methodological implications of her work for the study of organizational life, Riach et al. set out three characteristics of a Butler-inspired methodology as they see it: (i) 'anti-narrative' interviewing as a method of data generation and analysis; (ii) a methodological 'undoing' based on a performative ontology, and (iii) a commitment to a recognition-based, reflexive undoing premised upon an ethics of openness.

Developing a methodology that allows us to reflexively undo 'organizational undoings', as well as crafting a corresponding method that enables organizational researchers to appreciate the narratives on which the conferral or denial of recognition depends, is an endeavour that stands to benefit scholars, practitioners and activists with an interest in the complexity of organizational subjectivities, and in developing critical, reflexive analyses of their performance and management (see Borgerson, 2015; Fournier and Grey, 2000; Spicer et al., 2009; Wickert and Schaefer, 2014), particularly in understanding the work that goes into maintaining narrative coherence (Driver, 2015) and understanding the conditions of organizational becoming (Cabantous et al., 2015).

The methodology that Riach et al. (2016) outline constitutes, in Butler's terms, a reflexive 'undoing', not of organizational subjects, but rather of organizational subjectivities and the normative conditions upon which they depend. Hence, this reflexive rather than organizational undoing is designed, methodologically, to reveal the processes and governmental norms by which workplace subjectivities are shaped, as well as their consequences for lived experiences within organizations, enabling organizational researchers to understand more about the identity work that goes into presenting oneself as a viable, organizational subject. As such, a reflexive undoing is designed to contrast with a more performative, organizational undoing in revealing lived experiences of being subject to the narrow range of 'rules and norms' we are required to conform to 'if we are to exist' not simply in a physical sense, but as viable, social subjects, within and through organizational settings (Ford and Harding, 2011: 4). It also aims, in doing so, to show how accountability as a mode of organizational governance, when set within such a normative context, pre-empts the possibility of recognition, and of resistance (De Coster and Zanoni, 2019).

With this in mind, Riach et al. (2016) consider how organizational researchers might go about 'doing' a methodological undoing; how we might engage, in and through our research practice, in a self-reflexive undoing. The latter is specifically designed to reveal, rather than conceal, the complexities of lived experience that are constrained in the performance of viable, coherent organizational subjectivities, using Butler's critique of 'giving an account of oneself' as a theoretical resource. To illustrate their approach, Riach et al. draw on a series of anti-narrative interviews with older LGBTQ people within organizational settings, considering how narratives operate in the process of becoming a viable, workable subject. Drawing directly on Butler's notion (cited earlier), that narrative is not simply 'telling a story about oneself', but rather the response we are compelled to provide when being 'held to account' (Butler, 2005: 12), Riach et al. show how this takes place when being called to account for one's difference within socially normative organizational power relations.

Their interviews with LGBTQ people (see also Riach et al., 2014 and Chapter 3) emphasize how narrative functions as a process of organization through which the desire for recognition of oneself as a viable, coherent self is both compelled and constrained. This recognition-based understanding of narrative and its connection to subjective performativity is discernibly distinct from more theoretically and methodologically established approaches to narrative within organization studies. In the latter, narrative is arguably secondary or subsequent to the formation of the morally constituted self; that is, to presenting ourselves as capable of living an ethical life. In contrast, a performative approach influenced by Butler (drawing in turn on Althusser—discussed earlier), emphasizes that it is through narrating ourselves in a way that conforms to the normative conditions governing viable subjectivity that we are able to stake a credible claim to recognition.

Within organizational settings, and through organizational processes, the ability to provide a coherent narrative, and the capacity to give an account of one's ethical capability, arguably becomes conflated in the constitution of the self as a performative narration. It is this conflation, and its associated costs that, drawing on Butler (2004b, 2005), Riach et al. conceive as an organizational undoing, and which they suggest might be methodologically, reflexively, 'undone' through anti-narrative research.

Narrative analysis and storytelling research has made significant inroads into management and organization studies (see Boje, 2001, 2008; Czarniawska, 1998; Driver, 2015; Gabriel, 1991, 1995), particularly as a method of understanding 'organizational sense-making' (Weick, 1995). Yet the analytical emphasis within this literature has tended to be on understanding how knowledge is produced 'as individuals participate in the narration process' (Ainsworth and Hardy, 2012: 1696), with researchers attempting to develop ways of assembling coherence out of otherwise apparently fragmented accounts. In her discussion of narrative research, Czarniawska (1998: 19) reasons how, in this respect, organizational research often replicates organizational processes, as narrative modes of sense-making that tend to integrate a series of events into a coherent, linear 'plot' are reproduced rather than subject to reflexive critique.

The more performative approach to anti-narrative analysis that Riach et al. (2016) adopt draws on Butler's understanding of narrative as an attempt to give a coherent response to the experience of being called to account in emphasizing how the capacity to provide and sustain apparent narrative coherence is not just a sense-making process undertaken by organizational subjects, it is what constitutes the latter as we seek recognition of ourselves as organizationally viable.

Based on Butler's understanding of accounting for oneself, and on a commitment to 'undoing' as a methodological imperative as outlined above, what Riach et al. advocate as anti-narrative research is designed to reflexively unravel this process, the intention being to 'undo' apparent semblances of coherence in order to encourage critical reflection on the conditions of organizational recognition upon which they depend. In practice, this means that as a research method, anti-narrative interviewing is designed to put into practice a reflexive methodology that seeks to undo the conditions of subjective recognition within organizational processes and settings.

For clarification, Riach et al. (2016) use the term 'anti-narrative' to describe a methodological approach to research that seeks to unravel seemingly coherent narratives, including chronological ones, in order to reveal the labour that goes into producing and maintaining them. In addition, this approach encourages critical reflection on the consequences for those involved, of being unable or unwilling to conform to the conditions compelling the performativity required to sustain narrative coherence. Put simply, their approach encourages critical, reflexive evaluation of the conditions and consequences of narrative construction within organizational settings, through organizational process and according to organizational imperatives.[4]

Following Butler, this reflexive 'undoing' attempts to establish a methodological space in which to bring to the fore the otherwise occluded effort involved in maintaining a coherent, viable organizational self. If we recognise that organizations can effectively 'undo' us through the compulsion to perform and maintain subjective coherence in ways that often require that the complexities and contradictions underpinning them be concealed, a methodological undoing is designed to reflexively retrace the process and to 'recover', or in critical theoretical terms, 'remember' (see Honneth, 1995, 2008) the labour involved in producing semblances of coherence. As Cabantous et al. (2015: 14) emphasize in this respect, an approach to organizational research premised upon a critical performativity ideally proceeds from a shared recognition of 'the conditions of possibility for being and becoming organizational subjects' including, in a very practical sense, a mutual understanding of the various pressures and struggles engendered by those conditions.

As an illustrative example, one of Riach et al.'s (2014) participants, Chris (cited in Chapter 3), discussed what he described as the constant 'busyness' involved in negotiating recognition within organizational settings. Chris worked as a training consultant for a number of large organizations based in the United Kingdom, one of which has a reputation for particularly conservative attitudes towards LGBTQ people. As noted in Chapter 3, he explained, in a very practical sense, the identity work involved in managing what he perceived to be his subjective positioning as an 'outcast' because of his identity as an openly gay man within this environment.

The 'busyness' Chris describes (see Chapter 3) he relates specifically to the work involved in negotiating his need for belonging, for affection and intimacy, through the maintenance of a coherent, viable sense of self; in other words, one that is not, in Butler's terms, cast out (Butler, 1993) or rendered 'non-narratable' (Butler, 2005). In understanding this struggle, insights from Butler's writing are helpful in three important ways: first, in bringing the labour involved in continually striving for subjective coherence to the fore; second, in understanding how the ways in which the complexities of lived experience that are conflated through this labour constitute an organizational 'undoing' (Butler, 2004b), and, third, in creating a research space in which to reflect on the negating effects of being unable or unwilling to maintain subjective coherence, or on the sheer effort required to do so. This is precisely because, Riach et al. (2016) argue, Butler's writing opens up the methodological possibility of a critical, reflexive rather than an organizational 'undoing', one that seeks to reclaim the otherwise occluded processes and experiences such as the sense of perpetual 'busyness' that Chris describes and to understand them as a narrative response to the call, or 'hail' as Althusser puts it, to give an account of oneself. Hence, the aim of a reflexive 'undoing' is to reveal the complexities of lived experience that come to be conflated in the performance of the kind of viable, intelligible organizational subjectivities that Chris evokes.

In sum, Riach et al. (2014, 2016) explore the methodological potential that is opened up by Butler's writing on accountability, considering the latter as an organizational process, arguing that her work provides new and important ways of understanding and of studying the role that is played by organizations in compelling particular narrative performances and in constraining, or occluding, others. If, as Butler (2004b: 23) puts it, 'I tell a story about the relations I choose, only to expose, somewhere along the way, the way I am gripped and undone by these very relations', they ask:

> What does this tell us about how and why our subjectivities are compelled and *organized*? Why is it that the relations we live require us to 'tell a story'? How, and why, must our organizational settings result in us being 'undone by these very relations'?
>
> (Riach et al., 2016: 18)

Their discussion emphasizes that organizations play an important role in undoing the very narratives that they compel us to cohere on their behalf. They urge organizational scholars, practitioners and activists to interrogate this process and its consequences further, by providing critical, reflexive spaces in which to articulate how and why we continue to be 'gripped' by corporate narratives, and to consider what this means for us in terms of our lived experiences of organizational settings and relations.

In a second example of how organizational research has drawn on insights from Butler's writing in order to explain how giving an account of oneself constitutes an organizational imperative, Milroy et al. (2019) discuss the story of Bigali Hanlon, an indigenous Australian Yindji-barndi[5] woman who submitted an application to access her government files so that she could lodge a claim following the Western Australian government's announcement in 2010 that indigenous people would be compensated for unpaid wages. Milroy et al. explain how, at the age of four, Bigali was taken from her home in Mulga Downs, Western Australia, to live in a church-run hostel for 'fair-skinned' indigenous children until she was sent into indentured domestic service as a teenager. Like many other indigenous workers who were taken from their communities by the state, wages were collected on her behalf, but were never paid to Bigali. In reflecting on the issues raised by Bigali's story, Milroy et al. draw directly on Butler's (2005) writing on the costs associated with being called to give an account of oneself, considering how listening might form the basis of an ethics of recognition in feminist praxis.

The starting point for their discussion is Bigali's application to the Western Australian Stolen Wages Commission, which required documentary evidence to support claims from indigenous Australians for unpaid wages. These claims coalesced around the need to give a persuasive account on the part of indigenous people, but the effect of this process was that it positioned claimants in terms of a one-dimensional 'victim' subjectivity that replicates rather than recognizes and recompenses Bigali's earlier exploitation.

Milroy et al. show how Bigali and other indigenous people with similar stories to tell are effectively 'undone' by the Commissions to which they have made applications in a way that reduces the complexity of their lived experiences through the (self) production of coherent victim narratives.[6] Drawing on Butler (2005), their discussion of Bigali's story explores how the sharing of indigenous people's narratives might be opened up beyond 'giving an account' through a politics of listening premised upon an ethics of recognition.

Bigali's own narrative begins in *media res*, when many things have 'already taken place to make [her] story possible in language' (Butler, 2005: 39). Milroy et al.'s desire then isn't to retell Bigali's story but to unravel the coherence imposed on her narrative by a governmental process, and to emphasize how this process continues to act as an *organizing* one by compelling the conditional coherence of a 'victim' narrative on Bigali whilst purporting to offer the possibility of recognition and recompense. Bigali's account is part of a much wider story that constitutes a collective struggle for recognition. The compulsion to give a particular account of this in order to secure the possibility of compensation means that, for Bigali and many others in her position, this struggle is required to take a particular, one-dimensional narrative form.

As Butler (2005: 121, *emphasis added*) reminds us 'any discourse, any regime of intelligibility, *constitutes us at a cost*'. Milroy et al. consider Bigali's narrative as a poignant example of how the accounts that we give of ourselves to elicit recognition constitute powerful organizational processes that categorize difference and order it hierarchically at the cost of those subject to this organizing process. They also explore how feminist research and politics might listen to stories of lived experiences of this process, understanding more about its reifying effects and thinking through how stories such as Bigali's might be told differently. In other words, how narratives might be re-told to move beyond the subjective constraints of the accounts that we are compelled to give in order to be recognized as credible organizational subjects; in this instance, as those who might be recognized, respected and recompensed. In doing so, they consider what form recognition might take beyond a politics of accountability, and premised upon an understanding of difference beyond a relationship of appropriation.

For clarification, the term 'Stolen Generations' has come to represent one of the most oppressive of institutionalized dispossessions enacted by the white colonial administration in Australia from 1890s up to and including the 1970s (Milroy et al., 2019). Throughout this extensive period, Aboriginal people were subjected to extreme forms of 'governmentality' (Foucault, 1961). The constant surveillance and regulation to which they were subject was manifested in many ways, including the forced removal of children categorized as 'half-caste' from their Aboriginal families and placing them largely into state care where they could be taught proper 'civilized ways' under the protection of Aboriginal Welfare Boards. Bigali herself was caught up in this process, an experience she reflects on in the film, *Walking Tracks Back Home*[7] when she states that 'they [the state "protectors"] take you away from your family, your community, your language, your culture—it's genocide' (cited in Milroy et al., 2019).

The Australian Human Rights and Equality Opportunity Commission's report, *Bringing Them Home*, estimates that in the period 1910 to 1970 between 10 and 30 per cent of Aboriginal children were removed from their families (Langton and Barry, 1998). It highlights how in the early years the policy was explicitly directed at removing girls from Aboriginal communities before they reached puberty. Children as young as three or four were taken and adopted out to white families or were housed in dormitories, often hundreds of miles away from their families and communities. While concerns with 'racial purity' formed the basis of such policies, women and children especially also formed a pool of cheap (often unpaid) labour (Milroy et al., 2019). This further supported the racial project of 'settling' Australia by positioning white women's primary role as that of reproduction, at the same time as bolstering cultural superiority through the combined gendered and class connotations of freeing white women from domestic labour. Further, the legislation pertaining to Aboriginal people and the 'Protection Acts' enforced by the Australian government throughout the period of approximately 1890 to 1985 saw many Aboriginal people denied their entitlements to wages because of the control exercised by state and federal governments. Aboriginal people had the majority, if not all, of their wages sent to the relevant Department in their State who 'managed' their money (Milroy et al., 2019).

These wages, along with other State and Commonwealth entitlements such as maternity benefits, sickness payments and widow pensions, are collectively known as 'Stolen Wages'. In October 2006, the Australian Federal Government held a *Stolen Wages Senate Inquiry*. This inquiry received 128 submissions and published a report, *Unfinished Business: Indigenous Stolen Wages*. The report recommended that State governments allow better access to archives, fund education campaigns and provide legal research to support claimants in seeking compensation for wages or benefits never paid. Stolen Wages Commissions were established in four states: Western Australia, Queensland, Victoria and New South Wales (Milroy et al., 2019). While there were differences in the terms of reference of these Commissions, there were important similarities in the way that claimants were required to present a coherent account of their life histories, supported by documentary evidence.

In Butler's (2005) terms these accounts were given with the aim of persuading the Commissions of the intelligibility of claimants, and of the corresponding credibility of their claims, and in doing so, 'they reified the complexity of applicants' lived experience and life beyond "protection"' (Milroy et al., 2019). The accounts given to the Commissions in this sense, 'flatten' the complex layers that constitute life stories such as Bigali's in so far as they reduce the fragmentary recollections, often dependent upon aesthetic ways of knowing and understanding, to more 'factual', linear narratives that require applicants to unequivocally position themselves and each other as victims.

Bigali, like thousands of others, was called to give an account of herself as an indigenous child labourer. This required her to make her narrative cohere in order to make it intelligible in governmental terms,[8] as she was required to give coherence to the complexity of her lived experience. This meant assuming the subject position of a victim within the dominant terms of the account. A paradox of her life (and many others like her) is that Bigali has been called to account by the state, controlled and documented, indentured into a slave life, but at the same term rendered 'stateless' (Milroy et al., 2019). In order to be recognized, the State that had caused the trauma and stolen wages in the first place now required claimants such as Bigali to tell their story within the strictures of a pre-determined narrative, on their own terms and within their own timeframe, rather than hers. Further, telling the story was not in itself enough; applicants had to tell a verifiable story, supported by documentation which the State had compiled and would hand over only so that it could be re-presented in a way that lent credibility, in the form of recognition, to the claimants.[9] In this way, historical injustices associated with categorizing and classifying people, separating them off from their families and communities, alienating them from their land, ways of life and language, are effectively replicated in the governmental processes associated with the Commissions that simply position the claimants as 'victims' of workplace exploitation, as Milroy et al. (2019) emphasize in their reflections on this story.

The Stolen Wages Commissions required indigenous people to give an account of themselves. Drawing on Butler (2005) and Bigali's own reflections, Milroy et al. see two ethical problems arising from this process, both connected to what Butler (2005: 23) calls 'the social dimension of normativity that governs the scene of recognition'. First, the norms that govern the accounts that claimants were compelled to give had the power to either bequeath or withhold recognition according to normative terms set by the State, and not the claimants themselves, or their communities. Second, these normative frames of reference hold the potential to confer (or deny) the possibility of becoming a recognizable subject; in the case of the latter, the governmental process required assuming and attesting to a coherent 'victim' narrative, and providing evidence to support the credibility, or intelligibility in Butler's terms, of their claims.

In considering the first ethical concern, Milroy et al. (2019) propose moving from 'a need for coherence to embracing the incomplete, the not quite there, the unfixable'. As Bigali's story reminds us, giving an account of oneself is not simply 'telling a story', but rather constitutes the subject in a particular way; the particularity of this 'depends upon the ability to relay a set of sequential events with plausible transitions but also draws upon narrative voice and authority' (Butler, 2005: 12). Hence, subjects come into being in the context of establishing a plausible, coherent narrative account. However, as Butler has argued elsewhere (see Butler, 2004b), this coherence comes at the cost of complexity, as the account given is constrained and compelled by the norms governing subjective coherence, and the desire for recognition of oneself as socially viable.

Ahmed (2000) develops a similar critique, arguing that coherent accounts impose (or in Bigali's case, replicate) a reified order through their interpretation of lived experience; in other words, they are a *reorganization* of lived complexity. This means that the accounts that we give of ourselves can never fully express or 'carry' as Butler (2005: 36) puts it the fullness of lived experience. Requiring the Other to give a coherent account, knowing that this is impossible because the terms of impossibility have been established in advance, renders them 'non-recognizable' for which they are then condemned, as in the case of those claimants whose applications were rejected by the Commissions discussed earlier (Milroy et al., 2019). The paradox of this, the cruel ontological trick that it plays, is that producing coherence accentuates 'undoing' (Butler, 2004b) rather than alleviates it. This is because, as Bigali's story poignantly, painfully illustrates, coherent narratives can never do justice to the impossibility of communication that remains as a result of asymmetrical reciprocity.

Milroy et al. explain how, in telling her story in a way that brings this dispossession, and its histories, scars and traumas to the fore, Bigali reveals how the apparent coherence of the accounts required in governmental terms by the Commissions are just that—an imposition of coherence on an otherwise complex life story. Her story is not a coherent, linear narrative but rather a series of fragmented recollections, some of the most powerful of which are underpinned by Bigali's aesthetic experiences and sensory memories associated with the sounds and smells of her birthplace and 'home' community (Milroy et al., 2019).

For Butler (2005: 202) telling stories is a political act that can simply take the form of 'listening to, and recording, the details of the story that the other might tell'; this 'can come as the most extraordinary form of recognition'. What does Butler mean when she suggests that listening is a political act, embedded within a politics of recognition? Milroy et al. (2019) respond to this question by suggesting that a recognition-based ethical praxis of listening would require us to question 'the modes by which we are addressed and asked to take up the question of who we are' (Butler, 2005: 30). For Butler, it is the act of showing and telling, suffering and acting, within a 'crucible of social relations' that reveals how being called to account impinges upon, conditions and limits our intelligibility. Yet when we disclose ourselves, we are also, potentially, able to act on those schemes, 'undoing' them rather than being undone by them (Butler, 2004b), challenging the norms of intelligibility that govern who is allowed to be a speaking being, 'subjecting them to rupture or revision, consolidating their norms, or contesting their hegemony' (Butler, 2005: 132), as noted earlier.

Drawing on a project that highlighted the challenges associated with conducting transnational research such as that undertaken by Milroy et al. (2019), including the documenting and re-telling of a partial narrative of an woman who set herself on fire, Tiffany Page (2017) explores what it might mean to focus explicitly on explicating and recognizing vulnerability, responding to the demand that we do justice to the lives of others through the accounts that we give.

Page begins with an account of an incident that occurred in Lebanon in March 2014. Mariam al-Khawli had fled her home country of Syria with her husband and children after civil war broke out, arriving in Lebanon in early 2012. On the morning of 24 March 2014, Khawli stood outside the UN Refugee Agency office in Tripoli and set fire on herself. While her family had received food assistance from the World Food Programme since registering as refugees upon their arrival in Lebanon, sometime in August 2013 they had been deemed to be no longer eligible for the food vouchers they had been depending on. Khawli had been making regular visits to seek reinstatement of this eligibility; on the day in question, she stood outside the UN building and poured diesel over her head and clothes from a plastic bottle in her bag before setting herself on fire, resulting in her hospitalization with third-degree and deep second-degree burns. While she survived for an initial period, long enough to give some interviews to international news agencies, Khawli later died in hospital as a result of her injuries. Yet, as Page (2017: 14) explains, while her self-immolation generated global news attention, there was no reporting of her death by global media which, as she puts it, 'raises ethical questions . . . [about] our receptiveness to others'.

In her reflections on this event and the ways in which it was reported (or not), Page (2017) draws on Butler's writing on giving an account of oneself and on the political power of assemblies (see Chapter 6) to concur that 'sometimes deliberately exposing the body to possible harm is part of the very meaning of political resistance' (Butler, 2015a: 126). Like Milroy et al. (2019), Page is conscious of bringing a theoretical framework that has emerged predominantly in the (relatively privileged) United States and Western Europe into dialogue with a very particular practice of self-harm, or rather self-destruction that is very rare and enacted only under conditions of extreme precarity. At the very least, Khawli's actions leave those seeking to give an account of it on unstable epistemological ground, uncertain 'over how an act of self-harm involving an extreme form of violence could be narrated without enacting forms of epistemic and symbolic violence through the representation of Khawli's life and her self-immolation' (Page, 2017: 16).

To supplement insights from Butler (2005, 2015a), Page draws on Saba Mahmood's (2012: 199) argument that an assimilatory process of cultural 'translation', imposed in order to meet the demands for intelligibility in, for instance, academic modes of telling, means that 'inexplicable lifeworlds are rendered into certain "conceptual or communicable" forms, thereby taming and controlling that which exceeds hegemonic protocols of intelligibility'.

Page's discussion of her account of Khawli's actions and of her life before and immediately after 24 March 2014 emphasizes the importance of what she calls 'vulnerable writing' in opening up receptivity to not knowing, and to retaining uncertainty and hesitancy as integral to reflexive textual strategies and methodological approaches. Adapting questions that Mahmood (2012) raises, Page asks: What might it mean to not fully comprehend the lives upon which we make epistemic claims? And what kinds of analytical and hermeneutic resources might help us in thinking through such ethical concerns?

Responding to these questions, Page shows how as a mode of unsettled encountering, vulnerable writing requires that any move towards understanding different lifeworlds requires 'dislocating the certitude of one's own epistemological projections' (Page, 2017: 17). In practice, this involves working against dominant arrangements of temporal narratives and the compulsion to 'give an account' (Butler, 2005) by '*interrogating the organization of activities, scenes and events* into consequential sequences' (Page, 2017: 18, *emphasis added*). This method of working requires that we, as she puts it, slowly 'unstitch narratives', both pulling backwards to identify historical contexts and pushing forwards towards new modes of recognition and movements, a kind of 'undoing' narrative accountability in Butler's (2004b, 2005) terms, similar to that undertaken by Riach et al. (2016) and Milroy et al. (2019).

Drawing also on Povinelli (2011: 9), Page argues that attending to what tugs backwards within narratives can begin to illuminate how bodies, relations and attachments continue to engage in the struggle to endure, highlighting 'the effort it takes to persevere' within relations of precarity and when subject to organizational processes. In this sense, Page's account of Khawli's life shows how she had engaged in other forms of survival, and the everyday activities of care that had shaped her lifeworld, taking a 'backwards sweep' through her life using an analytical method that helps to make visible the layers of meaning and experience that are brought to the fore 'when the story is moved not only forwards but backwards, and slowed and quickened within each space' (Page, 2017: 18), crafting an epistemological 'undoing', in Butler's (2004b) sense.

For organizational scholars, practitioners and activists, Page shows how being vulnerable within research processes and accounts places unexpected affective and sensorial demands on researchers in representing the lives of others, and 'involves being receptive to the limits of *not* knowing' (Page, 2017: 18, *emphasis added*). This is a challenge for organization theorists in two important ways. First, as researchers, how do we remain open to what is not understood, to what unsettles, and to that which cannot be easily explained or articulated, or which moves us affectively? As Page (2017: 19) notes, these are questions that are not easily addressed in a context driven by performance outputs shaped by quantification and 'the need to say and declare something'. Second, it raises the question of how we can be simultaneously attentive to lived experiences of context, subjectivity and struggle, at the same time as connecting to the macro-politics of global economic systems, injustices and political processes.

As Butler emphasizes, the vulnerability engendered by precarity is always particular as it is shaped by our dependencies and attachments to contextually specific resources and support. Responding to both challenges, and to Butler's understanding of the particularity of precarity as well as its global resonances, Page's account of Khawli's life 'unstitches' a narrative composed of complex modes of endurance and resistance, showing what it means to keep holding on, '*situating her story* within the acute violence and impact of civil war, political unrest and poverty' (Page, 2017: 20, *emphasis added*).

Drawing from the particularities of Khawli's own life and the coverage of her self-immolation and resulting death in the news media, Page brings to the fore the extent to which some deaths that we think occur quickly may instead be 'slow and [are] eked out not over minutes but rather over months, years and generations' (Page, 2017: 21). As a means of attempting to disrupt erasures performed by linear narratives that strive for coherence, Page echoes Berlant's (2007) notion of the 'slow death' as she demonstrates how, in media responses to Khawli's decision to set herself alight, 'the complexity, materiality and temporality of suffering experienced within a long, drawn-out unspectacular time of precarity was . . . effaced through the singular, spectacular temporal moment of self-immolation' (Page, 2017: 21). Rather than focus on agency as a constant striving to better ourselves, Berlant suggests that we also consider agency as the capacity to endure, which, while preventing our immediate demise, slowly but surely wears us out. This attritional violence is not spectacular, but it is nevertheless destructive, and Page's argument is that the media focus on Khawli's dramatic self-immolation serves to detract from the slow death that her and her family and thousands of other refugees living unbearable lives similar to theirs have endured yet which 'struggles to be seen' (Page, 2017: 23). The task for organizational researchers, seen in this light, then becomes one of bringing this to account.

Organizational Recognition and Accountability

This kind of approach is adopted by Kate Kenny (2018) in her study of what happens to people who speak out about corruption in their organizations and who find themselves excluded from their livelihoods as a result. Kenny argues that whistleblowers experience exclusions because they have engaged in 'impossible speech'. In Butler's terms, this is an act or speech situation in which the subjectivity that is brought into being is unacceptable, illegitimate or 'unrecognizable'. Drawing on Butler's (1997a, 2005) theories of recognition, censorship and accountability, Kenny shows how norms of acceptable speech work through organizational practices such as recruitment and selection, alongside the actions of colleagues, in order to 'regulate subject positions and ultimately "undo" whistleblowers' (Kenny, 2018: 1025).

Based on a series of in-depth interviews with whistleblowers in the financial sector, Kenny's research contributes to debates on Butler's recognition-based critique of subjectivity in organizations, drawing on a performative ontology of excluded whistleblower subjects, considering how they are both 'de-realized' by organizational power relations and norms, and are compelled into ongoing and ambivalent negotiations in which they are required to give an account of themselves and their actions. In this sense, Kenny's research provides a nuanced understanding of the lived experiences and perceptions of excluded organizational subjects, focusing on so-called blacklisted whistleblowers.[10] In drawing on Butler, Kenny argues (2018: 1026) that:

> Butler's notion of censorship as a form of discursive power that produces particular kinds of subjects by instating a boundary separating legitimate from illegitimate utterances provides theoretical richness to our understanding of whistleblowing in organizations. Specifically, it shows how subjects are produced through regimes of censorship, how boundaries are created and illegitimate subjects excluded, and how people who speak out can find themselves actively contributing to this process.

In Butler's terms, de-realization occurs through the normative effects of power, producing certain subject positions by regulating the terms of intelligibility; 'de-realized subjects are not simply excluded but are unintelligible, *beyond recognition*' (Kenny, 2018: 1026, *emphasis added*). Drawing on this concept, Kenny shows how norms differentiating legitimate from impossible speech are used to control the terms of recognition, and to exercise power over the delineation of legitimate from illegitimate (and in this sense, unemployable) organizational subjects. Insights from Butler, Kenny argues, help to develop our theoretical understanding of 'blowing the whistle' on wronging; helping us to make sense of how those who speak out are excluded from their organizations and professions, Butler's writing sheds important light on 'how these exclusions relate to·one's act of speaking out, how power is implicated in this, and how this impacts upon people's subjective experiences' (Kenny, 2018: 1026).

Moving beyond 'hollow stereotypes' of a passive victim or a deserving traitor, Kenny seeks to recover the whistleblower as 'a full and complex human' (Kenny, 2018: 1026). She demonstrates, for instance, how whistleblowers experience de-realization, citing the experience of 'John', who spoke out about corruption in his bank's regional branches, where business clients were being overcharged because of pressures placed on local managers to meet impossible targets. John explained to Kenny that when his complaints to senior management amounted to nothing, he reported his concerns directly to the financial regulator, after which his colleagues marginalized him. As he put it:

> From an organizational point of view, there's a lot of ostracization [that] goes on. I think that is a common thing; you are made to feel isolated, you are made to feel outside. There's an in-group in the organization and somehow you're outside that and therefore. . . . You lose all your credibility by being outside the organization.
>
> ('John' cited in Kenny, 2018: 1038)

As their credibility is questioned, whistleblowers like John experience a process of de-realization, being called to account for their actions, and themselves. 'Peter' had been Head of Risk at a leading UK bank for a number of years before he realized that the culture in the mortgage sales department where he worked was 'dangerous' (Kenny, 2018: 1038) in its failure to adhere to basic prudence and ethics. He raised his concerns internally and was fired. What Kenny describes is an ensuing process through which Peter was called to give an account of himself. As she explains:

> When [Peter] challenged this decision through the courts, a formal investigation into his unfair dismissal claim was commissioned, although it used the firm's own auditors to carry out this apparently independent investigation. The report was based on interviews with former colleagues and bosses. The result was a document that disparaged Peter in no uncertain terms, concluding that he had been fired on personality issues, rather than his disclosures of wrongdoing.
>
> (Kenny, 2018: 1038)

Kenny cites Peter's own account of this process:

> I got a call from the editor of the *Financial Times*. He said, 'We have got the [audit firm] report. It says you are a lunatic, you are extraordinary, you ranted, you're prickly. . . . What have you got to say about that?' . . . It seemed like a disaster—it made me introvert on myself and question myself. . . . It was devastating. Can you imagine being described like that?
>
> (Peter, cited in Kenny, 2018: 1038)

In her analysis of examples such as these, Kenny demonstrates the value of insights from Butler's writing on de-realization and its connection to recognition as a way to understand how norms operate within and through organizational settings in the constitution of intelligible subjects. Butler's recognition-based critique, she argues, 'offers a rich understanding of the ways in which powerful discourses permeate the organizations we inhabit, and our vulnerability to these as subjects of recognition' (Kenny, 2018: 1029). Her focus is on developing accounts of organizational undoing, to shed light on the experiences of de-realized organizational subjects.

As Riach et al. (2014, 2016), Milroy et al. (2019), Page (2017) and Kenny (2018, 2019) all show, this process of organizational de-realization is a highly embodied one. A recent case involving a lactating mother being asked to prove that she was carrying expressed breast milk through airport security further illustrates this. In January 2017, Singaporean woman, Gayathiri Bose filed a complaint with German police alleging that she was told to squeeze her breast at airport security to prove that she was lactating. She reported being humiliated and traumatized by the experience that she was subject to because she was carrying a breast pump but was travelling without a baby.[11] Claiming the device to be suspicious, Ms Bose was required to 'account' for herself as a breastfeeding mother travelling without her baby in a way that left her feeling emotionally and physically exposed.

While Butler's analytical focus throughout *Giving an Account of Oneself* is largely on the costs attached to responding to calls to provide narrative coherence in accordance with the social norms governing recognition, or cultural intelligibility, it is with the ethical significance of the 'non-narratable' (Butler, 2005: 135) that she is, by implication, primarily concerned. Ethics requires us to constantly risk ourselves 'when what forms us diverges from what lies before us, when *our willingness to become undone in relation to others constitutes our chance of becoming human*' (Butler, 2005: 136, *emphasis added*). Returning once more to her Hegelian origins (Butler, 1987), she highlights how 'to be undone by another is a primary necessity'; it is both an ethical and an ontological endeavour, 'an aguish . . . but also a chance' (Butler, 2005: 136). In these closing lines of *Giving an Account of Oneself*, Butler connects her concern with undoing (Butler, 2004b) to the theme of precarity and dispossession that she turns to in her next substantive work, in which she considers performativity as a simultaneously ontological, ethical and political undertaking.

Notes

1. Butler herself reflects on this very point in an exchange with Vicki Kirby, when she says, 'I think perhaps mainly in *Gender Trouble* I overemphasize the priority of culture over nature, and I've tried to clear that up in subsequent writings' (Butler, in an interview with Kirby, 2006: 144).
2. By coincidence, although in a rather underdeveloped way, Althusser (2001: 119) illustrates this argument with reference to the example of individuals becoming subjects by being labelled, and related to, as either boys or girls, prior to being born. As he puts it, 'everyone knows . . . in what way an unborn child is expected. . . . Before its birth, the child is therefore always-already a subject, appointed as a subject in and by the specific familial ideological configuration in which it is "expected" once it has been conceived'.
3. See Butler (2015b: 46–47) for a discussion of the 'non-narratable'.
4. For clarification, this Butler-inspired method differs from Boje's (2001, 2008) concept of an 'ante-narrative', which emphasizes that in order to understand the full complexity of organizational storytelling it is important to examine the small, fragmented discourses that are told 'live', as events unfold, and to consider how these fragments result in stories that are complex and multiple. These fragmented, incoherent pieces of story are referred to as '*ante-narratives*' (*emphasis added*) in Boje's account and are viewed as stories told *before* narrative closure is achieved. Following Butler (2005), and emphasizing that because the (organizational) self requires constant narration as the struggle for recognition remains an on-going process, Riach et al.'s (2016) methodological premise precludes the possibility of narrative closure but instead, seeks to 'undo' the conditions compelling its pursuit. In practice, this opens up a critical space in which to reflect on the tensions, conflicts and compromises involved in becoming and maintaining viability at work through the narration of seemingly coherent, recognizable selves.
5. 'Yindjibarndi' is the name given to a distinct society of people who traditionally lived in the area near the town of Roebourne in the Pilbara region of Western Australia. The country of the Yindjibarndi people has been occupied for more than 40,000 years. It is in the Western Australian region of the Fortescue River. Over 300 indigenous Australian language groups and dialects covered the continent at the time of European settlement in 1788 (around 66 of which were in Western Australia). Today, only around 120 of those languages are still spoken and many are at risk of being lost as Elders pass away (Milroy et al., 2019).
6. See also Coulthard's (2014) critique of the 'discourse of healing' in Canada in the 1990s which, he argues, positioned indigenous people as needing to account for the harm done to them rather than interrogating a system of acculturative violence.
7. The film *Walking Tracks Back Home* is part of a larger project, *Indigenous Community Stories*, which has recorded 100 indigenous Elders from across Western Australia telling the stories of their accomplishments and reflecting on their lives and culture. The project aims to record

these oral histories for the nation to share. www.screenwest.com.au/news-events/2017/08/100th-indigenous-community-story-filmed-south-west/

8. Bigali was fortunate in that her case was well documented, and unlike many others' experiences, her documentation remained largely un-redacted (Milroy et al., 2019).

9. Despite the State being responsible for managing the wages of indigenous people under the Protection Act, many claims were rejected because of a lack of documentation. For example, in Queensland 3,200 applicants (37%) had their claims refused due to a lack of government records. Claimants' stories were not taken at face value, but required empirical substance that could be quantified. This, despite the fact that 'identity stripping' was part of the process of removal of indigenous people. Indigenous people (including Bigali) had their names changed, often several times, at the will of the State (Milroy et al., 2019).

10. Here, Kenny (2018, 2019) refers specifically to those who are excluded from their employing organization, or who are marginalized within the labour market, after speaking up about systematic corruption.

11. See www.bbc.co.uk/news/world-asia-38767588

5   Organized Dispossession
The Organizational Politics of Precarity

In *Undoing Gender* Butler (2004b: 33) emphasizes that 'the ek-static character of our existence is essential to the possibility of persisting as human'. In *Giving an Account of Oneself* (Butler, 2005: 115), she reaffirms this view, connecting it explicitly to the ontological vulnerability engendered by our primary relationality, emphasizing that it is through an 'ek-static movement', or struggle for recognition in the Hegelian sense, that the self emerges, by being drawn into a sphere of simultaneous dispossession and constitution. To recap, ek-statis is the term she uses to refer to the ethical state attached to living a life characterized by 'standing outside of oneself' (Butler, 2004a: 258).

In *Precarious Life* Butler (2004a) reminds us of the political and ethical significance of this, illustrating her argument with reference to the way in which ek-statis can denote both being 'transported beyond oneself in a passion' (Butler, 2004a: 24) and being beside oneself with grief, rage or humiliation. For Butler, two related factors shape this semantic and subjective ambiguity: the dialectical relationship between self and other, and the 'scene' of this dialectic as one in which we are situated in a world governed by norms that we have not fully chosen, in other words, that are 'beyond' us. As Lloyd (2007: 138) notes, this means that 'the ek-static character of existence . . . is inextricably tied to questions of recognition'. Butler once again 'fleshes out' what this means for how we live our lives in relation to others, against a scenography that is not entirely our own, in her discussion of precarious life. Her focus is underpinned by a question that has important resonance for organization theorists and activists: 'At what cost do I establish the familiar as the criterion by which a human life is grievable?' or liveable (Butler, 2004a: 38); in other words, what are the consequences of how the desire for recognition comes to be organized?

In the series of works in which she explores this question with reference to the theme of precarity (Butler, 2004a, 2009, Butler and Athanasiou, 2013), as Lloyd (2007: 138) outlines, Butler takes us back to arguments she developed in *The Psychic Life of Power* (Butler, 1997b) in order to do two things: first, to challenge an autonomous ontology of the subject, 'by demonstrating just how the other is a necessary condition for our persistence and survival'; and second, to explore the potential ethical (and later political) consequences of these bonds. Echoing her earliest preoccupations explored in *Subjects of Desire* (Butler, 1987) it is in *Psychic Life* that Butler emphasizes the extent to which the subject's existence depends upon this 'primary vulnerability' (Butler, 1997b: 21). All subjects emerge as a result of this mutual interdependency, but this relationality is then repressed ('forgotten'), or it is exploited and appropriated. This results in a politically induced condition, or a privative form of precarity in which certain populations 'become differentially exposed' or more vulnerable than others, 'to injury, violence and death' (Butler, 2009: xx). The context and consequences of this for social relations, and the capacity to secure and sustain a liveable life, are what concern her in *Precarious Life* (Butler, 2004a), a text that raises important questions for our understanding of the role that organizations play in responding to our primary vulnerability, and to inaugurating and perpetuating induced forms of precarity that capitalize on it, and of the consequences of this for those who have to endure unworkable lives.

Written in the aftermath of the attacks on the World Trade Centre on September 11, 2001 ('9/11') *Precarious Life* strives to re-imagine, in the context of a retaliatory 'war on terror', how the precarity of human life might become the basis for a shared radical, ethical project premised upon 'interdependency . . . as the basis for [a] global political community' (Butler, 2004a: xii–xiii). The question then becomes, as Lloyd (2007: 141) frames it, how might the experience of loss and vulnerability 'lend itself to a recognition of interdependence and community'?

Butler's response to this question is to emphasize that grief and mourning expose precarity and mutual vulnerability as signs of the inter-corporeal nature of existence. Through experiences of grief 'something about who we are is revealed, something that delineates the ties we have to others, that shows that these ties constitute who we are' (Butler, 2004a: 22); loss of another also becomes self loss as it reveals the self and other's mutual interdependence. In other words, mourning serves as a poignant reminder that inter-subjectivity is a life and death struggle. Grief and mourning are thus forms of dispossession that serve to 'remind' us of this; they are 'occasions when one body can be "undone" by another body, and it is the moment of undoing that reveals that our existence is always a being-with the other' (Lloyd, 2007: 142). For Butler, it is this 'moment' of mutual (self and other) loss when we are reminded of the primacy of our ethical relationality, of 'the condition of primary vulnerability' (Butler, 2004a: 31); at this point, being given over to the other becomes 'the source of my ethical connection' (Butler, 2004a: 46). Hence (paradoxically) loss is a transformative, affirmative experience; as Butler puts it, it is at this moment that we recognize 'we're undone by each other. And if we're not, we're missing something' (Butler, 2004a: 23).

Butler's contention that grief highlights how all fleshy, embodied existence is precarious means that all people will suffer; this is both the risk and the potential reward attached to self-loss, to being 'given over' to others. As Lloyd (2007: 142) notes, in the absence of a shared acknowledgement of this ethical primacy, however, 'political violence will be sanctioned and human lives will continue to be lost'; for Butler, violence is the most likely outcome when our primary ties to each other are forgotten, neglected or exploited. This has significant implications for the ways in which we understand human suffering within the context of organizational relations of production and consumption, particularly when set against Butler's concern that normativity governs the 'scene of recognition' (Butler, 2005: 23), shaping the terms of recognition in life and death. Hence, certain deaths count as 'mournable', worthy of grief, while others do not. In this sense, as well as our mutual vulnerability, grief and mourning remind us that while, precisely because of our primary relationality, we are all precarious, some lives are more precarious than others.

In considering these themes, as we do in this chapter, Butler returns to concerns with the social organization of the desire for recognition established through her earliest readings of Hegel (Butler, 1987). As Lloyd explains it, while Butler draws directly on Hegel she also suggests that his thinking is insufficiently attentive to two important points. First, the terms by which subjects are recognized are 'socially articulated and changeable' (Butler, 2004b: 2). Second, sometimes the terms that define what it means to be human for some are precisely those that deprive others of the possibility of achieving that status, of meeting the normative terms of 'mattering'—see Chapter 2. This endows some people with liveable, and grievable lives, while denying that possibility to others. As Lloyd (2007: 144) sums it up,

> In short, the point is that Hegel fails to acknowledge the fact that the scene of recognition itself assumes a set of cultural norms—or a normative horizon—that conditions who is recognizable as human.

This has, as Lloyd notes, profound implications for ethics and politics, as cultural normativity not only conditions who or what 'I' can be, but the terms on which 'I' might be recognized. This raises an important question: 'What happens if a life that is not recognized normatively *as a life* is violated in some way?' (Lloyd, 2007: 144, *emphasis added*). What, for Butler, is effectively a 'double negation' means that if harm is done to those who are 'unrecognized' or de-realized (see Chapter 4) then it fails to injure, since those effected are already negated (Butler, 2004a: 33).[1] This helps us to make sense, for instance, of why policies designed to offer protection from harm within organizational settings and contexts continue to be ineffective, as they fail to acknowledge the negation or misrecognition by which they are underpinned and, therefore, are undermined.

As a notable example, we might read instances of corporate man-slaughter such as the collapse of the Rana Plaza building in 2013 as examples of this double negation through which outsourced workers are harmed as a result of being situated in conditions that dehumanize and endanger them. On 24 April 2013, this building, that housed five garment factories, collapsed killing at least 1,132 people and injuring over 2,500 more, amounting to one of the worst industrial disasters on record. Negating the humanity of those whose lives were ended or destroyed effectively gives license to denying their rights to work in a safe environment, and for their deaths to be grieved, just as their working circumstances reinforce their disavowal as 'fully' human. Yet despite the scale of the collapse, reporting of the disaster at the time and since barely raised awareness of the poor working conditions faced by workers in outsourced garment factories supplying the so-called ultra-cheap fast fashion industry.[2]

As Lloyd notes, this 'double negation' presents the problem of how to identify with the suffering of those positioned as Other, including within and through organizational mechanisms. If, as Butler maintains, abject deaths constitute 'the melancholic background for my social world' (Butler, 2004a: 46), this relationship further negates the humanity of those whose lives are 'unrecognizable' and by the same token, whose deaths are ungrievable, or are grieved only in a reified way.

So-called 'Grenfell tourism' is another poignant example of this. In his account of the structural causes of the Grenfell Tower disaster, John Preston (2019) warns of the dangers of appropriating and ventriloquizing one of the most tragic events in British history, an approach that can 'misrecognize and commodify suffering'. On 14 June 2017, the twenty-four-story Grenfell Tower block of flats in North Kensington, London, caught fire, causing the deaths of seventy-two people. The rapid spread of the fire has been attributed to the cladding used on the outside of the building, resulting in the worst residential fire in the United Kingdom since the Second World War.[3] Preston's (2019: 55) account frames the disaster as a consequence of capitalism's 'everyday horrific functioning' and as a stark illustration of what he calls 'eliminationism': the decimation of populations for ideological purposes, notably on class or racial grounds.

The documentary film *The Trap* also attests to the differential distribution of precarity in the way that Butler (2009; Butler and Athanasiou, 2013) describes it, showing how US prisons have become lucrative recruiting grounds for a multi-billion dollar domestic sex trafficking industry that thrives on the lack of value placed on those whose vulnerability is exploited. All of the women the documentary makers spoke to had experienced histories of abuse and trauma: 'for many, the path into pimp-controlled prostitution had started with a need for love or a relationship which had been twisted through domestic violence, drug use and survival into something very different' (Kelly and McNamara, 2018: 53). The women were 'branded as outcasts'. Much of the filming took place in a Massachusetts jail in which many of the women serving were only in their twenties but had been in and out of prison throughout most of their adult lives, with a bleak resignation that things would be no different when they were released again. Their lack of hope that their lives could be otherwise is a recurring feature in the women's narratives, and the film shows how the prison system has become a lucrative hunting ground for sex traffickers seeking to capitalize on the women in question's isolation, sense of shame and vulnerability. The 'trap' of incarceration and exploitation that gives the film its name speaks to how precarious these women are; paradoxically, they are possessed in the sense of being reduced to the status of things because subjectively, socially, they are entirely dispossessed.

This film powerfully illustrates Butler's view that dependency (our primary, relational precarity) is not in itself exploitation (an imposed precarity), but it is 'a domain of dependency that is open to exploitation' (Butler, 2015b: 7). Susceptibility is not the same as subjugation, 'though it can clearly lead there'—the exploitation of vulnerable people's combined trust and dependency being a prime example. Being human, in this sense, carries with it the constant risk of dispossession simply because we are 'already undone, or undone from the start' (Butler, 2015b: 11) as she puts it; our condition of relationality means that 'we are never quite "done" with being undone' (Butler, 2015b: 16).

Dispossession and/as Organization

These themes are explored in a book co-authored in the form of a dialogue with Athena Athanasiou, in which Butler (2013) develops her performative ontology of gender (Butler, 1988, 1990/2000a), considered in Chapter 1 and throughout subsequent chapters. Performativity had hitherto in her writing tended to be conceived of largely as an individual, albeit it, inter-subjective process. In *Dispossession*, Butler lays the groundwork for a more plural (organized) theory of performativity, paving the way for the more collective, politicized themes explored in Chapter 6, on assemblage (Butler, 2015a) and vulnerability as resistance (Butler, 2016—see Postscript). It is here that she connects her thinking much more explicitly, arguably more so than ever before in her writing, to work, organizations and the labour market.

With this in mind, understanding her framing of dispossession as the political corollary of 'undoing' helps us to grasp the extent to which the displacements referred to above are collective, organizational processes of negation that poignantly illustrate the materiality of misrecognition. Once again, the theoretical basis of Butler's discussion of dispossession is a critical reading of the Hegelian dialectics of recognition, and a phenomenological understanding of the self as a situated, inter-corporeal 'relational sociality' (Butler and Athanasiou, 2013: 65), a theme that arguably underpins all of Butler's writing up to this point (see Butler, 2015b) and subsequently. As suggested earlier, it is in her writing on dispossession that she develops her understanding of performativity as a more political plurality. She does so by framing dispossession as the political parallel to 'undoing' as an ontological and organizational process, premised on the view that there is, on the one hand, a form of dispossession that we must value (a *relational* form—explored in *Giving an Account of Oneself*), and on the other, one that we must stand against, a *privative* form. The latter makes the full realization of the former impossible through its exploitation, as 'the power of dispossession works by rendering certain subjects, communities, or populations unintelligible' (Butler and Athanasiou, 2013: 20). In this sense, precarity as a relational, existential category is presumed to be primordial and socially shared, whilst 'precarity as a condition of induced inequality and destitution' is a way of exploiting this sociality, a process that is a profoundly organizational one. The latter is in part because this privative form of precarity, one situated within wider patterns of differential access to symbolic and material resources, means that discourses on vulnerability are used to 'shore up' paternalistic power, 'relegating the conditions of vulnerability to those who suffer discrimination, exploitation or violence' (Butler, 2016: 13).

For Butler and Athanasiou, this reification leads us to 'forget' the inter-corporeal nature of our primary, relational precarity through which we are all dispossessed:

> Through our bodies we are implicated in . . . intense social processes of relatedness and interdependence. . . . We are dispossessed by others, moved toward others and by others, affected by others and able to affect others.
>
> (Butler and Athanasiou, 2013: 55)

This 'forgetting' is because the differential allocation of resources and relations of recognition mean that dispossessed individuals and groups become subject to an additional, privative form of precarity, as

> We are dispossessed by normative powers that arrange the uneven distribution of freedoms; territorial displacement, evisceration of means of livelihood, racism, poverty, misogyny, homophobia, military violence.
>
> (Butler and Athanasiou, 2013: 55)

In contrast to what Athanasiou calls 'the governmental logics of tolerance' (Butler and Athanasiou, 2013: 66), which 'seeks to govern and enclose ontologically, possessively, the realm of human subjectivity and relationality' what is needed, Butler argues, is

> Not the creation of tolerant and tolerated identities, *susceptible to the market of recognition*, but rather the destabilization of the regulatory ideals that constitute the horizon of this susceptibility.
> (Butler and Athanasiou, 2013: 66, *emphasis added*)

Here Butler reminds us of Elizabeth Povinelli's (2002: 108) warnings about the 'cunning of recognition'—neo-liberalism's capacity to reproduce itself and its norms of recognition through a discourse of 'tolerance'. She argues that liberalism's cunning lies in its capacity to confer recognition through evoking the same governmental logic to ask and answer the question: 'who are you?' with the self-styled response 'you are one of us'.

Implicitly, pursuing a relational rather than a 'cunning', market-orientated form of recognition involves a mode of existence that involves 'risking intelligibility . . . living in a critical relation to the norms of the intelligible' (Butler and Athanasiou, 2013: 67)—moving from a norm of 'inclusivity' premised upon tolerance (risking over-inclusion, or conditional inclusion), to a recognition-based ethic of relationality, requiring us to take risks with intelligibility, living in a critical relation to social norms. Norms of inclusivity therefore threaten us with both unintelligibility (repression, exclusion), and with over-intelligibility (repetition, conditional inclusion). This leads us to the question of how to make way for an 'ethical relationality' (Butler and Athanasiou, 2013: 72) premised upon recognition.

Underlying these considerations is a very practical question: How do we survive liberal, organizational and organizing forms of recognition? Which is, of course, linked with another question—how do we survive without it? To paraphrase Spivak (1993), inclusion (in the form of employability, for instance) as an organizational form of liberal, market recognition becomes 'that which we cannot not want' (see Butler and Athanasiou, 2013: 76).

Moving away from the immanent critique of earlier work, Butler's aim in her discussion with Athanasiou is to 'formulate . . . a politics of the performative' (Butler and Athanasiou, 2013: x). With echoes of Honneth (1995), her focus on a political, reflexive form of dispossession emphasizes the latter as 'a form of responsiveness that gives rise to action and resistance' (Butler and Athanasiou, 2013: xi). This is distinguished throughout her analysis from a more systematic form of dispossession of people through, for example, forced migration, unemployment, homelessness, occupation and conquest (see Butler and Athanasiou, 2013: xi)—ways of being that 'systematically jettison populations from modes of collective belonging and justice' (Butler and Athanasiou, 2013: xi), as Preston (2019) describes in his discussion of 'eliminationism'.

The 'Trouble' With Dispossession

Butler's premise therefore is that, on the one hand, dispossession 'signifies an inaugural submission of the subject-to-be to norms of intelligibility'; this form of 'mastery' constitutes processes of subjection that resonate with the psychic foreclosures discussed in her critique of 'undoing' (determining the attachments that are possible and plausible to become a subject—see Butler and Athanasiou, 2013: 1). Here dispossession refers to an oppressive subjection to norms of social, political and organizational intelligibility and so to being 'undone' by them. In this sense,

> Being dispossessed refers to processes and ideologies by which persons are disowned and abjected by normative and normalizing power that define cultural intelligibility and that regulate the distribution of vulnerability.
>
> (Butler and Athanasiou, 2013: 2)

Drawing also on David Harvey's (2003) critique of the neo-liberal drive towards 'accumulation by dispossession', dispossession is framed as both existential (ontological) and ascribed (social) precarity, the latter as an exploitation of the former in the generation of human capital: 'we can only be dispossessed because we are *already* dispossessed. Our interdependency establishes our vulnerability to social forms of deprivation' (Butler and Athanasiou, 2013: 5, *emphasis added*), because of our 'primordial disposition to relationality' (Butler and Athanasiou, 2013: 5). This implies that the relational ethic explored and advocated in *Giving an Account of Oneself* (Butler, 2005) provides the ontological basis for dispossession, as well as the collective means to recognize and challenge it. The analytical tasks then become, first, how to think about dispossession outside of a logic of possession, and second, to explore how and why this more reflexive dispossession might be rendered socially and politically plausible, if it is the case, as Butler argues, that 'the privative form of dispossession makes the relational form of dispossession impossible' (Butler and Athanasiou, 2013: 9).

Dispossession is one of the few texts where Butler engages directly with work and the labour market, noting how among other manifestations of precarity, dispossession 'signifies the violent appropriation of labour and the wearing out of labouring and non-labouring bodies' (Butler and Athanasiou, 2013: 11), as forms of subjectivity are produced that transform human life into capital in a society in which being and having are constituted as ontologically akin to each other: 'being is defined as having; having is constructed as an essential prerequisite of proper human being' (Butler and Athanasiou, 2013: 13). This framing of dispossession as simultaneously referring to our undoing by social norms, and at the same time, our capacity to reflexively, critically 'undo' those norms (Butler, 2004b), extends the dynamic critique that underpins Butler's earlier writing on 'making trouble' with/through gender (Butler, 1988, 1990/2000a), beginning to shift (as signalled below) from a concern with mattering to the more political concept of 'appearing' (Arendt, 1958) that she focuses on in later work—see Chapter 6. As Butler puts it:

> Even though we are compelled to reiterate the norms by which we are produced as present subjects, this very reiteration poses a certain risk [being undone]. . . . But we might also start to performatively displace and reconfigure the contours of what matters, appears, and can be assumed as one's own intelligible presence.
>
> (Butler and Athanasiou, 2013: 15)

In essence, what this suggests is that relationality recognizes the spectral presence of what is materially present but subjectively and semiotically absent (see Butler and Athanasiou, 2013: 16). The spectre in this sense is not 'meant to conjure away corporeality' (Butler and Athanasiou, 2013: 16)—on the contrary, it is 'the trace that remains from the other's uncanny presence as absence—her present absence'. Here, drawing largely on Derrida (1994: 126), Butler argues that spectres occupy positions of 'invisible visibility' (a 'hyper-corporeality', existing in a physical but not subjective sense—see Butler and Athanasiou, 2013: 17). Her starting premise is how recognition of this spectral 'remainder' might function as a critique of ontology, or the conditions shaping ontology to be more precise, considering what possibilities for theory and practice this might open up. As Butler puts it, echoing her earlier concerns in *Gender Trouble*, but imbuing these with a more collective emphasis: 'How might we re-imagine performativity through this troubling of conventional categorizations of the ontological?' (Butler and Athanasiou, 2013: 17). This question continues an important thread opened up in *Precarious Life* in which Butler (2004a) discusses the 'derealization of the Other' as leading to the latter's interminably spectral presence, a point she illustrates with reference to deaths that remain unmarked and ungrieved.[4]

Butler's recognition-based critique of dispossession (and her response to the earlier question), developed in dialogue with Athanasiou once again strongly echoes her Hegelian influences, as illustrated by her acknowledgement that 'being dispossessed by the other's presence and by our own presence to the other *is the only way to be present to one another*' (Butler and Athanasiou, 2013: 17, *emphasis added*). The phenomenological starting premise of her analysis builds on this in two important respects. First, her concern with the problem of how to be present to one another, 'fully there', in ways 'not assimilated or submitted to the ontological presuppositions of normative authoritarian self-presence' (Butler and Athanasiou, 2013: 18). Second, her analysis of dispossession is more grounded than the ontological/subjective concerns of earlier works, including *Undoing Gender* (Butler, 2004b), articulated through a more explicitly phenomenological interest in the *situatedness* of precarity (in both its relational and reified forms). Here Butler takes situatedness to refer to the *emplacement* that produces and constrains intelligibility, arguing that

> The logic of dispossession is interminably mapped onto our bodies, onto particular bodies-in-place, through normative matrices but also through situated practices of raciality, gender, sexuality, intimacy, able-bodiedness, economy and citizenship.
>
> (Butler and Athanasiou, 2013: 18)

Emplacement therefore 'produces dispossessed subjectivities . . . putting them in their proper place' (Butler and Athanasiou, 2013: 18–19). *Taking place* refers therefore both to assuming a place and in some sense to happening/occurring in a situated way: we become/come to exist in a subjective sense by assuming a place, by becoming *emplaced*. Hence being kept out of place or in our 'proper place' precludes this (reducing us to a perpetual immanence) as, in an existential sense, for the human subject to emerge, the 'proper must be displaced' (Butler and Athanasiou, 2013: 21). Although Butler herself does not develop this line of thinking with reference to work and the labour market, this insight has important implications for how we think about being *emplaced* in and through organizational life, and for understanding the ways in which this process of emplacing reifies dispossession.

The relational critique of dispossession that she does develop, however, one that is premised upon a phenomenological approach that is reminiscent of much earlier work—see Butler, 1988), leads Butler to argue that the self-contained, proper(tied) liberal subject is

> Constituted through, and inhabited by, processes of de-subjectifying others, *rendering them usable, employable, but then eventually into waste matter*, or of no use: always available, always expendable.
>
> (Butler and Athanasiou, 2013: 27)

Consequently, 'the matter that must be addressed constantly and forcefully is the differential allocation of humanness' (Butler and Athanasiou, 2013: 31). For Butler, this is once again a question of 'mattering', but on a more collective scale than in earlier writing (Butler, 1993) whereby mattering here is taken to refer to having a material presence (being 'stuff') that is unable to signify anything of meaning or value, hence being simple 'waste matter'.

In this sense (and echoing Butler, 1993), the political emphasis of her critique of dispossession lies in its capacity to open up radical re-articulations of what it means to matter, 'rather than a rehabilitation of the humanist subject in the form of liberal tolerance or assimilatory inclusion of ready-made identities' (Butler and Athanasiou, 2013: 34). Her aim is to do so by 'moving toward a relational view' of human subjectivity (Butler and Athanasiou, 2013: 35), by finding ways to reinstate, or re-cognize our primary relationality.

In her dialogue with Butler, Athanasiou distinguishes between (i) 'that which gets abjected or foreclosed from the human'; and (ii) 'forms of life that are conferred recognition as human according to the established norms of recognizability, on the condition of and at the cost of conforming to these norms' (Butler and Athanasiou, 2013: 36), producing an 'exclusionary inclusion' (Butler and Athanasiou, 2013: 36). The latter involves being 'conditionally interpellated in the all-too-intelligible categories of the normative human' (Butler and Athanasiou, 2013: 36). Athanasiou maps this out in order to ask: Is it possible to 'trouble' this from the outside, that is, to establish a sustained challenge to the limits of the tolerable, through a communal performativity? This question raises the radical potential that emerges from loss, foreclosure and normative exclusion in a way that connects to Butler's (2008) engagement with Honneth, positing a relational enactment of struggle as one possible outcome of communities that are collectively negated (see Butler and Athanasiou, 2013: 36–37).

To set the groundwork for this shift towards a more collective understanding of a politics of 'mattering' and of a plural performativity in her work, Butler recaps on the basic premises of her writing, particularly her concern with 'the power relations that condition in advance who will count or matter as a recognizable, viable human subject and who will not' (Butler and Athanasiou, 2013: 78). Reminding us of her Foucauldian-infused Hegelian understanding of recognition as the normative, disciplinary regime through which human beings become social subjects, Butler's concern is with the regimes of power that regulate inter-subjectivity, 'defining what renders a subject legible, recognizable, desirable' (Butler and Athanasiou, 2013: 94).

Linking this later in the text specifically to embodiment, Athanasiou also emphasizes from Butler's work how 'normative ontologies of the body work to judge, adjudicate and demarcate which bodies matter' (Butler and Athanasiou, 2013: 97). Here mattering is developed into 'counting'; bodies matter because they have *enumerable value*, 'through current regimes of management, whereby bodies are measured and assessed through the governmentality of profitability, accumulation, auditability and indebtedness' (Butler and Athanasiou, 2013: 100). 'Fit' is also touched on here; Athanasiou notes how regulatory fictions and aesthetic ideals that no one would ever be able to embody

> Wield significant power and efficacy as they congeal over time to produce—or, to materialize—the effect of substance as the 'natural' grounds of identity coherence.
>
> (Butler and Athanasiou, 2013: 98)

It is thinking through these issues of embodiment, and of how to relate an ethics of corporeal vulnerability to a politics of autonomy and integrity, that leads Butler to consider a more collective politics of performativity, a 'plural performativity' as she puts it (Butler and Athanasiou, 2013: 157). This she develops largely in response to Athanasiou's question: 'How . . . might ideas of corporeal vulnerability resonate with social movement strategies and political claims of corporeal autonomy and self-determination?' (Butler and Athanasiou, 2013: 98).

This emphasis on plural performativity, prompted by her dialogue with Athanasiou, leads Butler to ask how the inter-corporeality and conviviality of assembled crowds opens up the potential for a radical critique of organized or imposed precarity in its 'privative' form. This is a theme she explores in more depth in her later work (see Chapter 6 and Postscript), but which she raises here as a significant concern underpinning the development of her thinking, particularly when she asks about what scope there might be for an 'alternative economy of bodies':

> How does this alternative economy of bodies offer space for effectual critique of the disembodied and affectively purified subject of conventional liberal democracy? How does this alternative economy of bodies offer space for objecting to neoliberal regimes of economization of life?
>
> (Butler and Athanasiou, 2013: 176)

Reiterating the rewards and not just the risks attached to ek-statis (Butler, 1987), she reminds us of how recognition 'designates the situation in which one is fundamentally dependent upon terms that one never chose in order to emerge as an intelligible being' (Butler and Athanasiou, 2013: 79). This means that recognition, particularly in its organized/organizational forms, 'is not in itself an unambiguous good, however desperate we are for its rewards' (Butler and Athanasiou, 2013: 82), because first, the terms are not of our own making, and second, because of the costs/conditions attached to such reified forms of recognition. However, in a non-reified form, one wrested from market orientation, recognition has the potential, she argues, to reinstate our primary relationality, not simply individually, but collectively. In practice this means that

> One of the most crucial challenges that we face today, both theoretically and politically, *is to think and put forward a politics of recognition that addresses, questions and unsettles . . . [market] mechanisms of recognition.*
>
> (Butler and Athanasiou, 2013: 83, *emphasis added*)

To paraphrase, this means that we ought to consider what needs to be done (or undone) in order to rearticulate, or re-signify, the discursive and normative apparatuses of organizations in order to be able to mobilize alternative versions of intelligibility and mechanisms of recognition. In other words, to put the issue rhetorically: How can we develop an ethical and political basis for a critical recognition, one that is reflexive and relational within/through organizational settings and processes? Responding to this kind of question, and drawing on Fanon's (1967) *Black Skin, White Masks*, Butler emphasizes her relational understanding of reflexivity, emphasizing that 'self-questioning is not merely an inward turn, but a mode of address' (Butler and Athanasiou, 2013: 81).

Again, thinking through the implications of this for organizational politics and practice, to paraphrase Butler (Butler and Athanasiou, 2013: 83), much depends on our ability to function as subjects who can engage organizational power without becoming subjugated by it (or allowing others to be). But—'can we pick and choose our involvement?' (Butler and Athanasiou, 2013: 83). One also needs to ask: To what extent are the regulatory discourses of organizations available to appropriation by radical strategies of resignification and subversion (Butler and Athanasiou, 2013: 84–85)? How might this be brought about, and how sustainable might it be if such critical engagements are constantly 'vulnerable to the co-opting forces of liberal, market recognition' (Butler and Athanasiou, 2013: 85)?

Butler and Athanasiou reflect on these dilemmas in their discussion entitled 'Relationality as self-dispossession'. Here Butler clarifies how dispossession implies our 'relationality and binding to others . . . but also our structural dependence on social norms that we neither choose nor control' (Butler and Athanasiou, 2013: 92). The *assigned* form of dispossession that results from this 'entails the different and differential manner in which the anxieties and the excitements of relationality are social distributed' (Butler and Athanasiou, 2013: 92).

Returning to Wendy Brown (2006) as a reference point, Butler emphasizes what we might think of as the paradox of inclusion, namely how a 'tolerant, inclusive ontology might work as the swiftest way to exclusion' (Butler and Athanasiou, 2013: 119). For Brown, tolerance or 'inclusion' as it is commonly articulated through organizational discourses, constitutes a governmental technique for regulating aversion and of managing the limits of the tolerable, forming the basis of an exclusionary inclusion. In her essay, 'The Political Affects of Plural Performativity', Butler explores this latter theme in more depth, further laying the groundwork for later work (Butler, 2015a) in which she develops a performative theory of assembly (see Chapter 6).

She does so, in part, by asking how a recognition of collective ek-statis might move us towards assembling and experiencing life beyond 'the normative operations of power that regulate the limits of the desirable, the sensible, and the intelligible' (Butler and Athanasiou, 2013: 177). Affect as an ek-static mode of being, one that 'signifies affecting *and* being affected by the corporeal dynamic of relatedness, mutual vulnerability, and endurance . . . being beside oneself' (Butler and Athanasiou, 2013: 177, *emphasis added*), is crucial to such an endeavour. Embodied assemblies potentially open up the possibility of a 'performative force in the public domain' (Butler and Athanasiou, 2013: 196), consisting of a collective bodily presence. This 'collective thereness' (Butler and Athanasiou, 2013: 197) enables bodies to 'enact a message, performatively' (Butler and Athanasiou, 2013: 197), articulating connections, a sensibility that is different from that of the market and an enactment of values, one that signals 'a defence of our collective precarity and persistence in . . . *refusing to become disposable*' (Butler and Athanasiou, 2013: 197, *emphasis added*).

In the final chapter of *Dispossession*, 'Spaces of Appearance, Politics of Exposure', Butler explores the importance of affective labour to critical agency (see Butler and Athanasiou, 2013: 193) in forging an alternative to the present. With careful wording that seems to (characteristically) hint at a radical reversal of the idea of 'accounting' as a disciplinary process of subjectification (Butler, 2005—see Chapter 4), she explains that for her, this question of futurity is

> The challenge of taking into account the politics of precarious and dispossessed subjectivity, in claiming the right and the desire to a political otherwise.
>
> (Butler and Athanasiou, 2013: 194)

In considering this issue, Butler develops a situated understanding of the affective politics of the performative that resonates with (and draws on) Arendt's (1958) formulation of the 'space of appearance'. Here Butler returns to her idea of 'taking place' as a performative process (both a happening and a possessing, a becoming in/through place, as noted earlier) as she considers this process in relation to the theme of who and what 'counts' as subjectively viable, particularly in relation to a consideration of the latter's aesthetics in a way that makes important empirical connections to organizational scholarship when she notes that

> It is through stabilizing norms of gender, sexuality, nationality, raciality, able-bodiedness, land and capital ownership that subjects are interpellated to fulfil the conditions of possibility for their appearance to be recognized.
>
> (Butler and Athanasiou, 2013: 195)

This reminds us of the fundamental question (regarding the social conditions and consequences of the power relations governing the conferral or denial of recognition): How do particular forms of 'corporeal engagement' (Butler and Athanasiou, 2013: 195) become intelligible, sensible, liveable, in other words, how do they become organizationally viable? And, more importantly, how do we challenge and change those conditions in order to broaden the range of possibilities? Organizational scholars and activists have begun to make important inroads into addressing these issues in recent years, drawing directly on Butler's writing on precarity and dispossession, exploring these themes as organizational phenomena and problems.

Precarity and Dispossession at Work

Kenny's (2010) discussion of Butler's notion of the ek-static self is an especially notable example, one that considers the influence of this particular aspect of Butler's thinking within work and organization studies. Kenny (2010: 1) focuses specifically on how sociality, as the basis of mutual recognition, is vulnerable to organizational processes of 'exclusion and policing'. The full implications of Butler's concept of passionate attachment[5] for understanding the management and experience of workplace identification, developed most notably in her emphasis on 'the fundamental sociality of embodied life' (Butler, 2004a: 22; cited in Kenny, 2010: 14), deserves a fuller consideration within work and organization studies, Kenny argues, and this is precisely what her own research picks up on.

In her discussion of whistleblowers, Kenny (2018: 1028) notes the importance for organizational scholars of engaging with those who are left out of processes of organizational recognition, 'whose very subjectivity has been foreclosed'. She reminds us that Butler's Hegelian understanding of subject formation means that this exclusion is inevitable in a process—organization—premised upon othering. As Butler puts it (noted earlier), the exclusionary matrix 'by which subjects are formed . . . requires the simultaneous production of a domain of abject beings, those who are not yet "subjects", but who form the constitutive outside of the domain of the subject' (Butler, 1993: 3). These 'de-realized' subjects are unrecognized by dominant normative frameworks and are therefore seen as invalid, lacking legitimacy; they are 'not-quite' lives (Butler, 2009; cited in Kenny, 2018: 1028).[6] The signifying capacity of those who count as human but not as subjects in this sense means that they cannot lay claim to rights and needs; as fundamentally unrecognizable, their lives are correspondingly ungrievable.

Kenny (2019) develops her analysis further in what is, to date, one of the most sustained applications of the full breadth of Butler's thinking to the analysis of organizational life, taking in her Hegelian and Foucauldian influences, her theory of performativity, precarity, psychic power, vulnerability, accountability and sociality in her discussion of 'affective recognition'. The latter draws in particular on Butler's writing on passionate attachment as a useful way to make sense of the precarity experienced by those who speak out about organizational wrongdoing. Kenny develops the idea of affective recognition to explain how, for whistleblowers, constituting a sense of self can involve subjection to norms and practices known to cause harm. Premised upon the idea of 'a radically social self', affective attachment offers, Kenny argues, a way to see how 'the norms at work in the organizations and institutions that dominate our lives affect our sense of who we are' (Kenny, 2019: 3–4), and by implication, who/what we are not.

Kenny draws on the concept of affective recognition to provide an account of the treatment and experiences of whistleblowers that illustrates processes of organizational subject formation beyond an (illusory) autonomous or discursive constitution of the self, one that is 'radically criss-crossed with desires for subjection to powerful discourses and histories of affective attachments' (Kenny, 2019: 48), premised upon an understanding of the self as the performative effect of ek-statis (Butler, 1987; Butler and Athanasiou, 2013). For Kenny, whistleblowing shows how the concept of the autonomous self as the basis of ethical relations is illusory as, in ways that are beyond our own constitution (or indeed, conscious awareness), we are embedded with others, ek-statically so. As Butler (1987; Butler and Athanasiou, 2013) emphasizes, our need for recognition means that our subjectivity is always in process, beyond itself. In organizational terms, this leads us to embrace harmful attachments that induce violence against us and others, at an individual level, in the case of abjected whistleblowers, and at a more social, structural level through the norms of global finance (or corporate or social disasters, such as those discussed earlier).

Against the backdrop of the personal accounts that Kenny draws on in her analysis of this, is a critique of our wider subjection to global finance norms. As she puts it, we are led to embrace terms of existence that cause harm because they are deeply entrenched in our sense of who we are and in our understanding of and engagement with the modes of organization that provide the structural and relational context for our lives; a set of circumstances that works to reinforce the prevailing authority of global finance and neo-liberal capitalism.

In her critique of this, Kenny (2019) draws on Butler and Athanasiou's (2013: 146) concern (one that takes Arendt (1958) as its reference point) with the relationship between dispossession and disposability, the latter framed as 'a contemporary characteristic of the human condition'. Connecting their dialogue on dispossession to themes in Butler's (1993) earlier writing on bodies that matter Butler and Athanasiou's (2013: 146) discussion of disposability revolves around practices that exploit bodies as resources on the basis of political power that operates 'along racial, gendered, economic, colonial and postcolonial lines', as noted earlier. As they put it, and influencing Kenny's (2018, 2019) account of the fate of whistleblowers, through practices that exploit abject and dispossessed bodies, 'people become expendable and disposable by forces of exploitation, poverty, machismo, homophobia, racism, and militarization'. This means that we can understand the politics of disposability as a way of abjecting those bodies that don't matter in terms of signifying value, but which matter just enough to be appropriated. In organizational terms, disposability therefore refers to an increasingly global scenario in which

> A body is hyper-instrumentalized for a brief period of employment and then arbitrarily deemed disposable, only then to be again taken up for instrumental purposes for another specific employment task and then once again abandoned.
>
> (Butler and Athanasiou, 2013: 147–148)

Butler alludes to the dialectical nature of this process with reference to the 'violent rhythms' of a labour market premised upon dispossession and disposability when she says:

> We have to be able to think about the arbitrary and violent rhythms of being instrumentalized as disposable labour: never knowing the future, being subjected to arbitrary hirings and firings, having one's labour intensively utilized and exploited and then enduring stretches of time, sometimes indefinite, in which one has no idea when work might come again. Subjection to such violent rhythms produces that pervasive sense of a 'damaged future' to which Lauren Berlant refers.
>
> (Butler and Athanasiou, 2013: 148)[7]

Lived experiences of undocumented, unprotected migrant labour are among the most notable examples of this attribution of disposability, the latter perhaps being explicated by Butler and Athanasiou as the labour market corollary of precarity in its broader sense. Global manifestations of imperialism, migration and the consequences of a rise of right-wing extremism are embodied at a local level by such workers, whose narratives foreground the currents of vulnerability that underpin Butler and Athanasiou's concerns. The precarious working conditions, not to mention the psychic harm inflicted by having to leave family behind and to work in unliveable conditions are increasingly recognized by organizational scholars and activists as shaping the dehumanizing effects of disposability. Ultimately, however, such dehumanization underpins disposability as it obfuscates recognition of the other's vulnerabilities, and therefore opens the way for the latter's exploitation, as Kenny's research shows. Indeed, work is perhaps the most significant aspect of life where vulnerability is especially apparent for undocumented migrant workers, for whom precarity is experienced not least through the constant threat of being deported. This 'deportation threat dynamic' (Fussell, 2011: 593), illustrative of the rhythmic nature of disposability to which

Butler and Athanasiou refer, allows (perhaps even encourages) migrant workers' exploitation by unscrupulous employers who are willing to take advantage of vulnerable workers for their own financial benefit. Undocumented migrant workers are particularly vulnerable to exploitation as such employers recognize their 'high tolerance' for abusive working conditions due to their pervasive fear of being reported, with wage theft being a particularly common mechanism of exploitation, as migrant workers lack any legitimate recourse, further accentuating their precarious labour market status and disposability (Segarra and Prasad, 2019).

The notion of a 'damaged future' also recurs as a motif in the accounts of the whistleblowers in Kenny's research. Underpinning their struggle for credible, recognition-based subjectivity are processes of subjection, namely to organizational terms of intelligibility as well as wider social norms, notably those 'global financial norms [that] give rise to certain kinds of subjecthood' (Kenny, 2019: 45) and abjection. The latter can involve a 'stark othering of those colleagues who also witnessed wrong-doing, but who stayed silent' (Kenny, 2019: 42).

Through engaging in speech about corrupt practices that were known about by many others in their employing organizations but which were rarely acknowledged or discussed, those who transgress corporate norms, including the terms of intelligibility operating in the wider sphere of global finance, are deemed illicit. The result, Kenny (2019) illustrates, is a denial of recognition for those transgressive speakers, one that is often violent. Kenny's account highlights how, as well as forms of physical and social exclusion, the latter also often involve psychic harm, often also involving practices of self-violence on the part of those who,

> Despite having left their organizations and being in dispute with them for long afterwards, remain deeply attached to them and to the norms therein. These norms include prescribed silence in the face of wrongdoing and the attendant exclusion of those who do not comply and speak up regardless. Paradoxically, whistleblowers are themselves not immune, because of their deep-seated organizational attachments. They can internalize this normative negation. Such aggression, turned inward, can lead to painful and anxiety inducing struggles . . . it can yield continual self-questioning about whether one had done the right thing.
>
> (Kenny, 2019: 45)

Connecting in-depth accounts of individual lived experience to organizational contexts and wider structural inequalities in her analysis of whistleblowing, Kenny shows how Butler's ideas about guilt, normative violence and recognition shed light on this complex and destructive process of self-questioning as one of de-realization. Yet Kenny also shows, drawing on Butler's (1988, 1990/2000a) performative theory of subjectivity, how something powerful can occur when the unintelligible, excluded other lays a claim to reality.

Varman and Al-Amoudi (2016) develop this particular line of argument further, exploring how as subaltern people, indigenous workers in the Indian village of Mehdigani, where an environmentally damaging bottling plant was set up in 1999, were 'de-realized' by the Coca-Cola corporation through practices that legitimated violence against them. They show how the workers' recourse was denied because of their designation as de-realized, ungrievable subjects or 'non-lives'. While their account also demonstrates how, in collaboration with local activist groups such as village councils, some workers attempted to resist the de-realisation to which they were subject through protest activities that raised awareness of their vulnerability, the corporation appropriated these claims 'through a paternalistic discourse' mobilized by Coca-Cola to justify violence and de-realisation practices, resulting in what Varman and Al-Amoudi (2016: 1909) call 'accumulation through derealization', and a perpetuation of violence against those most vulnerable to it.

Building on recent studies that have highlighted the centrality of capital accumulation through dispossession by multinational corporations across the world (Harvey, 2003), Varman and Al-Amoudi draw attention to the role of violence in profit extraction. A key issue for organizational scholarship, they note at the outset of their discussion, is the question of how we can explain the failure of a legislative framework, and activist protest, that promises to protect basic human needs and rights, and to raise awareness of violations. Their analysis draws attention to corporate violence not simply as acts of physical force that cause injury but also as 'more insidious—and equally harmful—forms of non-physical and symbolic violence that make coercion unaccountable' (Varman and Al-Amoudi, 2016: 1910). Drawing on Butler's concepts of de-realisation, ungrievable lives and dispossession (Butler, 2004a, 2004b, 2009; Butler and Athanasiou, 2013), they show how unchecked violence facilitates profit accumulation whilst allowing global corporations to slip into the role of both the vulnerable victim and the paternalistic protector of workers and local people.

In their account of the violence inflicted by the Coca-Cola plant on workers and local farming communities, Varman and Al-Amoudi (2016: 1910) ask: 'Through what practices is violence made possible in spite of a legal and administrative environment that should, in principle, protect the fundamental interests of local populations?'. In raising this question, their analysis hones in two wider problems for organizational analysis and activism, namely (i) how to tactically engage the very structures and sets of relations, not to mention resources, that perpetuate oppression: and (ii) how to respond to what, borrowing from Butler, we might think of as the 'double negation' through which harm inflicted on those designated as unintelligible others becomes occluded, even endorsed or actively pursued (Preston, 2019).

In thinking through these kinds of issues, the case of India is particularly telling Varman and Al-Amoudi (2016) argue, because with a population of over a billion people, it is widely considered to be the world's largest democracy, with labour laws to protect workers and institutions that profess to be the guarantors of accountability with regard to the social, economic and ecological impact of corporate practices. Yet, as Varman and Al-Amoudi's study shows, these mechanisms can be systematically ignored or undermined. As an instance of the violent co-optation of vulnerability, they argue that

> In the context of Mehdigani, resistance to derealisation reinforced, rather than replaced, the paternalist neo-liberal discourse through which villagers are de-realized, and violence is condoned or even justified.
>
> (Varman and Al-Amoudi, 2016: 1910)

Setting their analysis against a discussion of the contradictions underpinning this, they note how, on the one hand, corporate violence 'against people who count as humans creates grief and popular revulsion', leading to the formation of widespread discursive condemnation and regulatory structures in response (Butler, 2004a). Yet this creates a contradiction between the rejection of violence and the necessity of violence for profit accumulation. Corporations therefore face the problem of how to 'justify' the latter in order to sustain it, in other words, how to pursue violence legitimately. In their account of how organizations respond to this, Varman and Al-Amoudi (2016: 1911) show how 'corporations resolve this contradiction by relying on social and discursive processes of derealisation through which the lives of victims are made ungrievable and their sufferings impalpable'. Drawing on Butler, they do so by positioning those subject to violence either as 'deserving' victims, or as simply unreal, non-human.

In developing their argument, Varman and Al-Amoudi show how violence in Butler's writing on precarity and dispossession takes several forms that are important to organizational scholars and activists in understanding the complexities and contradictions at the heart of corporate violence. These include harm caused at the level of our most basic existential vulnerability (Butler, 2009); injurious speech (Butler, 1997a); exclusion from representation (Butler, 2004a), and through dispossession (Butler and Athanasiou, 2013). As they note, central to her analysis of each of these themes 'is the idea that violence is often inherent to normative or epistemic frameworks' (Varman and Al-Amoudi, 2016: 1911). Accordingly, normative and epistemic matrices of power differentiate lives that 'count' from those designated as ungrievable, and towards which 'violence becomes justified' (Butler, 2009: 156). This means that acts of violence such as those perpetrated by the Coca-Cola corporation towards local workers, farmers and activists, or those induced by the collapse of the Rana Plaza building discussed earlier, or those inflicted on residents of the Grenfell Tower (Preston, 2019) can be undertaken with 'indifference or even righteousness', because their lives have been negated and therefore cannot be harmed (Butler, 2009: 41, cited in Varman and Al-Amoudi, 2016: 1911).

To grasp the organizational processes at stake in the perpetuation of violence that Varman and Al-Amoudi describe, and the de-realisation on which it depends, it is important to keep in mind the distinction Butler makes between subjection and abjection. The former leads to the positioning of subordinate identities deemed inferior, but largely recognizable (even if only partially or narrowly, conditionally so) within the normative terms of intelligibility; whereas the latter are those 'de-realized identities [that] are even more fundamentally excluded because they do not fit recognizable categories through which subjects may vindicate rights, express needs *or even claim existence as human beings*' (Varman and Al-Amoudi, 2016: 1912, *emphasis added*). In her own writing, Butler refers to the de-realisation of prisoners at Guantanamo Bay (Butler, 2004a, 2009), and of trans people (Butler, 2004b) as examples of those who fall (or rather are pushed) into the category of the 'de-real'.

Varman and Al-Amoudi (2016: 1912) show how de-realisation is in itself an act of violence operating as a negation, criminalization or pathologization of 'unrecognizable identities'. Hence, those who are de-realized become abject, 'unethical' in so far as they are denied the possibility of being able to give an account of themselves (Butler, 2005). But, not surprisingly, de-realisation is also conducive to further forms of violence. Varman and Al-Amoudi (2016: 1912) map these out as including: (i) the *correctional* physical and symbolic violence that ensues from being perceived 'as a dangerous subversion of the social order'; and (ii) a *condoning* of violence so that even when state institutions such as the police or tribunals do not perform physically violent acts against those deemed unreal, 'they may allow such violence to remain unchecked'.

Yet Butler is conscious that de-realized persons are not passive victims; they challenge and resist violence in a number of possible ways. Elaborating on this realization, and 'reinstating' their humanness, Varman and Al-Amoudi (2016: 1913) note how

> Unreal people continue to breathe, to occupy a space, to speak, and to bond, even when their lives [and loves] are ignored, their bodies are segregated, their language remains unintelligible to the powerful, and their rights of association are negated. Moreover, de-realized persons produce resistance by forming associations through which they bond, develop counter-discourses that render them intelligible

(at least to each other), and through which they may countervail derealisation to claim their rights.

Resonating with Honneth's (1995, 2008) account of resistance to disrespect, Butler's (2016) writing emphasizes how actors resist de-realisation by collectively affirming vulnerability, through public displays for instance; in doing so, they 'reaffirm their reality as human subjects endowed with needs and desires, reflexivity and irony' (Varman and Al-Amoudi, 2016: 1913). Butler cautions, however, that vulnerability is open to co-optation and paternalistic appropriation; as she puts it, once marked as 'vulnerable' within human rights discourse and legal regimes, those who are positioned as abject, as dispossessed, become reified as vulnerable, fixed in a political position of powerlessness and constrained by a corresponding lack of agency (Butler, 2016—see Postscript).

To this list of appropriating discourses and regimes, we might add those organizational processes that reify vulnerability including, for instance, through accreditation practices that 'attest' to an organization's paternalistic benevolence while at the same time further disempowering de-realized groups and individuals. Through this kind of organizational response to vulnerability, agency gets further effaced and opposition is quelled through protective appropriations that amount to an 'ideological seizure and reversal' (Varman and Al-Amoudi, 2016: 1913) such as that described in relation to Coca-Cola, but many other examples could be cited by way of illustration, including subjection to discourses of 'inclusivity', for instance.

What Varman and Al-Amoudi (2016: 1913) argue is that Butler's framework is particularly relevant for studies of corporate violence 'as it provides a theoretical prism that highlights specific processes through which derealisation leads to unchecked violence, diffused resistance and paranoid reactions that generate, in turn, intensified violence'. India is the second most populated country in the world; it experienced considerable economic growth in the early 2000s, yet this was concentrated mainly in towns and cities, with rural poverty remaining widespread. Varman and Al-Amoudi cite a reported suicide rate of over 200,000 rural workers over a period of fifteen years from the 1990s, attesting to a sense of neglect, injustice and impoverishment across rural India. The setting of their study, the village of Mehdigani, consisted of a population of approximately 12,000 people, comprising mostly a community of weavers. Most farmers and activists were not protesting about the location of the Coca-Cola plant in their community, but rather its impact on irrigation in the area; farmers claimed that the company had been siphoning around 2.5 million litres of underground water every day, severely limiting local farmers' capacity to irrigate their land. Other concerns included poor waste management, pollution of neighbouring agricultural land, bribing of local officials and poor treatment of workers.

Butler's critique of de-realisation provides an important theoretical reference point for Varman and Al-Amoudi (2016: 1916) to highlight crucial, yet neglected, aspects of 'the violent practices performed, or mandated, by Coca-Cola to make profits and subdue resistance'. For example, when the alleged violations of labour and environmental protection laws led to protests by activist organizations within the local community, Coca-Cola responded by dismissing workers and by mobilizing state violence, using the caste divide in the region to the company's advantage.[8]

The initial perpetration of violence was therefore shown to be an important part of the operation of the Coca-Cola corporation in the area, enacted through the creation of exploitative working conditions, threatening workers, restricting access to water and polluting the rural environment. To understand not only how this was made possible but was facilitated by the relevant local authorities, Varman and Al-Amoudi (2016: 1919) turn to Butler's concept of de-realisation to emphasize that the local people's negation meant that the harm inflicted on them was effectively 'unreal', as a cause and consequence of a series of interrelated practices that systematically denied their rights and needs. These practices created what they describe as 'unchecked corporate violence through [the] derealisation of dispossessed farmers, protesting workers and active citizens', as well as what amounted to a de-realization of natural resources and local communities.

Turning, like Kenny (2018, 2019), to Butler's writing on the desperation that drives people to embrace norms that they know exploit and de-humanize them, Varman and Al-Amoudi cite the account of one particular ex-Coca-Cola worker, Prem, who describes the systematic negation of workers' rights in the area:

> If someone protests then he is told that he is indulging in union activities and is thrown out. . . . A lot of people come here for work, and sometimes they get work, but mostly they are made to stand in front of the gate [and are not given any job]. Workers work under contractors, and all contracts go to people who are very powerful. Coca-Cola exploits its workers. Instead of the usual eight hours, workers are forced to work for 12 hours [without any overtime payment]. Still, there is so much poverty and unemployment that people come here for work.
>
> (Prem, ex-Coca Cola worker, cited in Varman and Al-Amoudi, 2016: 1920)

As Varman and Al-Amoudi note, Prem's account suggests that corporations like Coca-Cola effectively get away with violence and appropriation because they are able to exploit poverty and unemployment in the local region. Workers believe that officials whose role it is to protect them are not only aware of this, but are complicit, choosing to overlook violations of their needs and rights in favour of global business interests, further undermining the agentic capacity of those who seek to protest, or simply raise awareness of the plight of local workers and farmers.

In what amounts to corporate abjection on a regional scale, Varman and Al-Amoudi (2016: 1925) describe Coca-Cola's 'two pronged attack' on the local economy: 'Coca-Cola is siphoning off the resources of the country by expatriating profits outside and is hurting the economic interests of the farming community by consuming millions of litres of water meant for irrigation of farms.' Coca-Cola's response, Varman and Al-Amoudi note, is congruent with Butler's (2016: 13) notion that powerful actors appropriate discourses of vulnerability to 'shore up their own privilege', reaffirming the various forms of violence to which dispossessed workers, communities and activists are subject. In sum, they show how these subaltern groups remain in a state of unreality, vulnerable to violent accumulation. Resistance to this, which invokes their vulnerability, is re-appropriated by the company, 'posing as a vulnerable entity that has to resort to police action, legal cases, spies and private guards to protect itself' (Varman and Al-Amoudi, 2016: 1929).

Varman and Al-Amoudi's account shows how Butler's writing offers insight into the consequences of processes of de-realisation, violent accumulation and re-appropriation in ways that considerably deepen our understanding of how corporate violence facilitates profit accumulation in situations of extreme dispossession. Their analysis ends by raising several important questions for future research, that Butler's later writing on assembly arguably begins to attend to (see Chapter 6), namely: How can dispossessed groups engage in meaningful resistance that can withstand attempts at corporate re-appropriation? What conditions of possibility are necessary for resistant invocations of vulnerability to become effective in countering dominance and exploitation? Further, 'how should resistance and vulnerability be articulated in alternative discourses that restrict rather than perpetuate paternalistic violence?' (Varman and Al-Amoudi, 2016: 1932). These are questions and issues to which we turn in Chapter 6.

Notes

1. This is an argument that Butler develops in her book, *Frames of War: When is Life Grievable?* (Butler, 2009) that examines the marking off of categories of personhood in the context of the US military's attacks in the Middle East, focusing particularly on the mainstream media's role in portraying Muslim people as deserving targets. Butler's point here is that the media 'frames' war in such a way that we do not recognize as fully human those who are harmed by it, in order to justify the actions of aggressors.
2. www.ilo.org/global/topics/geip/WCMS_614394/lang--en/index.htm
3. www.grenfelltowerinquiry.org.uk
4. A poignant example is New York's Hart Island (a 'potter's field') off the Bronx coast in Long Island Sound. Since 1869, over a million unclaimed bodies have been buried there in unmarked graves. What Butler means by

the de-realization of ungrievable lives is movingly illustrated in the unmarked space on the Island that was used to bury people who had died from AIDS-related illnesses in the 1980s.

5. Butler's theory of passionate attachments, a concept that draws together insights from Hegelian philosophy, poststructuralist ontologies of power and Freudian psychoanalysis, is developed most fully in her book *The Psychic Life of Power* (Butler, 1997b). Here she considers how the subject is produced through psychic attachments to the 'insidious' workings of power; at the risk of oversimplifying a complex explication of the processes involved, Butler's argument is essentially that the desire for recognition, the need 'to be' is 'a pervasively exploitable desire', resulting in a 'mandatory submission' that haunts us throughout our lives. Hegel (1977) himself emphasizes this when he notes that our lives are lived in perpetual servitude (see Butler, 1987). Butler illustrates what this means in her own writing with reference to the illustrative example of child sex abuse, arguing that the nature of this particular form of exploitation is such that it is not only the imposition of sexuality that is at stake but the exploitation of a love that is necessary for the child's existence, so that (at least in part) what is abused is the passionate attachment that a child has to an adult carer whom s/he trusts and depends upon (Butler, 1997b: 6, 7 and 8). Although the issues are of course complex, a similar point could arguably be made about the institutionalized forms of exploitation within the music and film industries, and particularly the 'casting couch' scenario, awareness of which, in the public consciousness at least, was raised by the Me Too movement.

6. In developing her ideas on de-realization, Butler draws on insights introduced much earlier in her writing. See, for instance, her reminder that it is important to remember that subjectivity is constituted through exclusion, 'that is, through the creation of a domain of de-authorized subjects, pre-subjects, figures of abjection, populations erased from view' (Butler, 1995a: 47) in *Feminist Contentions*.

7. See Berlant's (2011) account of what she calls the 'cruel optimism' attached to a damaged future.

8. In an analysis of a similar context, Annamma Joy et al. (2015) draw on Butler to show how the extreme divide between wealth and poverty and higher and lower castes in India impacts upon women's relative vulnerability. Their research demonstrates how, while lower class/caste women are undeniably at greater risk of sexual assault, even women of higher social status experience extreme precarity and high levels of embodied risk, particularly in more conservative rural areas. They document how, while structural changes and activist groups have encouraged increased collective awareness and resistance among women in India, a culture of condoned sexual violence is nonetheless an on-going and widespread reality.

6 Organizational (re)Assemblage
Towards a Plural Performativity

Despite her popularity across and beyond academia, Butler's writing has provoked anger and exasperation among her critics. On the one hand, for an intellectual project that aims to 'make trouble', this might be rather pleasing for its author, even taken as something of an endorsement of Butler's characteristic 'genius for insubordination' (Fraser, 1995a: 65). Yet the implied abrogation of social and political responsibility is clearly a cause of some on-going consternation both for Butler herself and for those who draw on her work, problematic as it is for the task of seeking to construct cultures of solidarity and collective ways of being that are not homogenizing or repressive, or easily reabsorbed into the mainstream. Although the lack of 'resolution' in her arguments, the 'alienating language',[1] and esoteric style are notorious criticisms, it is these more fundamental concerns that resonate most with the preoccupations of organizational scholars and activists. For the latter, the risks attached to 'making trouble' involve, on the one hand, accentuating an already precarious position for vulnerable groups and individuals and, on the other, a co-optation of critique with, for example, emancipatory language and endeavours being all too easily reabsorbed into oppressive practices and instrumental imperatives.

While most of Butler's critics are happy to attest to her work as 'among the most original and provocative writings by feminists' (Benhabib, 1995b: 108), her most vociferous—and personal—critic has arguably been the philosopher of law and ethics, Martha Nussbaum (1999: 13). The latter's critique in *The New Republic* described Butler as a pedlar of flimsy scholarship, whose political influence is 'dangerous' and who 'collaborates with evil'. As Kirby (2006: 131 and 132) has commented, the tone of Nussbaum's 'vitriolic outpouring' is one of outrage, and her attack is 'aggressively personal'. By sarcastically describing Butler's writing as 'sexy' no less than four times in one article, Nussbaum imposes on her 'the mythical powers of a Jezebel cum Pied-Piper of Hamlyn'. Yet the breadth and volume of Butler's writing attests, as Kirby retorts on her behalf, to the political concerns that are at the heart of her work, and to her 'enduring commitment to social change' (Kirby, 2006: 135); it is arguably for this reason in particular that her writing has been of sustained and growing interest to organizational scholars since the early 1990s.

A much more constructive (dialogical) critique of her work, one that relates more closely to the concerns of organization theorists and activists, comes from Butler's engagement with feminist theorist, Nancy Fraser. The latter is troubled that Butler's focus on performativity cuts her off from more everyday ways of talking and writing about ourselves, and that her writing constitutes a 'self-distancing idiom' (Fraser, 1995a: 67) as a result, one that has alarming theoretical and political consequences. In particular, Fraser is sceptical about Butler's faith in the political capacity of resignification, asking 'Why is resignification good? Can't there be bad (oppressive, reactionary) resignifications?' (Fraser, 1995a: 68). The hints at co-optation that Fraser raises here have important implications for organizational scholars drawing on Butler's work as work organizations are replete with discursive signifiers of ideas and idioms associated with social justice, 'inclusivity' perhaps being an obvious example, co-opted in the service of profit accumulation. How, drawing on Butler, can we develop a reflexive evaluation of such practices without resorting to a critique that relies on resignification, if the latter is the very object of our critical response?

In a pair of essays published in the mid-1990s, but which remain pertinent critical responses to Butler's work, Fraser (1995a, 1995b) argues that her refusal to offer some kind of political template that envisions how we might devise modes of critique and cultures of solidarity beyond resignification cuts her work adrift from her feminist origins and constituency. Arguably, as a result, this limits the analytical and political relevance of Butler's thinking for organization theorists and activists. In Fraser's view, this is largely because this refusal effectively removes Butler from an engagement with real life struggles whilst retaining a preoccupation with 'struggle' as an abstract, philosophical concept. For Fraser, this seems to be an inevitable consequence of Butler's over-attention to language, a point also made by Kirby (2006). It is in her more recent works, notably *Notes Towards a Performative Theory of Assembly* (Butler, 2015a) and *Vulnerability in Resistance* (Butler, 2016; Butler et al., 2016) that Butler strives to tackle the implications of Fraser's critique head on, and in doing so, responds eloquently to those of her other critics.

Indeed, it is in her development of a performative theory of assembly that Butler (2015a) once again 'fleshes out' ideas introduced in more abstract, theoretical forms in earlier writing, and in this text she does so more reflexively than before. In particular, it is to the idea of corporeal vulnerability that she turns her attention as she considers the politics of liveability in a more sustained, collective way than in earlier writing. To recap, liveability for Butler is what defines the ways of being that can be recognized as socially and culturally, and we might add organizationally, coherent, and it is to *how* a wider range of modes of living, working and being together in all our lived complexity might be 'recovered' beyond reified versions of ourselves that she turns her attention in her most recent books.

As outlined earlier, Butler (1988, 1990/2000a) places considerable ontological emphasis on the significance of the 'acts' through which gender subjectivities come into being. She does so to highlight the normative expectations governing the performance of such acts in order to broaden the sphere of recognition in which those acts can be culturally intelligible, and the lives of those who perform them can be liveable. In her earlier writing (Butler, 1988, 1990/2000a, 2004a, 2004b), these acts are largely individual in their orientation, even when analysed in relatively public forms such as in the case of drag performances, for instance. To be fair, however, even here it is not simply drag performances that are Butler's concern but rather, through her analysis of the drag and trans communities represented in the film *Paris is Burning*, shared enactments of drag that are experienced and embodied beyond individual acts. In her later work, she develops this orientation much more clearly, focusing on shared experiences of performativity, and on the latter as a form of collective action, beyond the individual or the local.

It is in *Notes Towards A Performative Theory of Assembly* (Butler, 2015a) that Butler explores the dynamics of public assembly most fully, understanding assemblies as plural forms of performative action. Echoing Honneth (1995, 2008), she extends her theory of performativity from its largely individual focus in earlier writing (see Butler, 1988, 1990/2000a) to argue that precarity (the destruction of the conditions of subjective relationality) has been a galvanizing force in contemporary social protest. Here she develops her earlier focus on performativity as containing within it the potential for social subversion through collective action. In this sense, Butler broadens her analysis of performativity, moving beyond speech acts in her discussion of the politics of the performative (Butler, 1997a) to argue for the significance of assemblies of bodies. Drawing also on Arendt (1958), she argues that plural and embodied performativity means that people 'are not just produced by their vocalized claims, but also by the conditions of possibility of their appearance . . . as part of embodied performance' (Butler, 2015a: 19). For Butler, when bodies assemble they are exercising

> A plural and performative right to appear, one that asserts and instates the body in the midst of the political field, and which, in its expressive and signifying function, delivers *a bodily demand for a more liveable set of economic, social and political conditions no longer afflicted by induced forms of precarity.*
>
> (Butler, 2015a: 11, *emphasis added*)

Linking the latter (induced forms of precarity) to post-Fordist forms of flexible working that rely on the substitution and disposability of working people, and to the individualization of responsibility brought about by 'the demand to become an entrepreneur of oneself under conditions that make that dubious vocation impossible' (Butler, 2015a: 15), Butler arguably gets much closer to a critical analysis of contemporary organizational life than in her previous works, a move signalled in her earlier dialogues with Athena Athanasiou (Butler and Athanasiou, 2013—see Chapter 5). She does so by reminding us how, on the one hand, everyone is dependent on social relations in order to maintain a liveable life. Yet at the same time, that dependency while not identical to subjugation can easily become its most effective medium. Hence, Butler emphasizes in this text that 'the organization of infrastructure' (Butler, 2015a: 21) is inescapably connected to the organization of the desire for recognition, as the former effectively constitutes an exploitation of the latter.

The basis of this final, substantive chapter is an extended discussion of the critical potential of Butler's faith in the political capacity of interdependency, and in the ways in which new social movements might constitute organizational forms that champion this interdependency, beyond exploitations of the desire for recognition. As she put it,

> Precarity is the condition against which several new social movements struggle; such movements do not seek to overcome interdependency or even vulnerability as they struggle against precarity; *rather, they seek to produce the conditions under which vulnerability and interdependency might become liveable.*
>
> (Butler, 2015a: 218, *emphasis added*)

For Butler, organizational forms that can 'avow the need we have for one another' (Butler, 2015a: 218) might pave the way for the conditions of a more liveable, and workable, life. A key problem, for organizational scholars, practitioners and activists, however, is first, how to go about bringing that about without putting oneself and others at risk, and second, how to safeguard against the possibility of a recognition of the need we have for one another becoming the basis of further subjugation, making our lives not more liveable and workable, but less so.

In Butler's frame of reference, embodied ethics broadly refers to the idea that the basis of our ethical relationship to one another is our embodied inter-connection and the mutual, corporeal vulnerability that arises from this. Recognition of the organizational potential and implications of this ethical relationship has been an important theme in work and organization studies in recent years (Dale and Latham, 2015; Hancock, 2008; Hancock et al., 2015). Much of this literature is either directly or indirectly premised upon a post-dualistic understanding of subjectivity (Merleau-Ponty, 2002), one that has a sustained presence in Butler's writing (see Butler, 2015b), and that thinks of embodied ethics not simply as a moral obligation but rather, an ontological compulsion. In other words, we exist in and through our own bodies but also those of others, because our mode of being, our embodied ontology, means that we encounter ourselves and others through the medium of our bodies, and because of this, we are inter-corporeally dependent upon each other (Hegel, 1977); we are 'intertwined' (Merleau Ponty, 2013 [1968]). This basic presupposition constitutes the philosophical and political basis of Butler's (2015a: 122, *emphasis added*) relational ethics emphasizing that 'it is not from pervasive love for humanity or a pure desire for peace that we strive to live together. We live together *because we have no choice.*'

For Butler (2015a: 197), assemblies (the shorthand term she uses to describe 'assembled bodies') consist simply of a recognition-based bodily presence, a 'collective thereness', enabling those involved to 'enact a message, performatively' in a way that connects this relational ethics to politics. Assemblies are premised, she argues, on a mutual recognition of our shared inter-corporeal vulnerability, the basic need that we have for reciprocation, rather than some reified notion of ascribed characteristics. As a reminder of themes explored in her writing on precarity (see Chapter 5), for Butler, our mutual, inter-corporeal dependency means that we are all vulnerable, but in a hierarchically organized society, some people are clearly much more vulnerable than others. In practice, this means that while we are all ontologically 'dispossessed' by our dependency upon one another, and by our need for mutual recognition, the materialities of our social, political and economic circumstances mean that we are not all equally or homogeneously so (Butler and Athanasiou, 2013).

These are themes and concepts that are particularly important for critical organization theory, given the latter's concern with understanding and addressing enduring inequalities, and with exploring the political potential of embodied assemblies to challenge them. Butler (2015a) considers a question posed by Adorno (2005: 39) when he asserts that a 'wrong life cannot be lived rightly'. Thinking of this as an organizational problem raises some important questions such as: Is it possible to live an inclusive life in an exclusionary one (in other words, a life in which the inclusion of some is premised upon the exclusion of others)? What might this mean, in terms of the conditions of inclusion? How might these conditions be subject to critique, and re-thought, through the lens of feminist writing on embodied ethics? And how might this theoretical critique inform feminist activism and organizational practice in the future? These questions are explored in Butler's writing on assembly as a form of political engagement and activism, and in her more recent discussion of vulnerability in resistance (Butler, 2016).[2] Framing these questions as organizational challenges requires us to consider how themes such as inclusion might be thought about and practiced beyond, on the one hand, a logic of exclusion, and on the other, an instrumental co-optation of difference, of our primary relationality and the vulnerability engendered by our desire for recognition. It also requires us to think about what organizational forms an embodied, relational ethics might take.

To recap, the basic premise of Butler's writing is that everyone is dependent on each other in order to maintain a liveable life (Butler, 1987, 2015a). Yet at the same time, that dependency is vulnerable to appropriation[3] when recognition is conditional (on organizational imperatives such as 'fit' for instance). This implies, as considered thus far, that instrumental commitments such as inclusion are simply an organizational exploitation of our need to belong (Ahmed, 2012), that is, of our basic need for recognition.

To reiterate, the theoretical basis of Butler's discussion of assembly is a critical, feminist reading of the Hegelian (1977) dialectics of recognition[4] and a phenomenological understanding of the self as a situated, inter-corporeal 'relational sociality' (Butler and Athanasiou, 2013: 65). The latter leads Butler to argue that it is our ethical relationality—our embodied relationship of mutual interdependency—that defines us (Butler, 2000a, 2000b). It is her critical reflections on the differentiating effects of the normative regimes governing this relationality that resonate strongly with the critical concerns of organization theorists, notably when Butler argues that rather than mutual recognition, these regimes render others usable, exploitable and 'eventually into waste matter, or of no use: always available, always expendable' (Butler, 2015a: 27). The political potential of this critique for organizational scholars and activists lies in its capacity to open up radical re-articulations of what it means to matter: *'rather than a rehabilitation of* the humanist subject in the form of liberal tolerance or *assimilatory inclusion* of ready-made identities' (Butler, 2015a: 34, *emphasis added*), Butler's explicit aim is to move us towards a relational ethics and politics premised upon recognition (see Tyler, 2019).

It is in this respect that, in dialogue with Athanasiou (Butler and Athanasiou, 2013) and developing themes introduced in her earlier work (Butler, 1988, 1990, 1993), Butler introduced the concept of 'dispossession' to her critique. For Butler, dispossession is the collective, political corollary of undoing that she explored at a more individual level in her earlier writing (Butler, 2004b). To recap, her account is premised on the view that there is, on the one hand, a *relational* form of dispossession that must be valued,[5] and on the other, a *privative* form that ought to be opposed. In this sense, it is presumed that the former, a relational precarity, is shared equally as part of the human condition (as a consequence of our need for recognition), while the latter, 'precarity as a condition of induced inequality and destitution . . . is a way of exploiting [this] existential condition' (Butler and Athanasiou, 2013: 20). In practice, this means that, on the one hand, 'the self is always in relational sociality' (Butler and Athanasiou, 2013: 65). As discussed earlier, this is because, through our inter-corporeality, 'we are implicated in . . . intense social processes of relatedness and interdependence' (Butler and Athanasiou,

2013: 55), so that, in this sense, we are always 'dispossessed' by others as we are affected by them, and in turn affect others through our basic need for mutual recognition. Yet at the same time, we are also dispossessed, in a more 'privative' way, by normative powers that serve to exploit and oppress our desire to be recognized.

In contrast to 'the governmental logics of tolerance' (Butler and Athanasiou, 2013: 66) that 'seek to govern and enclose' our basic relationality 'ontologically, possessively', what is needed, Butler argues, is not a politics of inclusion. The latter, she emphasizes, is far too susceptible to what she calls 'the market of recognition'. Rather, we should work to destabilize (or 'make trouble' with, to borrow from her earlier writing, see Butler, 1990/2000a) the regulatory ideals that constitute this susceptibility. In other words, we should look to find ways to draw on the collective, political potential of relationality in order to recognize, and address, more privative forms of dispossession. In effect, this suggests turning inclusion back on itself, revealing its tendency to appropriate and exploit our need for recognition while professing to do precisely the opposite.

In organizational terms, and with the questions outlined earlier in mind, this raises two important issues for organizational researchers to consider. First, *lived experiences* of the dynamics of exclusion and inclusion shaping the pursuit of recognition, as well as the performative labour—the work involved in bringing particular subjectivities into being in order to conform to normative regimes of intelligibility and recognition—must be acknowledged and understood. Thanem and Wallenberg (2016) describe very poignantly the emotional strain and pain of this kind of labour when it involves, for instance, repressing transgender, as well as the effort and concentration (the performative labour)[6] involved in conforming to organizational/organizing gender norms and expectations (see also O'Shea, 2018). Second, *the significatory processes* through which patterns of exclusion and over-inclusion come to shape lived experiences of organizational settings and processes must also be subject to critique, including those that Butler might mark as 're-significatory', but about which organizational scholars and activists need to be reflexively cautious, for the reasons already outlined. The latter in particular help us to understand more about how organizations that formally proclaim a commitment to equality continue to practice inclusion is a way that simply perpetuates exclusion. As Thanem and Wallenberg (2016: 268) emphasize in their discussion of gender fluidity, while organizations may formally, rhetorically espouse an ethos of openness to difference they 'typically *depict* people who do gender appropriately'. Ahmed (2012) reaches a similar conclusion in her critique of institutional racism showing how organizations discursively co-opt commitments to social justice as their actions continue to perpetuate inequalities and cause harm.

To sum up thus far, Butler distinguishes between (i) the exclusion of 'that which gets abjected or foreclosed'; and (ii) the over- or conditional inclusion of 'forms of life that are conferred recognition . . . according to the established norms of recognizability, on the condition of and at the cost of conforming to these norms' (Butler and Athanasiou, 2013: 36). In organizational terms, this produces an alienating, abjecting exclusion, on the one hand, and an 'assimilatory inclusion' (Butler and Athanasiou, 2013: 34), on the other. The latter Povinelli (2002) has described as a compulsion to embody an ascribed 'authenticity' that effectively converts recognition into nothing more than a reified form of difference articulated through a rhetorical commitment to inclusion; the 'stranger fetish', in Ahmed's (2000) terms.

Proceeding from this critique requires careful thinking about how organizational life might be made not more 'inclusive', risking with it a perpetuation of exclusion or (conditional) over-inclusion and a reification of difference, but *relational* where the latter is taken to mean open to difference, rather than seeking to control or contain it. It is in thinking this through that Butler's writing on assembly (Butler, 2015a), and on resistance in vulnerability (Butler, 2016) has much to offer organization theorists, practitioners and activists.

Drawing together insights from Butler's writing considered thus far, an important first step towards developing a reflexive critique of organizational encounters with difference has to be to explore how the twin strategies of exclusion and over-inclusion outlined earlier might be unsettled, ruptured or 'troubled' (Butler, 1990/2000a). In some of her most recent work, Butler (2015a) emphasizes that this unsettling can take the form of a radical, affective solidarity enacted in opposition to the precarious effects of contemporary political and economic forces, enabling a new sense of mattering to emerge—interdependent, relational and persistent (see Tyler, 2019).

As Lloyd (2007) notes in her critical commentary of what were Butler's most recent texts at the time she was writing, namely *Precarious Life, Undoing Gender* and *Giving an Account of Oneself*, Butler appeared to be setting the groundwork for taking her interest, even investment, in the idea of primary vulnerability in important directions. As Lloyd notes, in these significant texts Butler argues that the subject's primary dependency on others and its ensuing opacity to itself are precisely what 'incurs and sustains some of its most important *ethical* bonds' (Butler, 2005: 20, cited in Lloyd, 2007: 139, *my own emphasis added*).

In her later works, Butler also considers this primary interdependency not simply as an ethical bond but also as a *political* capacity. This development in her thinking owes a great deal to her reading of Hegel's (1977) narration of the 'primary enthrallment' with the other, and with the body as the medium through which the self and other encounter one another (Butler, 1987, 1993). It is also influenced by her more recent engagement with Honneth's (2008) critique of reification (Butler, 2008).

For Honneth (drawing on Lukács, 1971 [1923]), as a 'distortion' of recognition, reification is the condition in which attitudes, entities and practices, as well as other people and environments are treated instrumentally as objects. Through Butler's dialogue with Honneth on the relationship between recognition and reification, she reminds us that recognition is the 'condition of possibility for human exchange, for communication, and for acknowledging the existence of others' (Butler, 2008: 99—see also Introduction). Recognition is an affirmative process based upon reciprocity and relationality, providing the basis for what she refers to (albeit in passing) as 'genuine praxis' (Butler, 2008: 101). Her critique of Honneth is premised largely on what Butler sees as his teleological reading of Hegel; as she puts it, 'the dynamics of subjugation' so central to her own engagement with *The Phenomenology of Spirit* (see Butler, 1987) are, in her view, 'nowhere to be found' in Honneth's account. More fruitful, she emphasizes, is Honneth's critical emphasis on the relationship between recognition and reification. For Honneth, we take up social life by placing ourselves in the position of the other; if we fail to do so, the other remains reified to/for us, or 'perhaps better said, we maintain . . . a set of reifying relations to the other' (Butler, 2008: 102). Without reciprocity, the other remains merely 'an instrument for the satisfaction of our aims' (Butler, 2008: 102), a critical concern with which was, of course, one of the signature contributions to critical theory of the Frankfurt School.

An interesting quandary that Honneth's work on recognition raises for Butler is the question of how to overcome this reification by remaining attached to the other, whilst also maintaining a bounded or distinctive self as the basis of praxis. This is a problem that she frames thus: 'How do I live this boundary that both closes me off to others and opens me to them?' (Butler, 2008: 106). In part, this is an ontological question about the nature of our bonds with others, as suggested when Butler asks: 'What distinguishes attachment from fusion?' To a degree, Butler answers this question herself by turning back to Honneth's emphasis on recognition as a 'reminder' of our primary, or primordial relationality, one that resonates with other critical theorists' understanding of reification as a 'forgetting' of this relationality as the antecedent mode of recognition.[7]

Echoing her earlier concerns with the accounts we give of ourselves that bring our subjectivities into being as attempts to cohere lived complexities (see Chapter 4), Butler (2008: 118) notes that, from Honneth's perspective, 'reification . . . can only be a kind of semblance'. In contrast, recognition is 'a condition of possibility, a relationality that is coextensive with human sociality' (Butler, 2008: 118), or rather, which is the precondition for it.

Recognition of this, that is, of the political capacity engendered by the primacy of our mutual interdependence as an ethical bond is a theme that runs throughout Butler's work, in one form or another, tying most of her texts together, but it is explicated in the most sustained way in her more recent writing. As Lloyd (2007) sums it up, in *Gender Trouble* (1990/2000a, building on Butler, 1988), Butler's primary aim is to de-naturalize the gendered, sexed body. In *Bodies That Matter* (Butler, 1993), she extends this project to consider how particular bodily ontologies, namely those that conform to the heteronormative expectations shaping the terms of recognition, come to 'matter' more than others. Here she examines the processes of subjection and abjection through which significatory capacity is either invested or denied, respectively, in bodies that matter and those that don't. In her discussion of passionate attachments and psychic power (Butler, 1995c, 1997a, 1997b), Butler hints at her later explication of assembly as a collective performativity when she draws (in relative passing) on Agamben's (1993) writing on the possibility or potentiality of existence. As Butler puts it, what this opens up is a rereading of 'being' as that which exceeds normative interpellation such that a failure of interpellation both puts the subject's coherence at risk (undermining the possibility of being in a self-identical sense), and at the same time, also potentially marks the path 'toward a more open, even more ethical, kind of being, one of or for the future' (Butler, 1997b: 131).

In her works published in the mid- to late 2000s, Butler (2004a, 2004b, 2005, 2008, 2009) considers how bodily vulnerability shapes the terms of liveability, emphasizing how our bodies are exposed by simultaneously opening up to the possibility of recognition, and in doing so, rendering us at risk of misrecognition. It is in this discussion that she (literally) begins to flesh out this politically charged, dynamic understanding of the subject as 'undone'. For Butler, the latter is much more than simply a subjective predicament; it carries the full weight of normative and physical violence but also (as hinted at in Butler's earlier citation of Agamben, 1993) the promise of reciprocal recognition.[8] Our state of being 'given over to others' (Butler, 2005: 92) is both our potential promise and our perpetual problem, and it is precisely this porosity that establishes the terms of the 'field of ethical enmeshment with others' (Butler, 2004b: 25) that shapes the scenography of subject formation as a moral dilemma for Butler. Like Levinas (1961), and Hegel (1977), Butler is fully committed to an ethics, and by implication a politics, that is shaped by a recognition of the mutual vulnerability of embodied subjects.

As Lloyd (2007) explains, this puts her at odds both with feminist attempts to instate women's corporeal integrity and shared right to bodily self-determination, and at the same time, out of step with feminist arguments (popular in the 1980s, and contra De Beauvoir) that women's bodies, rather than a source of constraint, are a locus of power and capability. The latter is of course premised on the view that women's bodies are 'special', or at least distinctive, in their capacity to give and nurture life. As Lloyd (2007: 140) notes, this is not an ontological or ethical position that Butler shares; for her, it is not bodies *per se* that are important but rather the relationship between bodies that, to borrow Butler's (1993) own term, 'matters'. This being the case, it is hard to disagree with Lloyd (2007: 140) when she says that Butler's contention that bodies are vulnerable to and dependent upon others 'offers a profound challenge to [the] idea of bodily autonomy'.

However, it is important to note that Butler herself is adamant that acknowledging the co-constitution and mutual vulnerability of embodied subjects does not mean that feminists and other groups should cease to campaign for shared rights to corporeal self-determination and integrity. Her aim, it seems, is to supplement this position rather than replace or somehow override it. Butler does so, as Lloyd explains it, by asking if there might not be 'another normative aspiration that we must also seek to articulate and defend' (Butler, 2004a: 26), one that recognizes and reinstates the primary relationality that the ek-static subject embodies. Anticipating Butler's work to come, Lloyd (2007: 140) surmises: 'Here, I think, there is a way to align the . . . feminist campaign with Butler's project'. It is arguably precisely this challenge that Butler picks up in her recent writing, both independently (Butler, 2015a, 2016) and in dialogue with others (Butler and Athanasiou, 2013, Butler et al., 2016), in which vulnerability is recognized as carrying with it the constant prospect of violation yet at the same time, also opening up the social, political capacity for connection in a collective 'struggle with the norm' (Butler, 2004b: 13).

Re/Assembling as a Plural Performativity

In *Notes Toward a Performative Theory of Assembly*, Butler (2015a) explores the dynamics of public assembly, understanding assemblies as plural forms of performative action. She extends her theory of performativity to argue that precarity (the destruction of the conditions of subjective viability) has been a galvanizing force in contemporary protest (see also Honneth, 1995). Butler broadens her analysis of performativity moving beyond individual speech acts to argue for the significance of collective assemblies of bodies, for the very fact of assembling together says something beyond speech, something agentive and affective. A plural and embodied performativity means that people

> Are not just produced by their vocalized claims, but also by the conditions of possibility of their appearance . . . as part of embodied performance.
>
> (Butler, 2015a: 19)

Drawing on Arendt's (1958) views on action and appearance, she argues that by enacting a radical, affective solidarity in opposition to the precarious effects of contemporary political and economic forces, a new sense of 'mattering' potentially emerges. The point of the latter is not simply to extend social [organizational] inclusion but to reconfigure the nature of the relationship 'between the recognizable and the unrecognizable'

(Butler, 2015a: 5). Butler argues that forms of assembly have the capacity to signify an 'embodied and plural performativity' (Butler, 2015a: 8), materializing an assertion of the right to appear.[9] The freedom of assembly is important, she reminds us, because the power to gather together is a political prerogative distinct from the right to say something—the gathering itself (the assertion of appearance) itself constitutes a plural performativity that has signifying capacity beyond speech but in a way that connects the immediacy of bodies asserting the right simply to be; to occupy conceptual and physical, including public space, that has been hitherto denied.

With this in mind, Butler outlines her intention to develop a theory of performativity beyond individual performance, noting the importance of considering forms of performativity that operate through coordinated action, 'whose condition and aim is the reconstitution of plural forms of agency and social practices of resistance' (Butler, 2015a: 9). Here more than in earlier texts Butler situates performativity and induced precarity in its socio-economic, political context, emphasizing for instance, that when bodies assemble

> They are exercising a plural and performative right to appear, one that asserts and instates the body in the midst of the political field, and which, in its expressive and signifying function, delivers a bodily demand for a more liveable set of economic, social, and political conditions no longer afflicted by induced forms of precarity.
>
> (Butler, 2015a: 11)

Developing her discussion of disposability and its links to dispossession (Butler and Athanasiou, 2013), she goes on to connect induced forms of precarity explicitly to post-Fordist forms of flexible working, those modes of organization 'that rely on the substitution and dispensability of working people' (Butler, 2015a: 11). She also links this to the individualization of responsibility (self-reliance) brought about by induced precarity and 'the demand to become an entrepreneur of oneself under conditions that make that dubious vocation impossible' (Butler, 2015a: 15), as noted earlier.

Getting much closer to a critical organizational analysis than ever before, she reminds us here how, on the one hand, everyone is dependent on social relations in order to maintain a liveable life ('there is no getting rid of that dependency', Butler, 2015a: 21). Yet, at the same time, because 'the organization of infrastructure' (Butler, 2015a: 21) is inescapably connected to the organization of the desire for recognition, the former, to recap, thrives on an exploitation of the latter.

Against this backdrop, the question becomes: What function does assembly serve, and what form of ethics might it embody? In responding to this question, Butler argues that a collective recognition of our mutual interdependency has the potential to reaffirm the basis of a politics of solidarity and to work as a mechanism for 'devising collective and institutional ways of addressing induced precarity' (Butler, 2015a: 22).

With this in mind, much of her argument in *Notes Towards a Performative Theory of Assembly* seeks to understand the expressive or signifying capacity of assembly as both an embodied and plural performativity, based on 'an ethical conception of human relationality' (Butler, 2015a: 22). In this sense, Butler extends her political and theoretical ideas by returning to her earliest interests in Hegelian philosophy (Butler, 1987), connecting her faith in the potentially transformative effects of a plural performativity with an ethics premised upon mutual recognition *en masse*.

Organizing the Right to 'Appear'

Recognition is a theme that runs throughout Butler's work, particularly through the ways in which she explores the relationship between performativity, precarity and the norms governing the right to 'appear' (Arendt, 1958). Echoing Honneth, she argues that precarity is a mediating or middle term between 'performativity and alliance', the latter constituting a plural performativity (Butler, 2015a: 27.) As well as *Subjects of Desire*, her discussion of assembly also returns Butler to themes explored in *Gender Trouble* (Butler 1990/2000a) as she restates her performative theory of gender, noting how: 'the possibility of missing the mark is always there in the enactment of gender; in fact, gender may be that enactment in which *missing the mark is the defining feature*' (Butler, 2015a: 30, *emphasis added*). By reiterating her framing of gender as a perpetually elusive, aspirational process, one charged with normative expectations associated with performativity's reception rather than inscription, she reminds us of the extent to which performativity is enacted through a set of interpellations, including organizational ones. This raises the question of how we can make room for 'ways of living gender that challenge prevailing norms of recognition' (Butler, 2015a: 33).

By returning to a specific focus on gender in this way, Butler adds empirical substance to her discussion, reminding us that her normative critique is underpinned by a concern to understand, and address, the governmental [organizational] regimes through which our gendered selves are 'hailed' or interpellated into being (see Butler, 2005). As she put it, these categorize gender, conflating the complexity of our lived experiences into a narrow range of templates that are culturally intelligible, or recognizable; classified in binary terms and ordered hierarchically, these mean that we become gendered 'prompted by obligatory norms that demand that we become one gender or the other' (Butler, 2015a: 32). But because the reproduction of gender 'is always a negotiation with power' (Butler, 2015a: 32), in the course of its repeated re-enactments the possibility of doing gender 'in unexpected ways . . . remaking gendered reality' (Butler, 2015a: 32) is opened up. Crucially, Butler reminds us, in the context of her discussion of assembly and plurality, that the political aspiration of this performative ontology (its 'normative aim'—Butler, 2015a: 32) 'is to let the lives of gender and sexual minorities become *more possible and more liveable*' (Butler, 2015a: 32, *emphasis added*). To open up this possibility, as she puts it rather whimsically, 'the world as it should be would have to safeguard breaks with normality, and offer support and affirmation for those who make those breaks' (Butler, 2015a: 33).

Gender performativity is restated therefore, as both a theory and a practice that is opposed to the unliveable conditions that govern those who pass as 'normal'. Taking her underlying conviction that 'the question of recognition is an important one' (Butler, 2015a: 35) as her starting point, Butler emphasizes how 'the highly regulated field of appearance does not admit everyone' (Butler, 2015a: 35). Drawing directly on Arendt (1958), the 'field of appearance' is taken to refer to both a corporeal, bodily aesthetic as well as a political one, underpinning an affective politics. Butler frames her concerns through a series of interrelated questions, beginning with: 'Why is that field regulated in such a way that only certain kinds of beings can appear as recognizable subjects, and others cannot?' (Butler, 2015a: 35). Further: Which humans are eligible for recognition within the sphere of appearance, and which are not, and why? What norms operate in shaping the conferral or denial of recognition within the sphere of appearance?

Responding to these questions, Butler reminds us that for her, 'naming' is much more than a linguistic quandary; what we call those who do not and cannot appear as 'subjects' within hegemonic discourse is a vital political and ethical question. One obvious response is to repose the question (as Butler often does), and ask: 'What do the excluded call themselves?' (Butler, 2015a: 37).

Developing her earlier discussions in *Undoing Gender* (Butler, 2004b), Butler responds to these questions by considering the relationship between the ideal and the lived, arguing that 'ideals . . . are never fully inhabitable' (Butler, 2015a: 39). To become a normative ideal would involve 'overcoming all striving, all inconsistency, all complexity' (Butler, 2015a: 39). She addresses this with yet another question, asking 'Is there a way of closing that gap so that the gender ones feels oneself to be becomes the gender by which one is recognized?', framing this as marking 'the precondition of a liveable life' (Butler, 2015a: 39).

Exploring the theme of recognition further she argues that 'to be . . . deprived of recognition threatens the very possibility of existing' (Butler, 2015a: 40). The cultural context and power of recognition is such that

> To be a subject at all requires first finding one's way with certain norms that govern recognition, norms we never chose, and that

found their way to us and enveloped us with their structuring and animating cultural power.

(Butler, 2015a: 40)

This raises the question particularly of 'what it means to be [to live and work] at the limits of recognizability' (Butler, 2015a: 40), existing with and through a social conditioning of agency 'at the threshold of developing the terms that allow us to live' (Butler, 2015a: 40). Butler's contention is that 'ways of avowing and showing certain forms of interdependency stand a chance of transforming the field of appearance itself' (Butler, 2015a: 43), yet she is sketchy at best on the substantive details of what this might entail, and what form it might take. In terms of the ethics (and affective politics) of appearance, she argues that 'there has to be a way to find and forge a set of bonds and alliances [that enable us] to link interdependency to the principle of equal value, and to do this in a way that opposes those powers that differentially allocate recognizability' (Butler, 2015a: 43) but (as with earlier work, see Fraser, 1995a, 1995b) Butler remains frustratingly non-committal over what this might involve and how it might be undertaken.

In working towards an ethic of relationality, she emphasizes how a basic principle of liveability presumes recognition of the extent to which, 'in a common world . . . one's own prospects for living are invariably linked with everyone else's' (Butler, 2015a: 44).[10] Despite her lack of substantive detail, Butler arguably comes closer here to posing this as an organizational question than previously (developing some of the inroads made in Butler and Athanasiou, 2013), noting how:

> The ethical question, how ought I to live? or even the political question, how ought we to live together? *depends upon an organization of life that makes it possible to entertain those questions meaningfully.*
>
> (Butler, 2015a: 44, *emphasis added*)

Going back to the example of trans people that she cited in earlier writing (Butler, 1990/2000a, 1993), Butler argues that if trans people must sometimes pass through a pathologization as a way to realize and to establish an embodied way of life that is liveable, 'What kind of enfranchisement is this?', and how might it be possible *not* to pay such a costly price? (Butler, 2015a: 54–55). This question raises others that are fundamental to a critical, reflexive understanding of the organization of recognition more widely, particularly if assembly is 'a way of acting from and against precarity' (Butler, 2015a: 58). To recap, for Butler, precarity is both an economic and a social *condition* (but not an identity, see Butler, 2015a: 58). Those on the margins of recognizability can also be 'on the critical edge of the recognizable' (Butler, 2015a: 59).

Here she returns to her earlier faith in queer as 'a movement of thought, language, and action' that moves 'in directions quite contrary to those explicitly recognized' (Butler, 2015a: 62), framing queer as a necessary escape from the normative conditions of recognition, emphasizing its radical potential as a form of undoing through which the emergent subject is 'held to account' (see Butler, 2004b, 2005). As she puts it:

> As much as recognition seems to be a precondition of liveable life, it can serve the purposes of *scrutiny, surveillance, and normalization* from which a queer escape may prove necessary precisely to achieve liveability outside its terms.
>
> (Butler, 2015a: 62, *emphasis added*)

Developing the theme of bodies in/as alliance, Butler makes her faith in collective social struggle clear, emphasizing that 'the rights for which we struggle are plural rights' (Butler, 2015a: 66), so that our struggle 'seeks to expand what we mean when we say "we"' (Butler, 2015a: 66). This sets the basis and political context for a plural performativity in response to the neoliberal, entrepreneurial ethic of which she is explicitly critical (see Butler, 2015a: 67). For Butler, the latter has staged a 'war on the idea of interdependency', the foundation of her relational ethics. In contrast, she emphasizes how plural rights are collective and embodied, emerging from 'an understanding that the condition of precarity is differentially distributed [so that] the struggle against . . . precarity has to be based on the demand that lives should be treated equally and that they should be equally liveable' (Butler, 2015a: 67). What she calls alliance is not only a social form, 'sometimes it actually *is* the structure of our own subject formation', meaning that alliances form when

> The 'I' in question refuses to background one minority status or lived site of precarity in favour of any other; it is a way of saying, 'I am the complexity that I am'.
>
> (Butler, 2015a: 68)

This social relationality challenges autonomous, coherent or categorical ontologies of assembly and subjectivity, yet in doing so, appears to reinstate a reworked liberal, democratic ideal emphasizing 'not that I am a collection of identities, but that *I am already an assembly . . .* or an assemblage' (Butler, 2015a: 68, *emphasis added*). However, in pursuing a liveable life, the point is not to court market recognition, or to fall for what Brown (2006) calls the 'cunning of recognition', and hence not 'to rally for modes of equality that would plunge us all into equally unliveable conditions' (Butler, 2015a: 69). The opposite of precarity is not independence, or security (or not just security), but 'a *liveable interdependency*' (Butler, 2015a: 69, *emphasis added*); what Butler calls a 'politics of alliance . . . rests upon, and requires, an ethics of cohabitation' (Butler, 2015a: 70). Queer connects to this if

> We remember that the term queer does not designate identity, *but alliance*, and it is a good term to invoke as we make uneasy and unpredictable alliances in the struggle for social, political and economic justice.
>
> (Butler, 2015a: 70, *emphasis added*)

Again drawing on Arendt's (1958) commitment to a politics of appearance, Butler develops her argument that simply appearing constitutes a form of assemblage through which the (collective) body shows both its precarity and its persistence; what she alludes to as queer alliances constitute a mode of being together that requires 'breaking into' the established regime of space (and thereby challenging the space of appearance in Arendt's terms). On the one hand then, 'bodies are productive and performative' (Butler, 2015a: 84), yet they are also mutually interdependent, and are vulnerable in being so: 'they can persist and act only when they are supported, by environments, by nutrition, by work, by modes of sociality and belonging' (Butler, 2015a: 84). In organizational terms therefore, 'there can be no embodied life without social and institutional support' (Butler, 2015a: 70).

In this sense, and at this stage in her work, Butler's relationship to both organizations as entities and organization as a process is complex. On the one hand, she is of course critical of the organization of recognition, and of the organizational processes and imperatives that differentially impose and exploit our need for recognition, yet at the same time, she acknowledges both our need for organizational processes and structures, as well as resources, *and* has considerable faith in the radical, democratic potential of social modes of organization. The latter, she argues, have the capacity to act as 'the space of sociality' (Butler, 2015a: 84). An ongoing thread in her discussion of organizational resources is her concern with the labouring body as both an exploited precarity *and* as a political capacity. Indeed, the inter-corporeality of working bodies is positioned as the ontological basis of her relational ethic articulated and developed throughout her discussion of assembly. As she puts it:

> If we are living organisms who speak and act, then we are clearly related to a vast continuum or network of living beings; we not only live among them, but our persistence as living organisms depends on that matrix of sustaining interdependent relations.
>
> (Butler, 2015a: 86)

Here Butler's post-dualistic phenomenological influences, notably Merleau Ponty (2002; see Butler, 2015b), lead her to be particularly critical of

Arendt's (1958) political separation of the public and private, emphasizing how 'it is a kind of fantasy that one dimension of bodily life can and must remain out of sight, and yet another, fully distinct, appears in public' (Butler, 2015a: 87). Her phenomenological understanding of appearance as perception (distinct from but related to Arendt's more political notion) emphasizes how appearing in the world constitutes 'a morphological moment' (Butler, 2015a: 87), one that involves 'engaging others' bodies, to negotiate an environment on which one depends, *to establish a social organization for the satisfaction of needs*' (Butler, 2015a: 87, *emphasis added*).

Butler takes and develops from Arendt (1958) then the notion that the human as a social and relational being can never be truly alone because of our reliance on corporeal interdependency or 'entwinement' (Butler, 2015a: 97), a term she borrows from Merleau Ponty (2013). This means that our bodies are constituted through perspectives they can never fully inhabit, 'and this dispossession marks the sociality to which we belong' (Butler, 2015a: 97), because 'as located beings, we are . . . constituted in a sociality that exceeds us' (Butler, 2015a: 97). This ek-static understanding of our way of being in the world as enacted through a primary dispossession (Butler and Athanasiou, 2013) constitutes the philosophical and political basis of Butler's relational ethics, and of her critique of dispossession as the basis of a plural performativity.

This position very much sets the scene for Butler's articulation of an ethics of cohabitation and its connection to precarious life, itself a play on Hegel's (1977) ethical life. Here she focuses specifically on how ethical obligations emerge within relations of proximity that are not simply physical, but social, developing a relational as opposed to a contractual ethics premised upon cohabitation. By the latter she means those obligations in which we are enmeshed regardless of choice that emerge from our social conditions and 'not from any agreement we have made or from any deliberate choice' (Butler, 2015a: 121). These conditions not only imply relationality but also differential exposure to precarity, underpinning a global obligation to find 'political and economic forms that minimize precarity and establish political equality' (Butler, 2015a: 122), in other words (to put it very simply) to identify organizational solutions to organizational problems. As a reminder, for Butler,

> It is not from pervasive love for humanity or a pure desire for peace that we strive to live together. *We live together because we have no choice.*
>
> (Butler, 2015a: 122, *emphasis added*)

Part of what the body is, she emphasizes, is an ontological claim to interdependency on other bodies and networks of support: 'the body is entered into social life first and foremost under conditions of dependency'

(Butler, 2015a: 130). For organizational scholars, this has two important implications. First, that the conditions of support for the most vulnerable moments of life are themselves vulnerable, and second, that 'no one, however old, ever grows out of this particular condition, characterized as dependent and susceptible' (Butler, 2015a: 131), i.e. dependency is not an infant condition that we 'grow out of' as we become social [organizational] subjects. This implies an ontological rather than a biological essentialism, premised upon shared vulnerability, and a politics based on mutual recognition of that shared vulnerability, or on existential dispossession as our way of being (see Butler and Athanasiou, 2013). And it is the ontological basis of an ethics-politics that calls into question the discreetness and self-sufficiency of the human condition and of recognition systems, or conditions of inclusion, premised upon this perspective. Rather, the human body (and social existence) is framed as intertwined with *organizational life*, where the latter is taken to mean:

> A certain kind of dependency on infrastructure, understood complexly as environment, social relations, and networks of support and sustenance that cross the human, animal and technical divides.
> (Butler, 2015a: 133)

If we have to have a definition of what it means to be human contra to the discreet, self-sufficient (fallacy) of neo-liberalism, 'let it be one that connects vulnerability and agency' Butler (2015a: 139) argues, as the basis for a theoretical analysis that enables us to understand and respond to the positioning of social groups as differentially vulnerable (and therefore more or less able to exercise their capacity for agency) within this organizational complexity. Mobilizing vulnerability, 'the moment of actively appearing' (Butler, 2015a: 140) involves a deliberate risk of exposure, including for example, in an organizational politics of inclusion, which always carries with it the risk of exposure to appropriation, essentialism and reductionism. 'Vulnerability implicates us in what is beyond us yet part of us' (Butler, 2015a: 149); this is the basis of Butler's understanding of embodiment as our lived experience of social life, and of its connection to assembly, as an 'ecstatic relationality' (Butler, 2015a: 149), but which also carries with it the risk of that vulnerability being exploited.

This raises the question of what kind of recognition-based inclusion or liveable life might be possible, if individualism were minimized, within the organizational complexity referred to above. This is a question that leads Butler to focus explicitly on the political capacity of precarity to provide a meaningful basis for assembly, putting her faith in the political possibilities opened up by 'the collective assembling of bodies . . . that press up against the limits of social recognizability' (Butler, 2015a: 153). Yet the body 'as a resource' (Butler, 2015a: 153) is 'not an endless or a magical one' (Butler, 2015a: 153), it has to be supported to act, hence the significance of social networks and organizations. This accentuates the body's vulnerability, for this secondary (political) vulnerability is always, also grounded in its more phenomenological, ontological susceptibility:

> The body is always exposed to people and impressions it does not have a say about, does not get to predict or fully control, and . . . these conditions of social embodiment are those we have not fully brokered.
>
> (Butler, 2015a: 152)

This means that we are vulnerable because, on the one hand, organizations exclude us or, on the other, exploit our need for inclusion, yet at the same time, they are the very mechanisms through which we seek—and need—to address that vulnerability. What conditions does this impose upon us? Butler suggests that social solidarity emerges from recognition of our shared vulnerability rather than from deliberate agreements that we enter into knowingly, contractually, or even choices that we make. Such recognition can provide the basis for a way to enact the world we wish to see, 'or to refuse the one that is doing us in' (Butler, 2015a: 153). This form of deliberate exposure or persistence, 'the embodied demand for a liveable life', shows us the simultaneity of precarity and performativity, she argues, representing an important collective, political extension of her earlier critique of un/doing (Butler, 2004b).

Also revising her earlier writing on speech acts (Butler, 1997a), Butler develops her reading of Arendt's writing on the space of appearance in developing a critique of what she calls 'the standardization of the excellence protocols' (Butler, 2015a: 154). Here she explicitly emphasizes how

> *The assembly is already speaking before it utters any words* . . . by coming together it is *already* an enactment of popular will [a plural performativity].
>
> (Butler, 2015a: 156, original emphasis)

In other words, the 'we' voiced in language is already enacted by the gathering of bodies. A difficult and persistent question remains in considering this democratic project, however, namely: 'Any designation of the people works through delimiting a boundary that sets up terms of inclusion and exclusion' (Butler, 2015a: 164), risking an infinite regression. What is needed, Butler argues, is 'a check on the exclusionary logic by which any designation proceeds' (Butler, 2015a: 164), including we might surmise, in organizational terms and settings but, again, *how* this might be brought about remains open.

Speaking of 'the people' as a normative composition, Butler notes how representations function as potentially exclusionary designations that 'start and end somewhere, composing a sequence' (Butler, 2015a: 165).

This sequencing (and sequestering) is 'always limited by the perspective by which its object is selected, crafted and conveyed' (Butler, 2015a: 165). This effectively frames both collective and individual subjectivity as a reflection of 'ways of editing and selecting what and who will count' (Butler, 2015a: 165). Butler considers collective utterances such as 'we the people' as a 'strategy of containment' (Butler, 2015a: 165), a performative speech act that qualifies who has the right to appear, and on what basis. Butler's question (in response to Arendt) is: What are the bodily conditions for the enunciation of this?

For her, 'the assembly of bodies [is] a performative enactment' (Butler, 2015a: 177); it is a performative, political undoing, one that when mobilized, seeks to 'ward off the prospect of oblivion' (Butler, 2015a: 181). In sum, 'bodies require other bodies for support and survival' (Butler, 2015a: 182). But crucially, they require not just one another, but organizational 'social systems of support that are complexly human and technical' (Butler, 2015a: 182). Vulnerability is emphasized as the condition of resistance, as the basis of assembly to the way in which these exploit and appropriate our primary relationality, seeking to reinstate the latter in a radical, recognition-based form:

> In resistance, vulnerability is not precisely converted into agency—it remains the condition of resistance, a condition of the life from which it emerges, the condition that, rendered as precarity, has to be opposed, and is opposed.
>
> (Butler, 2015a: 184)

Resistance involves exposing vulnerability but also '*mobilizing that vulnerability as a deliberate and active form of political resistance*, an exposure of the body to power in the plural action of resistance' (Butler, 2015a: 184, *emphasis added*), a theme Butler explicates in more detail in her most recent work on this (Butler, 2016, see Postscript).

It is in her final essay in *Notes Towards a Performative Theory of Assembly*, 'Can One Lead a Good Life in a Bad Life?', that Butler follows up on Adorno's (2005) question of how we can live with ourselves if that life is at the expense of others. Adorno himself underscores the difficulty of finding a way to pursue a good life for oneself, as oneself, in the context of a broader world that is structured by inequality, exploitation and effacement. This question takes new forms depending on where and when it is posed, but it generally raises two problems for organizational scholars and activists that Butler herself brings to the fore; first, how to live one's own life well in a world in which a good life is foreclosed to so many, and second, what form does this question take for us now?

There are clearly many different views on what the good life might be—many have taken it to mean economic well-being, prosperity and security (but many claim to live a good life such as this while prospering on the exploitation, or profiting from the labour of others, entrenching inequality, living a good life not just in, but because of, a bad life). So the good life has to be defined and lived so that it does not presuppose inequality or cause harm, and this helps Butler to address the liberal connotations of her desire to proliferate the range of ways of living and being that might be accorded recognition.

When Adorno (2005) raises his question, he is asking us to think about the relationship between moral conduct and social conditions. But he is also asking us to consider, as Butler puts it, 'how the broader operations of power and domination enter into, or disrupt, our individual reflections on how best to live' (Butler, 2015a: 195). For Butler, this question is bound up with further questions: Whose lives matter? [And] on what grounds? These are simultaneously questions of recognition and of organization, of bearing 'the status of a subject who is worthy of rights and protections, with freedom and a sense of political belonging' (Butler, 2015a: 196).

In response, Butler's concern is 'to understand the differential way that [recognition] is allocated' (Butler, 2015a: 196); her ethical and political preoccupation is with both how recognition organizes, and with how it comes to be organized. Precarity involves living a 'shadow life' (Butler, 2015a: 197), in 'the shadowy domain of existence' (Butler, 2015a: 198), as 'a modality of nonbeing' (Butler, 2015a: 198), and ultimately, Butler strives to understand the ways in which the desire for recognition comes to be organized in order to *re*organize the terms on which it is accorded to some but remains perpetually elusive for others. Adorno himself acknowledges the bind in which we are situated as this project is pursued *within* the very settings, and drawing on the very resources, it seeks to address. He reminds us of the need to undertake reflexive self-criticism of our own need to establish ourselves in terms that make our own lives recognizable, while at the same time as offering a critique of the reigning order of values: 'the question of how to live the good life, then, is already . . . bound up with a living practice of critique' (Butler, 2015a: 200). As Adorno puts it, 'we ought also to mobilize our own powers of resistance in order to resist those parts of us that are tempted to join in' (cited in Butler, 2015a: 216); in other words, we need to keep the temptations of complicity continually in check, a poignant reminder when situated within the context of organizational power relations and of the need to maintain a liveable and sustainable working life.

So what to do for those of us concerned, on the one hand, to understand and address the physical and psychic harms caused by organizational phenomena and processes, and on the other, who maintain an emancipatory faith in the capacity of 'organization' as a collective response to those harms. Butler herself is well aware of this dilemma, noting how

> If one sphere of inequality is disavowed in order to justify and promote another sphere of equality, then. . . *we need a politics that can*

> name and expose that very contradiction and the operation of dis-
> avowal by which it is sustained.
>
> (Butler, 2015a: 206, *emphasis added*)

Again, Butler is vague (thus far) on the precise detail of what form this might take, and how it might proceed; what she does emphasize is that such a recognition-based politics must 'begin with an understanding of human dependency and interdependency, one that, in other words, can account for the relation between precarity and performativity' (Butler, 2015a: 206–207). For her, social forms of relationality require economic forms that presume and structure interdependency: 'only through a concept of interdependency . . . can we think a social and political world that seeks to overcome precarity in the name of liveable lives' (Butler, 2015a: 211).

A relational ethic means that the question of morality cannot be posed outside of the context of who or what counts as a liveable [workable] life. For Butler, Adorno's (2005) claim 'doubles' the meaning of life, to refer to (i) life as it is lived and experienced ('my life'); and (ii) 'life as socially and economically organized' (Butler, 2015a: 213). In Butler's analysis, the latter is 'bad' precisely because it does not provide the conditions for a liveable life for all, not only because that liveability is unequally distributed but, further, because it exploits our very need for liveability, for 'a good life'. But the reverse is also the case; the life that I am living is inextricable from the broader networks and social organization of life: 'if I were not connected with such networks, I could not actually live' (Butler, 2015a: 213), 'so my own life depends on a life that is not mine, not just the life of the other, but *a broader social and economic organization of life*' (Butler, 2015a: 213–214, *emphasis added*). Framed in this way, our ek-statis is shaped not simply by the struggle for recognition that characterizes the relationship between self and other (Hegel, 1977; Butler, 1987) but also by the complex ways in which we are intertwined with the organizational lifeworld (Butler, 2015a). If there are two parallel 'lives'—the individual and the collective—then one is entirely implicated in the other and this is both an organizational process and an organizational problem, in terms of the harm it causes, yet paradoxically, it is a problem that also has organizational solutions, or so Butler suggests.

Here Butler's Hegelian reading of Adorno means that her focus is very much on the social conditions shaping what she calls the '*mediation* of recognition' (see Butler, 2015a: 214, *emphasis added*). The reason these two lives (the I and the you, the individual and the social/collective) are so bound up is that they are interrelated in a system of mutual interdependency so that, 'although I perform . . . some set of social norms is being worked out in the course of that performance . . . and whatever is being worked out does not originate with me' (Butler, 2015a: 214). Butler ends her discussion of this by emphasizing the political capacity of precarity; writing in the aftermath of the Occupy movements, she frames the latter as an empirical example of the political mobilization of our mutual interdependency when she notes that

> Precarity is the condition against which several new social movements struggle; such movements do not seek to overcome interdependency or even vulnerability as they struggle against precarity; rather, they seek to produce *the conditions under which vulnerability and interdependency become liveable.*
>
> (Butler, 2015a: 218, *emphasis added*)

Our shared exposure to precarity is, for Butler, but one ground of our potential equality, and of our 'reciprocal obligations to produce together conditions of a liveable life' (Butler, 2015a: 218), so that 'in avowing the need we have for one another' (Butler, 2015a: 218) we might pave the way for the conditions of a liveable (good, ethical) life. For Butler, these conditions belong to 'a form of thinking and acting that responds to the urgencies of our time' (Butler, 2015a: 219).

Again, however, Butler is implicit at best on the details of how we might bring this about, and what form it might take. While she has clear respect for a body politics premised upon the assumption of autonomy (see Lloyd, 2007), her desire is to supplement this with an acknowledgement of mutual interdependency, not simply as a mere 'fact' of bodily existence, but normatively, politically. She hints at later interests to come, in this respect, in *Precarious Life* (Butler, 2004a: 28) when she asks whether a collective recognition of the primacy of mutual vulnerability might lead to a 'normative reorientation for politics'. Lloyd (2007: 141) adds to this question by asking: 'Could it, moreover, lead to a more ethical relation with the other?' A further question, one that Butler has begun to engage with more directly in her most recent writing, is: What role might organizational life play in this reinstatement of an ethics and politics of relationality?

Organizations and/as Assemblies

As Lloyd (2007: 146–147) notes, one of the ways in which social theorists and feminists have argued that recognition might be universalized is through a framework of equal rights, 'organized . . . as the mechanism through which recognition is conferred and/or resources are made available to ensure equal participation in democratic governance'. Yet until recently, at least, Butler has remained a staunch critic of institutions such as the state, which she sees primarily as a regulatory body intent on consolidating its own power and normalizing regimes, determining not just how subjects might be recognized, but on what basis, whilst at the same time, failing to support those not accorded recognition. Organizations such as the state therefore monopolize, in Butler's view, both recognition and the resources attached to it. In her most recent writing, however, she seems to have tempered or re-thought this position (see Butler, 2016 and Postscript).

The problem it raises, one that is particularly significant for organizational scholars, practitioners and activists, is the question of what other ways of securing recognition might be possible? In other words, how might we be able to pursue recognition without reifying established norms, lending credence to the latter, and without further strengthening the normalizing power of institutions including but also beyond, the state? These are not simply questions of what form struggles for recognition, and recognition itself might take, but of how that latter might be brought about. As noted by her critics, Butler is frustratingly non-committal (at least to date) on a way forward. For her, there is little point in pursuing 'a single political direction' (Butler, 2004b: 226) in order to realize a feminist commitment to expanding the terms of recognition, or to broadening the range of possibilities attached to the governance of a liveable life.

Not surprisingly, the radical political struggles that Butler envisages are those that tend to be enacted in civil society, beyond the remit and reach of the state. She sees non-state organizations and social movements as having the capacity to mobilize around issues of concern and to bring about necessary changes. For her, the arena of civil society is the optimum site for democratic struggle; the politics of the everyday are where she sees a transformation of social life being possible, through a re-articulation of social relations, an opening up of new conceptual horizons, and through collective enactments of subversive practices. In particular, she highlights the transformative potential attached to the crises evoked when those who are denied recognition demand it. Such scenarios, she argues, require a process of cultural translation,[11] one that *potentially* forces the current terms of recognition into question and opens up the possibility of new sets of norms being developed (Butler, 2005: 24). Recent debates in the United Kingdom over amendments to the Gender Recognition Act perhaps illustrate Butler's faith in this process, and the political capacity attached to demanding recognition in instances, and conceptual (including legislative) spaces, where it has hitherto been denied. But perhaps a better example of what she means by performative assemblies can be found in the Women's Marches that took place across the world when Donald Trump began his US presidency in January 2017 (Tyler, 2019).

As Sang and Lyon (2017) outline, over 600 marches were organized in dozens of countries, with an estimated participation in excess of 4.5 million people. Many of the symbols used in the Marches drew attention to the 'double otherness' of the different groups of people who took part, including Muslim women. What the Marches also highlighted, however, were the difficulties associated with assembling on such a mass scale, including the effects of crowd sizes and fears about personal safety in areas of the United States, for instance, in which those opposed to the Marches have ready access to firearms. Against this backdrop, the value of virtual assemblies such as Me Too is also illustrated, as is the importance of all forms of feminist writing to protest, think about and resist widespread physical and psychic harm. In particular, the Marches and responses to them in social media and academic forums emphasized the re-significatory power of humour in taking oppressive power and language and turning it against itself as 'an insider joke for the marginalized' (Sang and Lyon, 2017: 2) *en masse*. The 'Pussy Power' hats and ears were a prime example, amongst many others that could be noted here.

In her discussion of the 2017 Marches, Maggie Humm (2017) cites an interview that Butler gave in which she commented on the ways in which the demonstrations had brought about an alteration in the public understanding of who 'we the people' are through a collective, corporeal claim to public space.[12] Referring to an *unphilosophe.com* interview in which Butler suggests that 'forms of assembly and resistance [are] sites for imagining and enacting that alternative imaginary',[13] Humm argues that the wearing of pink pussy hats by marchers exemplified how performing gender differently on such a mass scale could act in a subversive way, 'undoing' Trump's ideas and articulations on women's bodies (Butler herself also praised the subversive potential of placards such as those declaring 'Nasty women vote', turning the misogynistic and personal tone of Trump's insults to Hillary Clinton on its head). As Butler puts it, 'the huge numbers of marches across the world, combined with largely supportive media coverage, enacted an alternative bodily imaginary both in public and digital spaces' (Humm, 2017: 5).

In what seems like a concession to the state, Butler goes on to argue in the same interview that demonstrations, along with occupations and encampments, work most effectively in political terms when the police are aligned with the demonstrators, as happened in London and Washington, where police assisted the organisers and policed with a 'light touch', making no arrests in either city (Humm, 2017). At the risk of idealization, I would agree with Humm's account of her personal experience, when she says 'the London March rendered visible . . . intersectional social groupings and, through homemade pink hats, speech acts and placards, gave demonstrators a sense of political and cultural power encouraging us to further challenges' (Humm, 2017: 7). In particular, the speed of assembly brought about by social media illustrated, as noted earlier, the value of the latter in bringing together unprecedented numbers of people, many of whom were new to political action, and who were drawn in by the focus on women, as well as the significance of virtual assemblies as a complement to the mass occupation of public space; what these marches illustrated, in Butler's terms, is the political capacity of a non-violent, recognition-based ethics as the basis of assembly, mobilizing vulnerability in resistance and evoking resignificatory powers.

As Rumens (2018) discusses in *Queer Business*, human vulnerability is, for Butler, the potential basis for a non-violent ethics and politics (see also Rumens and Tyler, 2015, 2016). In Butler's terms, this would be grounded in recognition of mutual relationality, rather than reified notions of tolerance or inclusion, or of democratic participation in the form of 'giving voice'. Political struggles against the norm, such as those enacted by queer theorists and activists, or by the women's marchers, Occupy protestors or Me Too campaigners are important ways to pursue the possibility of ethical relations that she opens up.

When Lloyd (2007) was writing her commentary on Butler, the idea of an ethically relational politics was still largely embryonic in Butler's thinking. Lloyd sees Butler's *Precarious Life, Undoing Gender* and *Giving and Account of Oneself* (Butler, 2004a, 2004b and 2005) as signalling an important ethical turn in her work based on an ontology of inter-corporeal vulnerability that returns Butler to her earliest Hegelian concerns (Butler, 1987). In the texts that she has written since, Butler has begun to flesh out her thinking on ethics and politics, with the concept of assembly being an important link between the two.

In her earlier work, Butler focused largely on sex, gender and sexuality. In subsequent writing, she has situated her discussions more broadly in the 'human' and so the appeal of her work has extended. She has also begun to engage more explicitly with questions of the economy, work and organizational life. An enduring concern with the organization of the desire for recognition connects these various thematic phases and philosophical preoccupations in her writing. While performativity will, as Lloyd (2007: 156) notes, 'almost certainly be the concept for which Butler is best remembered', as her work becomes more socially and organizationally grounded, it has increasing resonance with the concerns of sociologists of work and organization theorists, yet the latter have only recently begun to engage with the full breadth of Butler's writing (see Kenny, 2019 for a notable example) and to recognize its implications for the ways in which we 'do' organizations, as well as the ways in which we continue to be 'undone' by them. Butler's writing on assembly, in particular, opens up important ways of thinking about the ethical and political potential attached to our capacity for connection, for connections, to simply standing together as a mode of organization that materializes the relational power of mutual vulnerability.

Rhodes (2017) discusses these themes in his consideration of ethical praxis and LGBTQ organizational activism, drawing on insights from Butler's recent writing as well as her engagement with Levinas (1961), in an analysis that emphasizes the political possibilities attached to mobilizing and tactically exploiting a business case logic for ethical ends. This implied undoing of, or making trouble with, the business case starts from the premise that hetero- and cis-normative exclusion and LGBTQ workplace activism as it relates to ethics and politics can be 'fruitfully understood through

Judith Butler's more recent work' (Rhodes, 2017: 5). Rhodes reminds us that it is, in Levinasian terms, an ethical acknowledgement of the otherness of the Other that is 'precluded organizationally by hetero- and cisnormativity'. As an example of how this is played out, Rhodes outlines how the business case rests on two distinct, but related, modes of alterity. The first casts the LGBTQ other as abnormal, resulting in the latter's marginalization and subjection to discrimination. The second regards the other as 'unique, irreplaceable and deserving of respect and devotion'. While Rhodes suggests that if the latter means responding to the other with 'genuine care and respect, then alterity is a prompt to humanization' (Rhodes, 2017: 5). Yet Butler's reading of Levinas highlights—in organizational terms—how *both* forms of alterity are modes of de-humanization through which the other's difference from what is reinstated as the norm is used as the basis of either negation or co-optation. This is a perpetual problem for organizational theorists, practitioners and activists if we accept that othering is the outcome of either an abjectifying exclusion, as Rhodes (2017) notes in relation to LGBTQ people subject to hetero- and cis-normativity, but also a process of over-inclusion, or conditional inclusion. What Rhodes alerts us to is how discourses of categorization produce social norms that perpetuate discrimination but also to how we might re-signify these, in Butler's terms, in the service of an ethics and politics of alterity.

Rumens (2018: 176) explores this in more depth, considering how the accentuated vulnerability experienced by LGBTQ people in the workplace, the 'constant foreclosure of a collective recognition of the mutual vulnerability engendered by our inter-corporeal dependency' eradicates what for Butler is one of the most important resources 'from which we take our bearings and find our way in the world'. Considering how management and organizational scholars might pursue a queering of organizational sexualities in order to 'critically evaluate and oppose' this (Butler, 2004b: 30, cited in Rumens, 2018: 177) is a challenge that Rumens takes up in his discussion of LGBTQ workplace friendships and/as an ethics of non-violence.

For Rumens, if workplace friendships, as everyday ways of relating to each other within and through organizational life, open up the possibility of soliciting alternative ways of making lives more liveable, 'then this is an ethical endeavour that necessitates being open to the Other' (Rumens, 2018: 177). Mobilizing Butler's ethics of non-violence, he argues that one possibility for organizational scholars is to explore how friends are 'given over' to each other, hinting at the radical potential of a queer futurity in which our vulnerability is protected without being annihilated or exploited, acting as the starting point for what Butler (rather idealistically in his view), calls a 'sensate democracy' (Butler, 2004a: 151). In this sense,

Queer . . . steers us away from an ethic of tolerance (putting up with the Other) as well as of generosity (giving oneself to the Other), ever

mindful of the risks of appropriation, exploitation and normaliza-
tion . . . associated with both strategies, towards an ethic of openness
to the Other (being given over to the Other).

(Rumens, 2018: 177)

The latter, an ethics of openness, is premised upon a mutual recognition of the artifice of ethical boundaries between oneself and others (a
reconciliation with the other's otherness in Levinasian terms), and of
the political consequences of those boundaries. In this respect, Rumens
(2018) connects the performative ontology and political emphasis on a
perpetual undoing set out in Butler's earlier writing (see Chapters 1 and 3)
to a queer ethics and politics. In Butler's (2004a: 44) own hands, this
takes the form of a 'petition', a hint at the more collective assemblage in
her later work (Butler, 2015a), when she argues that

> When we ask for recognition for ourselves, we are not asking for
> another to see us as we are . . . [but] to solicit a becoming, to instigate
> a transformation, to petition the future always in relation to the Other.
>
> (Butler, 2004a: 44)

In other words, responding non-violently to the other's vulnerability is
not simply a question of treating the other as we might wish to be treated
ourselves, but rather of recognizing our mutual vulnerability within a
shared scene of recognition in the hope that we might be able to recon-
stitute that scene in order to distribute the possibilities of liveability more
ethically. In this sense, recognition for Butler is simultaneously a political
and ethical act. As Rumens (2018) emphasizes, this non-violent version
of ethics is premised upon recognizing not simply the other's sameness or
difference, but rather the common vulnerability engendered by us living
perpetually 'outside ourselves, constituted in cultural norms that precede
and exceed us . . . that condition us fundamentally' (Butler, 2004a: 45).
Rumens (2018: 178, *emphasis added*) explores workplace friendships as
'a way of proceeding, *of organizing ourselves and others*, based upon this
complex yet enormously appealing ethic-political imperative', one that
involves negotiating an ethics of openness at work.

By way of illustration, Rumens cites an account shared with him by
Leonard, a gay man working as a hospital-based occupational therapist,
about his relationship with his straight male friend, Will. Leonard recalls:

> The other day I was talking to Will in the office canteen, he was
> telling me how self-conscious he is because he is constantly peeing
> at work . . . people are noticing, and it's because he's got prostate
> problems, and what's worse is his GP can't do anything for him . . . *it
> broke my heart to hear him struggling* . . . like when he wet himself
> at work because he couldn't get to the loo in time . . . later that day

he heard a couple of patients talking about him . . . one referred to him as that old codger who pissed his pants. No doubt they thought it was a joke but it's hardly a joke is it? . . . *It struck me how vulnerable he is, for all to see.*

(Leonard, in Rumens, 2018: 178, *emphasis added*)

Rumens (2018: 178) reads this account as an insight into the corporeal vulnerability that is central to a Butlerian ethics of non-violence in which Will's disclosure is pivotal to Leonard's recognition of shared vulnerability, 'acknowledging his friend's concerns about his failure at being able to performatively constitute a viable organizational subject whose body is fit for work'. Yet we can also read here a recognition of the simultaneous opportunity for connection and exposure engendered by that vulnerability, 'for all to see'. For Rumens (2018: 179), this account has an 'arresting quality' in its portrayal of a recognition-based relationship between two men, one that enables both to seek 'non-normative alternatives, perhaps queer futures' beyond their ascribed 'ageing gay' and 'straight man' subject positions. For him, it is one that provides a glimpse into possibilities and nuances attached to an ethics based on recognition and relationality, one that has the capacity to disrupt heteronormative discourses about male workplace relationships as 'guarded, blighted by homophobia and thus carefully choreographed' (Rumens, 2018: 179).[14]

Drawing on Butler's writing on an ethics and politics of assembly, Rumens indicates how queer futures premised upon a non-violent relationality might bring greater possibilities for recognition on a more collective scale. His discussion of male friendships hints at how an ethics premised upon a non-sovereign subject, decentred within a field of relationality by recognition of our mutual inter-corporeal vulnerability, potentially creates the possibility for 'more democratic organizational worlds'. As he puts it,

> Recognition of our mutual vulnerability is a potent statement about the importance of relationality in providing the social conditions that are the crux to our very existence. . . . It is this sense of mutual dependency that facilitates an ethics of non-violence to emerge that can enable us to petition for queerer futures in which we might be extended recognition in ways not presently afforded to us.
>
> (Rumens, 2018: 180)

These are issues that Marianna Fotaki (2019) also turns to in her recent work. Drawing on Butler, she explores how Butler's notions of precarity and embodied vulnerability provide a focal point for making ethical connections with the unknown other based on trust relations. As she puts it, 'Butler's understanding of the human as a relational social being who craves recognition by others allows us to appreciate the role of social [organizational] norms in the subject's formation' (Fotaki, 2019: 16). Yet at the same time, Butler's focus on our primary relationality highlights why public policies and forms of collective action might *and must* emerge from a shared recognition that all our lives are precarious, and that we all depend upon each other for our survival. How to bring this collective recognition about, and what form it might take, within and through organizations remains a salient concern, perhaps more so now than ever, for organizational scholars, practitioners and activists.

Notes

1. In 1998, Butler was notoriously awarded first prize in the fourth 'Bad Writing' contest, sponsored by the conservative academic journal, *Philosophy and Literature*. See Butler (1999) for her response, cited in Kirby (2006). The passage of text that earned her this dubious honour was: 'The move from a structuralist account in which capital is understood to structure social relations in relatively homologous ways to a view of hegemony in which power relations are subject to repetition, convergence, and rearticulation brought the question of temporality into the thinking of structure, and marked a shift from a form of Althusserian theory that takes structural totalities as theoretical objects to one in which the insights into the contingent possibility of structure inaugurate a renewed conception of hegemony as bound up with the contingent sites and strategies of the rearticulation of power' (Butler, 1997a: 13).
2. Butler's discussion on this reflects her earlier insistence that 'inclusion' is not the opposite to the negative forms of exclusion or abjection (Butler, 2004b: 149).
3. These ideas draw heavily on De Beauvoir's (1976: 82) argument that our interdependence 'explains why oppression is possible and why it is hateful'; it is an exploitation of our mutual, but socially situated (and therefore hierarchically organized), vulnerability.
4. To illustrate, Butler's recognition-based critique of dispossession proceeds from her acknowledgement that 'being dispossessed by the other's presence and by our own presence to the other is the only way to be present to one another' (Butler and Athanasiou, 2013: 17). We can also see strong echoes of Butler's Hegelian thinking here when she describes recognition as the process by which human beings are construed as social subjects on 'normative and disciplinary terms' with the latter regulating inter-subjectivity by defining 'what renders a subject legible, recognizable, desirable' (Butler and Athanasiou, 2013: 90).
5. See *Giving an Account of Oneself* (Butler, 2005) for a more sustained discussion of relationality and ethics.
6. Drawing on Butler, I use the term 'performative labour' here to refer to the expenditure of time, effort and skills required in order to bring particular subjectivities into being, and to sustain them, through the work involved in conforming to normative regimes of intelligibility and recognition (see Tyler, 2019).
7. Indeed, perhaps one of the most oft-quoted lines from Adorno and Horkheimer's (1997 [1947]) *Dialectic of Enlightenment* is the point that 'all reification is a forgetting' (cited in Honneth, 2008: 17). This is clearly a view that Butler shares, when she argues, for instance, that what we call modernity is 'a form of forgetfulness and cultural erasure' (Butler, 2004b: 231).

196 Organizational (re)Assemblage

8. To understand the dynamics of this, it is important to keep in mind Butler's starting premise, namely the Hegelian idea that the moment of self-loss marks 'the beginning of community' (Butler, 2004b: 250), or at least opens up the possibility of communal connections and ways of living to emerge. She sought, in the context of the heightened vulnerability and aggression that emerged after the terrorist attacks on September 11, 2001 (9/11), to find 'a basis for community' premised upon a mutual recognition of our exposure to violence and our complicity in it (Butler, 2004a: 19).

9. This emphasis is a development of Butler's growing interest in the idea that the public sphere is constituted in part 'by what can appear', and her conviction that 'the regulation of the sphere of appearance is one way to establish what will count as reality, and what will not', and further 'it is also a way of establishing whose lives can be marked as lives, and whose deaths will count as deaths' (Butler, 2004a: xxi).

10. Velicu and Garcia-López (2018) draw directly from this in their discussion of common experiences of being mutually vulnerable in power relations which are enabling as being akin to a 'politics of commoning', where the latter is taken to refer not simply to the allocation or management of resources but to a common struggle to experience liveable lives.

11. Butler borrows the term 'cultural translation' from Homi Bhabha (1994), who in turn derives it from Walter Benjamin (1972; see Lloyd, 2007: 151).

12. A version of the interview cited by Humm is on the Verso website: www.versobooks.com/blogs/3025-trump-fascism-and-the-construction-of-the-people-an-interview-with-judith-butler

13. Interview with Judith Butler, 19 December 2016, on *unphilosophe.com*.

14. A similar view is expressed by the trans artist and activist Grayson Perry (2018) in an essay written in association with an exhibition of work on the history of cross dressers at the Photographers' Gallery, London, in which he reflects on some photographs he took of himself between 1979 and 1984 when he was an art school student. As he put it, 'there is a sense of poignancy about these images that I used to get when I went to transvestite gatherings. It came from a group of men trying to find and express something quite tender and vulnerable about themselves: burly truck drivers, engineers, architects or whatever all dressed up as their fantasy woman. There is still something very touching about it' (Perry, 2018: 34).

Postscript

Organizing a/as Non-Violent Ethics and Politics

I have written this section as a 'postscript' because it seemed odd to add a Conclusion to a body of work that continues to evolve and which has increasing resonance for organizational theory, practice and activism. As Lloyd (2007) notes, performativity may well be the idea for which Butler is best known; however, her performative ontology has been a 'way in' to a complex body of ideas that, at its heart, is concerned with how the desire for recognition comes to be organized, and what the consequences of those modes of organization might be both for those subject to them, and for those rendered abject by dominant organizational ways of being and relating to one another.

It is both unsurprising and to be applauded, but perhaps problematically premature to declare *Gender Trouble* out dated (see Fischer, 2016).[1] Thirty years after its first publication we find ourselves 'poised someplace between gender mattering tremendously and mattering not very much at all' (Fischer, 2016). In 2014, Facebook stopped limiting its gender options to 'male' or 'female' and began to give users some fifty other choices. In 2015, it abandoned a pre-set menu altogether, and gave users the option of selecting up to ten words of their own choosing, a fluidity materialized in the ubiquity of gender neutral toilets and changing facilities. As performers sharing cramped dressing rooms have long since known, gender is simply 'all part of the show'.

If the aim of *Gender Trouble* was to open the door for 'cultural configurations of sex and gender [to] proliferate', as Butler (1990) put it in the book's conclusion, 'confounding the very binarism of sex, and exposing its fundamental unnaturalness' then in many ways, job done. And yet, to take gender fluidity and sexual freedom for granted would be un-reflexive and ethnocentric in the extreme as individuals, groups, organizations and communities across the world continue to struggle for something so basic yet complex, so immediate yet elusive: recognition.

At the time of writing, Butler is developing her thinking on non-violent ethics and public assembly in important and interesting directions that connect to feminist politics and campaigns for gender recognition, yet which also (in doing so) have much wider appeal, speaking to a broad range of struggles. Butler's writing is complex, rich and evolving, but throughout the range of texts considered here she maintains a constant commitment to securing intelligibility and legitimacy for those denied recognition on the basis of hegemonic social, political and legal norms. What concerns Butler most, as Lloyd (2007: 133) has summed it up, is 'their freedom to live a liveable life, a freedom presently restricted by the operation of norms defining the terms of such a life'. Underpinning this preoccupation, and therefore Butler's wider political project, are the largely sociological connections between normative violence, cultural intelligibility, and the dialectics of recognition. Connecting all of these is an enduring focus on the social, cultural and we might argue, organizational particularity of norms that define the parameters of who and what 'counts', or matters.

It is a concern with this relationship and its implications for the capacity to live a liveable (and workable) life that shapes Butler's earliest writing on Hegel (Butler, 1987) and its articulation in her views on performativity (Butler, 1988, 1990/2000a), and which continues to evolve in her most recent work (Butler, 2015a; Butler, 2016; Butler et al., 2016) at the time of writing. In various theoretical and thematic forms, it has underpinned each of her key publications in the intervening period on which scholars in the arts, humanities and social sciences, and increasingly in the field of work and organization studies have drawn and which have been considered here.

While Butler's most recent writing gets much closer to organization theory than her previous work, it is clear that she develops themes here that have always been present in her thinking. Namely, that we need to articulate a normative critique of exclusion that strives, as she puts it, to 'expose and ameliorate those cruelties by which subjects are produced and differentiated', and to set political goals designed to address 'questions of social and economic justice which are not primarily concerned with questions of subject formation' but which cannot be extricated from them (Butler, 1995b: 141). To this end, Butler has long since argued that it is crucial for us to rethink social relations premised upon an appropriation or exploitation of our basic inter-connectedness as a matter of political and ethical urgency. Butler framed this latter issue as follows, in earlier writing in which she introduced themes explored in her most recent preoccupations; that is, with an ethics and politics designed to recuperate our basic, primal precarity, when she asked:

> Will what appears radically Other, as pure exteriority, be that which we refuse and abject as that which is unspeakably 'Other', or will it constitute the limit that actively contests what we already comprehend and already are?
>
> (Butler, 1995b: 143)

Butler posed this question to herself back in 1995 when she considered it in relation to our potential transformation by virtue of self-limiting encounters with difference; but here she seemed to still be working largely at the level of the individual subject. Nancy Fraser (1995b: 163) picked up on this in her critique, noting that while feminist politics requires a more comprehensive moral-political vision than a mere de-reification of performativity, in its form at the time, Butler's framework privileged 'the local, the discrete and the specific' with 'large scale institutions such as states and economies' remaining either deliberately or developmentally beyond its reach.

Responding to this in her more recent writing, Butler has turned to this proposition as a more collective phenomenon, recuperating the political in a de-reified, collaborative performativity, and as she does so, attempting to think through what form this might take, and what critical capacities it might open up. It is worth noting that Fraser also accused Butler of overestimating the emancipatory potential of 'gender-bending' (the term she used in 1995b: 163) in relation to structural dynamics, and of missing the latter's susceptibility to 'commodification, recuperation, and de-politicization—especially in the absence of strong social movements struggling for social justice'. Nor were we given, in Butler's earlier writing, 'a means to theorize inter-subjectivity . . . [our] relations to one another' (Fraser, 1995b: 163).

It is arguable that developments in Butler's own work, and in the wider social sphere since have begun to address each of these concerns. In short, Butler's ideas seem to be more capable than ever of helping us to understand, engage with and address issues relating to 'the social totality' (Fraser, 1995b: 164) and to tackle questions of social justice played out at 'the macro level, the inter-subjective, and the normative'. Yet (thus far), as noted in Chapter 6, she is tantalizingly, frustratingly even, hesitant to set out the forms that a recognition-based ethics and politics might take, and to be clear on how it might be enacted. In this sense, much of her work continues to hover around the margins of organization theory and politics, as a kind of open invitation to organizational scholars, practitioners and activists to further 'flesh out' what her work means for how we experience, think about and engage with organizational life, possibly in transformative ways. In this sense, the continuing influence of her work, in scholarship and activism, affirms how 'undoing' the violent accumulation engendered by organizational processes, settings, power relations and imperatives is a collective political and intellectual task.

As Butler shifts her focus towards explicating a non-violent ethics premised upon vulnerability in (rather than as distinct from) resistance a timely challenge becomes how to pursue a plural performativity that links the particularities of individual lives to the collective demand for recognition without risking fragmentation at one extreme or homogenization at the other, to bring about 'a performativity in plurality' (Butler and Athanasiou, 2013: 157).

It is with this issue that her current writing seems to be grappling. Written in the months after the Occupy Gezi movement in Turkey, her edited collection with Zeynep Gambetti and Leticia Sabsay (Butler et al., 2016), and her essay within this collection, 'Rethinking Vulnerability and Resistance' (Butler, 2016), takes up the challenge of rethinking vulnerability *as* resistance. The collection emerges from a series of conversations trying to make sense of the Occupy movement, and the events leading up to it and in its aftermath, registering the combination of 'exhilaration and sorrow' experienced and enacted by bodies on the streets (where 'bodies' is taken to mean both individuals and collectives), who together enact the promise of an alternative society in which vulnerability 'would cease to be a curse and would instead constitute the very ground for modes of solidarity' (Butler et al., 2016: x).

In their introductory discussion, Butler et al. set out their approach to reformulating vulnerability and resistance beyond two pervasive assumptions prevalent in popular and theoretical discourses and interventions: first, that vulnerability—as a passive site of inactivity—is the opposite of resistance and cannot be conceived of as part of collective action; and second, that vulnerability needs and deserves protection, a presumption that shores up paternalistic forms of power and (by implication) philanthropic subject positions. Both assumptions are at the expense of understanding how vulnerability relates to collective forms of resistance and possible social (organizational) transformation, and both reify vulnerability and those designated as 'vulnerable' by fixing them into a position of powerlessness, in need of protection and advocacy. Through an analysis of concrete contexts, Butler et al. (2016: 1) call into question the basic assumption that vulnerability and resistance are 'mutually oppositional' in order to open up the potentially transformative relationship between the two, reimagining vulnerability as the basis of political action, asking: What forms of subjectivity might emerge outside of, or against, this binary? This is a question that has important and exciting possibilities for rethinking organizational life, including potentially opening up 'queer futures' (Rumens, 2018).

To consider this question, Butler et al. further unpack the relationship between vulnerability and precarity revisiting some of Butler's earlier discussions (see Butler and Athanasiou, 2013), affirming precarity as a social relation induced by the ethical primacy of mutual vulnerability. For Butler, precarity emerges when social and political arrangements produce unequal distributions of vulnerability.[2] The problem, Butler et al. (2016) note is that those positioned as vulnerable, such as those subject to sexual violence, or living as refugees for instance, are deemed to be entirely without agency and consequently, become subject to protective discourses and practises. Wresting collective agency from this positioning is a political challenge but also a necessity if alternative resources for self-empowerment, collective resistance and solidarity are to be mobilized. Examples given include, for instance, feminist forms of self-defence, self-organized networks and shelters and 'grass roots modes of organizing within civil society or outside its established norms' (Butler et al., 2016: 2). This rethinking or reclaiming of vulnerability is crucial, they argue, to overcoming the difficulties that result from being stuck in a situation in which paternalism and vulnerability are the two opposing alternatives to collective agency and resistance.

The dialectical account of vulnerability and resistance that Butler et al. (2016: 4) offer brings to the fore, for critical reflection and resistance, the ways in which encounters with vulnerability function, for dominant social groups, as an expulsion or projection of relationality (and hence a negation of our primary, mutual vulnerability). As they put it, 'when vulnerability is projected onto another, it seems as if the first subject is fully divested of vulnerability, having expelled it externally onto the other'. Not only does this projection shore up the myth of the invulnerable, autonomous subject, it also becomes a licence to either indifference at one extreme, or exercises in paternalistic power at the other. The latter becomes a kind of epistemic violence that reinforces the other's precarity, as mutual vulnerability mutates into a powerful patronage articulated through claims to 'know better' what the other needs and wants.

At stake for Butler et al. (2016: 50, *emphasis added*) is whether this 'dialectical inversion', one that relies on 'the *presumptive invulnerability* of those with power', can be refuted. Further, can this refutation open up the possibility of linking mutual vulnerability to practices of resistance in the service of social and political justice? The condition of precarity, as the result of an 'unequal distribution of vulnerability' (Butler et al., 2016: 5), often works in tandem with the discursive management of those designated as vulnerable individuals, groups and populations. While not explicit, Butler et al. suggest that this is an organizational process, one through which governmental regimes designate vulnerable groups as 'in need of protection', a process that not only negates the agentic capacity of those rendered vulnerable to act politically, but which also, in doing so, re-affirms the forms of regulation and control to which they are subject, positioning those dispensing protection as simultaneously pseudo vulnerable (as 'givers', 'carers') and invulnerable (not themselves 'in need' of protection but rather, as capable of giving it).

The strategies Butler et al. (2016: 6) propose involve a rethinking of human relations and what they call 'infrastructural mobilizations' such as barricades, hunger strikes, improvised gatherings, modes of deliberate exposure and artistic forms of intervention, including in public spaces. These forms of resistance challenge and oppose a more neo-liberal notion of 'resilience' premised upon an attempt to 'cover over the structural conditions of accelerated precarity, inequality, statelessness, and occupation' (Butler et al., 2016: 6). A challenge for how this endeavour relates to feminist and/or organizational politics revolves around, on the one hand, breaking with dominant (masculinist, managerialist) models of autonomy without essentializing or homogenizing femininity or idealizing vulnerability 'as an ultimate value' (Butler et al., 2016: 7). The aim is for vulnerability to be made manifest by means of 'new forms of embodied political interventions and modes of alliance that are *characterized by interdependency and public action*' (Butler et al., 2016: 7, *emphasis added*) rather than striving to somehow overcome it.

As noted in Chapter 6, those who gather to resist various forms of state and economic power take risks with their own bodies and those of others, exposing themselves to possible harm so that vulnerability is literally 'enacted by assembling' (Butler, 2016: 12). For Butler, the important question becomes: Does resistance overcome this vulnerability, or does it mobilize it, and if the latter, what might this open up, politically and ethically? To this we might add, what could this imply 'organizationally' if organization is both a mechanism for reaffirming induced precarity and potentially resisting and rethinking it?

In her essay on 'Rethinking Vulnerability and Resistance', Butler returns once again to Arendt (1958, see Butler, 2015a) to explore the forms of media through and within which the space of appearance is constituted. She notes how the public space of the media is denied to some, 'those who are, through coercion, fear, or necessity, living outside the reach of the visual frame' or made available to others, 'those who *can appear* within the visual images of the public', but only on the basis of their willingness to continually subject themselves to its normative parameters, forming virtual, digital 'passionate attachments', so to speak. Yet Butler also notes how the media can function as an infrastructural support 'when it facilitates modes of solidarity and establishes new spatio-temporal dimensions of the public sphere' (Butler, 2016: 14), as was arguably the case in instances such as Me Too, the Occupy movements and the Women's Marches discussed in Chapter 6.

These examples suggest that, to borrow from Butler's earlier phrasing, the media as the 'visual frame' of the public sphere, or the space of appearance in Arendt's (1958) terms, might—could—be both the scenography of abjection and assembly. Within and through instances of the latter, the embodied demand to recognize and address induced precarity is 'enacted publically by those who expose their vulnerability to failing infrastructural conditions'; in such moments, there is arguably 'plural and performative bodily resistance at work' (Butler, 2016: 15), showing how such modes of assembly might work to recognize—reorganize and reinstate—our primary relationality.

Connecting this to queer politics, Butler (2016: 18) notes that it is in domains such as these that 'something queer can happen', where norms are refuted or revised, breaking what she calls 'citational chains of . . . normativity' potentially paving the way for more liveable and workable forms of life to emerge as viable, not by overcoming vulnerability but by recognizing and reinstating ('reminding' ourselves of) it. This links 'the intersubjective and infrastructural conditions of a liveable life' in so far as the aim is not to somehow resiliently 'overcome' the social and material conditions of our primary vulnerability but instead to 'make them more just, more equal, and more enabling' (Butler, 2016: 19). Crucially,

> We are embodied creatures . . . exposed to what we are called and *dependent on the structures that let us live*. So whatever performative agency might mean, it cannot overcome these prior and constituting dimensions of social normativity.
>
> (Butler, 2016: 19, *emphasis added*)

Overcoming vulnerability is not the issue, then; rethinking and reorganizing it is, but as Butler is well aware, this carries with it the risk of exposure to physical and psychic harm. But it also acknowledges our vulnerability to organization as our mode of being, attributable to our mutual vulnerability and our dependency on complex social, political and economic infrastructures. By bringing this to the fore, Butler focuses on organizational life in its broadest sense—as both an organization of inter-subjective relationality, and of resources, the latter understood as 'environment, social relations, and networks of support and sustenance by which the human . . . proves not to be divided from the animal or the technical world' (Butler, 2016: 21), as noted in Chapter 6.

Yet our primary vulnerability is increasingly exploited and appropriated by decimated or disappearing infrastructures of environmental, social and economic support, and the extent to which secure, fairly compensated labour is increasingly elusive for large numbers of people at the same time as we are interpellated into subject positions premised upon self-reliance and resilience as the basis of recognition and as a (reified) replacement for relationality. Not only are we then vulnerable to one another, an inevitable feature of social relations if understood dialectically; this vulnerability is accentuated by the very systems of support on which we depend.

In response to this predicament, Butler's argument is that as a deliberate exposure to power, vulnerability is not the opposite of resistance, but embodies it. At the risk of 'smuggling in discounted paradigms for reconsideration', as she puts it (alluding to an ethics of care or generosity), with its essentialist connotations, Butler contends that a view that positions resistance *as opposed* to vulnerability effectively 'shores up paternalistic power, relegating the condition of vulnerability to those who suffer discrimination, exploitation or violence' (Butler, 2016: 22). But what about the power of those who are oppressed? What about the vulnerability of those who exercise paternalistic power, and of paternalistic institutions? If the latter can be 'brought down, or rebuilt on egalitarian grounds, then paternalism itself is vulnerable to a dismantling that would undo its very form of power' (Butler, 2016: 23). When subjugated people bring this about, do they overcome their vulnerability, if/as the latter is converted into agency? Butler argues that in such instances, vulnerability takes a different form, one that *reminds* us of our relationality, the primacy of our shared vulnerability, reinstating this 'forgotten' mutual dependency. When we oppose this, Butler notes, it is usually because our dominant social norms hail us into seeing ourselves as agentic only if we 'overcome' vulnerability; opposing relationality in the name of agency implies that we prefer to see ourselves as those who act rather than as those who are acted upon—as organizers rather than as the organized. But (to borrow from Butler, 2016: 24) what form of organizational life is supported by this 'posture of control', this adamant disavowal of mutual connection and dependency? And what possibilities might thinking about and enacting organizational life differently bring about?

Butler's contention is that one of the important features of recent examples of public assembly is that we see enacted and embodied within them a mobilization of resistance *as* (rather than as opposed to) vulnerability, showing how the latter 'can be a way of being exposed and agentic *at the same time*' (Butler, 2016: 24, *emphasis added*). Such modes of assembly are organized differently to the idea that political agency derives from vanquishing vulnerability,[3] affirming the latter as an 'existential condition' (Butler, 2016: 25), as well as a socially induced one of 'disproportionate exposure to suffering'. Once we understand the relationship between vulnerability and resistance in this way, our engagement with both terms changes, Butler argues, 'and the binary opposition between them can be undone'. For her, this is 'a feminist task' (Butler, 2016: 25), but it is also an organizational one.

Our dependency on each other and on infrastructural support makes this clear. While this may take the form of political action as non-violent protest in the traditional way in which that has been understood, it can also involve simply asserting the right to appear. Under such conditions, 'continuing to exist, to move and to breathe are forms of resistance', and Butler cites placards in Palestine with the slogan 'We still exist!' as but one example. Such instances might be shorn of political and legal protection, and risk injury and exposure in being so, but they show how vulnerability can affirm relationality in/through resistance as a mode of reorganization, one that reveals our mutual vulnerability as it reinstates it. At its most basic level, this emphasizes how simply exercising the right to appear (otherwise) constitutes an audacious act of defiance and affirmation, one that can be enacted in and through organizational life on an individual, day-to-day level, or collectively *en masse*. In organizations that hail us into a culture of presence, for instance, or which compel or constrain us into narrowly defined ways of being on which our recognition, our capacity to sustain liveable, workable lives depends, exercising the right *not* to appear, not to embody and enact corporate life on its own terms, can also open up the possibility of living, working and organizing differently—of making trouble, undoing and reassembling the organizational lives that, albeit in different ways and to different degrees, render us beside ourselves.

Notes

1. Butler herself acknowledges that 'in many ways, *Gender Trouble* is a very dated book'; perhaps most notably it does not engage with trans experiences and identifications for instance (in an interview with Fischer, 2016).
2. This is a slightly confusing shift in terminology from Butler and Athanasiou (2013), in which Butler distinguishes between a primal, existential precarity and an induced, unequally distributed precarity with the latter being, effectively, an exploitation or appropriation of the former. Butler (2016: 12) slightly shifts this, when she argues that it is 'important to establish a more precise relationship between vulnerability and precarity'. This is more than a semantic slippage, however, and signals an important development in Butler's thinking as she begins to refine her framing of the relationship between our primary, ethical vulnerability—the premise of her thinking on recognition derived from Hegel (1977), see Butler (1987)—and the social arrangements that exploit that vulnerability. My sense is that to signal this shift from a more individual to collective understanding of this relationship, Butler (2016) begins to distinguish between precarity and vulnerability with more precision. It is confusing, however, as she also refers to 'induced vulnerability' when she seems to be referring to socially situated precarity (Butler et al., 2016: 2). Yet Butler's view that vulnerability is the 'sense of exposure' that makes precarity possible is important for organization theorists as it brings to the fore our inability to resist, collectively but also day-to-day, regimes that we know to exploit and harm ourselves and others (see Kenny, 2018, 2019).
3. This, Butler argues, is a masculinist ideal that we ought to continue to oppose (Butler, 2016: 24).

References

Adorno, T. (1973) First published 1966. *Negative Dialectics*. London: Continuum.
Adorno, T. (2005) First published 1951. *Minima Moralia: Reflections on a Damaged Life*. London: Verso.
Adorno, T. and Horkheimer, T. (1997) First published 1947. *Dialectic of Enlightenment*. London: Verso.
Agamben, G. (1993) *The Coming Community*. Minneapolis: University of Minnesota Press.
Ahmed, S. (2000) *Strange Encounters*. London: Routledge.
Ahmed, S. (2012) *On Being Included: Racism and Diversity in Institutional Life*. London: Duke University Press.
Ainsworth, S. and Hardy, C. (2012) 'Subjects on Inquiry: Statistics, Stories and the Production of Knowledge', *Organization Studies*. 33(12): 1693–1714.
Althusser, L. (2001) *Lenin and Philosophy and Other Essays*. London: Monthly Review Press.
Amsterdam, van N. and Eck, van D. (2018) ' "I Have to Go the Extra Mile": How Fat Female Employees Manage Their Stigmatized Identity at Work', *Scandinavian Journal of Management*. 35(1): 46–55.
Arendt, H. (1958) *The Human Condition*. Chicago: Chicago University Press.
Austin, J. L. (1955) *How to Do Things with Words*. Cambridge, MA: Harvard University Press.
Benhabib, S. (1992) *Situating the Self: Gender, Community and Postmodernism in Contemporary Ethics*. London: Routledge.
Benhabib, S. (1995a) 'Feminism and Postmodernism: An Uneasy Alliance', in S. Benhabib, J. Butler, D. Cornell and N. Fraser (eds.) *Feminist Contentions: A Philosophical Exchange*. London: Routledge, pp. 17–34.
Benhabib, S. (1995b) 'Subjectivity, Historiography, and Politics: Reflections on the "Feminism/Postmodernism Exchange" ', in S. Benhabib, J. Butler, D. Cornell and N. Fraser (eds.) *Feminist Contentions: A Philosophical Exchange*. London: Routledge, pp. 107–125.
Benjamin, J. (1988) *The Bonds of Love: Psychoanalysis, Feminism and the Problem of Domination*. New York: Pantheon.
Benjamin, W. (1972) *Illuminations*. London: Fontana.
Berlant, L. (2007) 'Slow Death (Sovereignty, Obesity, Lateral Agency)', *Critical Inquiry*. 33(4): 754–780.
Berlant, L. (2011) *Cruel Optimism*. Durham, NC: Duke University Press.
Bhabha, Homi K. (1994) *The Location of Culture*. London: Routledge.

Boje, D. (1995) 'Stories of the Storytelling Organization: A Post-Modern Analysis of Disney at "Tamara-Land"', *Academy of Management Journal.* 38: 997–1035.

Boje, D. (2001) *Narrative Methods for Organizational and Communication Research.* London: Sage.

Boje, D. (2008) *Storytelling Organizations.* London: Sage.

Borgerson, J. (2005) 'Judith Butler: On Organizing Subjectivities', *Sociological Review.* 53(1): 63–79.

Borgerson, J. (2015) 'Humility and the Challenge to Decolonize the "Critical" in Critical Management Studies', in A. Mills, J. Mills, P. Prasad and A. Prasad (eds.) *The Routledge Companion to Critical Management Studies.* London: Routledge, pp. 107–123.

Brown, W. (2006) *Regulating Aversion: Tolerance in the Age of Identity and Empire.* Princeton: Princeton University Press.

Butler, J. (1987) *Subjects of Desire: Hegelian Reflections in Twentieth-Century France.* New York: Columbia University Press.

Butler, J. (1988) 'Performative Acts and Gender Constitution: An Essay in Phenomenology and Feminist Theory', *Theater Journal.* 40(4): 519–531.

Butler, J. (1990) *Gender Trouble: Feminism and the Subversion of Identity.* London: Routledge.

Butler, J. (1993) *Bodies That Matter: On the Discursive Limits of 'Sex'.* London: Routledge.

Butler, J. (1995a) 'Contingent Foundations: Feminism and the Question of "Postmodernism"', in S. Benhabib, J. Butler, D. Cornell and N. Fraser (eds.) *Feminist Contentions: A Philosophical Exchange.* London: Routledge, pp. 35–57.

Butler, J. (1995b) 'For a Careful Reading', in S. Benhabib, J. Butler, D. Cornell and N. Fraser (eds.) *Feminist Contentions: A Philosophical Exchange.* London: Routledge, pp. 127–143.

Butler, J. (1995c) 'Burning Acts—Injurious Speech', in A. Parker and E. K. Sedgwick (eds.) *Performativity and Performance.* London: Routledge, pp. 197–227.

Butler, J. (1997a) *Excitable Speech: A Politics of the Performative.* London: Routledge.

Butler, J. (1997b) *The Psychic Life of Power: Theories in Subjection.* Stanford, CA: Stanford University Press.

Butler, J. (1997c) 'Further Reflections on Conversations of Our Time', *Diacritics.* 27(1): 13–15.

Butler, J. (1999) 'A "Bad Writer" Bites Back', *New York Times.* 20 March, p. 15.

Butler, J. (2000a) *Gender Trouble: Feminism and the Subversion of Identity*, 10th anniversary edition. London: Routledge.

Butler, J. (2000b) 'Longing for Recognition: Commentary on the Work of Jessica Benjamin', *Studies in Gender and Sexuality.* 1(3): 271–290.

Butler, J. (2004a) *Precarious Life: The Powers of Mourning and Violence.* London: Verso.

Butler, J. (2004b) *Undoing Gender.* London: Routledge.

Butler, J. (2005) *Giving an Account of Oneself.* New York: Fordham University Press.

Butler, J. (2008) 'Taking Another's View: Ambivalent Implications', in M. Jay, A. Honneth, J. Butler, R. Geuss and J. Lear (eds.) *Reification: A New Look at an Old Idea.* Oxford: Oxford University Press, pp. 97–119.

Butler, J. (2009) *Frames of Work: When Is Life Grievable?* London: Verso.

Butler, J. (2010) 'Performative Agency', *Journal of Cultural Economy*. 3(2): 147–161.

Butler, J. (2015a) *Notes Towards a Performative Theory of Assembly*. Cambridge, MA: Harvard University Press.

Butler, J. (2015b) *Senses of the Subject*. London: Fordham University Press.

Butler, J. (2016) 'Rethinking Vulnerability and Resistance', in J. Butler, Z. Gambetti and L. Sabsay (eds.) *Vulnerability in Resistance*. London: Duke University Press, pp. 12–27.

Butler, J. and Athanasiou, A. (2013) *Dispossession: The Performative in the Political*. Cambridge: Polity.

Butler, J. and Bell, V. (1999) 'Interview: On Speech, Race and Melancholia', *Theory, Culture and Society*. 16(2): 163–174.

Butler, J., Gambetti, Z. and Sabsay, L. (eds.) (2016) 'Acknowledgements' and 'Introduction', in *Vulnerability in Resistance*. London: Duke University Press, pp. ix–x, 1–11,

Cabantous, L., Gond, J-P., Harding, N. and Learmonth, M. (2015) 'Critical Essay: Reconsidering Critical Performativity', *Human Relations*. 69(2): 197–213.

Cheah, P. (1996) 'Mattering', *Diacritics*. 26(1): 108–139.

Coulthard, G. (2014) *Red Skin, White Masks: Rejecting the Colonial Politics of Recognition*. Minneapolis, MN: University of Minnesota Press.

Cremin, C. (2010) 'Never Employable Enough: The (Im)possibility of Satisfying the Boss's Desire', Organization. 17(2): 131–149.

Czarniawska, B. (1998) *A Narrative Approach to Organization Studies*. Thousand Oaks, CA: Sage.

Dale, K. and Latham, Y. (2015) 'Ethics and Entangled Embodiment: Bodies-Materialities-Organization', *Organization*. 22(2): 166–182.

De Beauvoir, S. (1976) First published 1948. *The Ethics of Ambiguity*. Trans. B. Frechtman. New York: Citadel Press.

De Beauvoir, S. (2011) First published 1949. *The Second Sex*. Trans. C. Borde and S. Malovany-Chevallier. London: Vintage.

De Coster, M. and Zanoni, P. (2019) 'Governing Through Accountability: Gendered Moral Selves and the (Im)possibilities of Resistance in the Neoliberal University', *Gender, Work and Organization*. 26(4): 411–429.

De Souza A E, Souza v. Primark Stores Ltd. (2018) *Employment Tribunal Case Number: 2206063/2017*. London: Employment Tribunals Service.

de Souza, E. M., Brewis, J. and Rumens, N. (2016) 'Gender, the Body and Organization Studies: Que(e)rying Empirical Research', *Gender, Work and Organization*. 23(6): 600–613.

Derrida, J. (1979) 'Signature Event Context', *Glyph*. 1: 172–197.

Derrida, J. (1994) *Specters of Marx*. London: Routledge.

Diprose, R. (2012) First published 2002. Corporeal Generosity: On Giving with Nietzsche, Merleau Ponty and Levinas. Albany, NY: State University of New York Press.

Douglas, M. (1966) *Purity and Danger*. London: Routledge.

Driver, M. (2015) 'How Trust Functions in the Context of Identity Work', *Human Relations*. 68(6): 899–923.

Duffy, K., Hancock, P. and Tyler, M. (2017) 'Still Red Hot? Postfeminism and Gender Subjectivity in the Airline Industry', *Gender, Work and Organization*. 24(3): 260–273.

Fairclough, N. (2013) *Critical Discourse Analysis: The Critical Study of Language*, 2nd edition. London: Routledge.

Fanon, F. (1967) *Black Skin, White Masks*. London: Routledge.

Fine, L. (2016) 'Judith Butler and Leadership: Reimagining Intelligibility, Social Change and Leadership Discourse', *Journal of Leadership Studies*. 10(2): 69–81.

Fischer, M. (2016) 'Think Gender Is a Performative? You Have Judith Butler to Thank for That', *New York Times Magazine*. 13 June.

Ford, J. and Harding, N. (2011) 'The Impossibility of the "True" Self of Authentic Leadership', *Leadership*. 7(4): 463–479.

Ford, J., Harding, N. and Learmonth, P. (2010) 'Who Is it That Would Make Business Schools More Critical? Critical Reflections on Critical Management Studies', *British Journal of Management*. 21(1): 571–581.

Fotaki, M. (2019) 'Feminist Ethics: Embodied Relationality as a Normative Guide for Management and Organizations', in C. Neesham and S. Segal (eds.) *The Handbook of Philosophy of Management*. London: Springer (online).

Fotaki, M. and Harding, N. (2017) *Gender and the Organization: Women at Work in the Twenty First Century*. London: Routledge.

Foucault, M. (1961) *The History of Madness*. London: Routledge.

Foucault, M. (1980) *The History of Sexuality, Volume One: An Introduction*. Trans. R. Hurley. London: Random House.

Foucault, M. (1991) *Discipline and Punish: The Birth of the Prison*. London: Penguin.

Foucault, M. (2002) *Archaeology of Knowledge*. London: Routledge.

Fournier, V. and Grey, C. (2000) 'At the Critical Moment: Conditions and Prospects for Critical Management Studies', *Human Relations*. 53: 7–32.

Fraser, N. (1995a) 'False Antitheses: A Response to Seyla Benhabib and Judith Butler', in S. Benhabib, J. Butler, D. Cornell and N. Fraser (eds.) *Feminist Contentions: A Philosophical Exchange*. London: Routledge, pp. 59–74.

Fraser, N. (1995b) 'Pragmatism, Feminism and the Linguistic Turn', in S. Benhabib, J. Butler, D. Cornell and N. Fraser (eds.) *Feminist Contentions: A Philosophical Exchange*. London: Routledge, pp. 157–171.

Fraser, N. (1997) *Justice Interruptus: Critical Reflections on the 'Postsocialist' Condition*. London: Routledge.

Freeman, E. (2010) *Time Binds: Queer Temporalities, Queer Histories*. Durham, NC: Duke University Press.

Fussell, E. (2011) 'The Deportation Threat Dynamic and Victimization of Latino Migrants: Wage Theft and Robbery', *The Sociological Quarterly*. 52(4): 593–615.

Gabriel, Y. (1991) 'Turning Facts into Stories and Stories into Facts: A Hermeneutic Exploration of Organizational Folklore', *Human Relations*. 44(8): 857–875.

Gabriel, Y. (1995) 'The Unmanaged Organization: Stories, Fantasies and Subjectivities', *Organization Studies*. 16(3): 477–501.

Glick, E. (2000) 'Sex Positive: Feminism, Queer Theory and the Politics of Transgression', *Feminist Review*. 64: 19–45.

Goffman, E. (1956) *The Presentation of Self in Everyday Life*. New York: Doubleday.

Goffman, E. (1963) *Behaviour in Public Places*. New York: The Free Press of Glencoe.

Goffman, E. (1967) *Interaction Ritual: Essays on Face-to-Face Behaviour*. New York: Doubleday.

Gond, J-P., Cabantous, L., Harding, N. and Learmonth, M. (2016) 'What Do We Mean by Performativity in Organizational and Management Theory? The Uses and Abuses of Performativity', *International Journal of Management Reviews*. 18: 440–463.

Gregson, N. and Rose, G. (2000) 'Taking Butler Elsewhere: Performativities, Spatialities and Subjectivities', *Environment and Planning D: Society and Space*. 18: 433–452.

Haas, B. (2018) 'Escape the Corset: South Korean Women Rebel Against Strict Beauty Standards', *The Guardian*. 26 October.

Habermas, J. (1979a) *The Theory of Communicative Action*, Volume One. Trans. T. McCarthy. Boston, MA: Beacon Press.

Habermas, J. (1979b) *The Theory of Communicative Action*, Volume Two. Trans. T. McCarthy. Boston, MA: Beacon Press.

Hall, A., Hockey, J. and Robinson, V. (2007) 'Occupational Cultures and the Embodiment of Masculinity: Hairdressing, Estate Agency and Firefighting', *Gender, Work and Organization*. 14(6): 534–551.

Hancock, P. (2008) 'Embodied Generosity and an Ethics of Organization', *Organization Studies*. 29(10): 1357–1373.

Hancock, P. and Tyler, M. (2001) 'Managing Subjectivity and the Dialectic of Self-Consciousness: Hegel and Organization Theory', *Organization*. 8(4): 565–585.

Hancock, P. and Tyler, M. (2007) 'Un/Doing Gender and the Aesthetics of Organizational Performance', *Gender, Work and Organization*. 14(6): 512–533.

Hancock, P., Sullivan, K. and Tyler, M. (2015) 'A Touch Too Much: Negotiating Masculinity, Propriety and Proximity in Intimate Labour', *Organization Studies*. 36(12): 1715–1739.

Harding, N. (2003) *The Social Construction of Management*. London: Routledge.

Harding, N. (2007) 'On Lacan and the "Becoming-ness" of Organizations/Selves', *Organization Studies*. 28(11): 1761–1773.

Harding, N. (2013) *On Being at Work: The Social Construction of the Employee*. London: Routledge.

Harding, N., Ford, J. and Fotaki, M. (2013) 'Is the "F"-Word Still Dirty? A Past, Present and Future of/for Feminist and Gender Studies in Organization', *Organization*. 20(1): 51–65.

Harding, N., Ford, J. and Lee, H. (2017) 'Towards a Performative Theory of Resistance: Senior Managers and Revolting Subject(ivitie)s', *Organization Studies*. 38(9): 1209–1232.

Harding, N., Lee, H. and Ford, J. (2014) 'Who Is the Middle Manager?', *Human Relations*. 67(10): 1213–1237.

Harding, N., Lee, H., Ford, J. and Learmonth, M. (2011) 'Leadership and Charisma: A Desire That Cannot Speak Its Name?' *Human Relations*. 64(7): 927–949.

Harvey, D. (2003) *The New Imperialism*. Oxford: Oxford University Press.

Haynes, K. (2012) 'Body Beautiful? Gender, Identity and the Body in Professional Services Firms', *Gender, Work and Organization*. 19(5): 489–507.

Hegel, G.W.F. (1977) First published 1807. *Phenomenology of Spirit*. Oxford: Oxford University Press.

Hicklin, A. (2017) 'Intersex and Proud: Model Hanne Gaby Odiele on Finally Celebrating Her Body', *The Guardian*. 23 April.

Hirst, A. and Schwabenland, C. (2018) 'Doing Gender in the "New Office"', *Gender, Work and Organization*. 25(2): 159–176.

Hodgson, D. (2005) 'Putting on a Professional Performance: Performativity, Subversion and Project Management', *Organization*. 12(1): 51–68.

Honneth, A. (1995) *The Struggle for Recognition: The Moral Grammar of Social Conflicts*. Cambridge: Polity.

Honneth, A. (2008) 'Reification and Recognition: A New Look at an Old Idea', in M. Jay, A. Honneth, J. Butler, R. Geuss and J. Lear (eds.) *Reification: A New Look at an Old Idea*. Oxford: Oxford University Press, pp. 15–94.

Höpfl, H. (2007) 'The Codex, the Codicil and the Codpiece: Some Thoughts on Diminution and Elaboration in Identity Formation', *Gender, Work and Organization*. 14(6): 619–632.

Humm, M. (2017) 'The Women's March on London: Virginia Woolf, John Berger, Judith Butler and Intersectionality', *Interdisciplinary Perspectives on Equality and Diversity*. 3(1): 1–14.

Irigaray, L. (1985a) *Speculum of the Other Woman*. Trans. G. C. Gill. Ithaca, NY: Cornell University Press.

Irigaray, L. (1985b) *This Sex Which Is Not One*. Trans. C. Porter and C. Burke. Ithaca, NY: Cornell University Press.

Jack, G., Riach, K. and Bariola, E. (2019) 'Temporality and Gendered Agency: Menopausal Subjectivities in Women's Work', *Human Relations*. 72(1): 122–143.

Jameson, F. (2001) 'Introduction', in L. Althusser (ed.) *Lenin and Philosophy and Other Essays*. London: Monthly Review Press, pp. vii–xiv.

Jeanes, E. (2007) 'The Doing and Undoing of Gender: The Importance of Being a Credible Female Victim', *Gender, Work and Organization*. 14(6): 552–571.

Jenkins, J. and Finneman, T. (2017) 'Gender Trouble in the Workplace: Applying Judith Butler's Theory of Performativity to News Organizations', *Feminist Media Studies*. 18(2): 157–172.

Joy, A., Belk, R. and Bhardwaj, R. (2015) 'Judith Butler on Performativity and Precarity: Exploratory Thoughts on Gender and Violence in India', *Journal of Marketing Management*. 31(15–16): 1739–1745.

Kelan, E. (2009) *Performing Gender at Work*. London: Palgrave.

Kelan, E. (2010) 'Gender Logic and (Un)Doing Gender at Work', *Gender, Work and Organization*. 17(2): 174–194.

Kelly, A. and McNamara, M.-L. (2018) 'Modern Slavery: How We Exposed Sex Trafficking in American Prisons', *The Guardian*. 7 July.

Kenny, K. (2009) 'The Performative Surprise: Parody, Documentary and Critique', *Culture and Organization*. 15(2): 221–235.

Kenny, K. (2010) 'Beyond Ourselves: Passion and the Dark Side of Identification in an Ethical Organization', *Human Relations*. 63(6): 857–873.

Kenny, K. (2018) 'Whistleblowers and Impossible Speech', *Human Relations*. 71(8): 1025–1048.

Kenny, K. (2019) *Whistleblowing: Toward a New Theory*. Cambridge, MA: Harvard University Press.

Kenny, K., Whittle, A. and Willmott, H. (2011) *Understanding Identity and Organizations*. London: Sage.

Kirby, V. (2006) *Judith Butler: Live Theory*. London: Continuum.

Kotz, L. (1992) 'The Body You Want: Liz Kotz Interviews Judith Butler', *Artform*. 31(3): 82–89.

Kristeva, J. (1982) *Powers of Horror: An Essay on Abjection*. New York: Columbia Press.

Kruks, S. (1992) 'Gender and Subjectivity: Simone de Beauvoir and Contemporary Feminism', *Signs: Journal of Women in Culture and Society*. 18(1): 89–110.

Laclau, E. and Mouffe, C. (1985) *Hegemony and Socialist Strategy: Towards a Radical Democratic Politics*. London: Verso.

Laine, P.-M., Meriläinen, S., Tienari, J. and Vaara, E. (2016) 'Mastery, Submission and Subversion: On the Performative Construction of Strategist Identity', *Organization*. 23(4): 505–524.

Langton, M. and Barry, K. (1998) 'Aboriginal Women and Economic Ingenuity', in M. Gatens and B. Caine (eds.) *Australian Feminism: A Companion*. Oxford: Oxford University Press, pp. 3–11.

Law, J. (2008) 'On Sociology and STS', *The Sociological Review*. 56(4): 623–649.

Learmonth, M. (2005) 'Doing Things with Words: The Case of "Management" and "Administration"', *Public Administration*. 83(3): 617–637.

Lee, R. (2018) 'Breastfeeding Bodies: Intimacies at Work', *Gender, Work and Organization*. 25(1): 77–90.

Levinas, E. (1961) *Totality and Infinity*. Pittsburgh: Duquesne University Press.

Lloyd, M. (2007) *Judith Butler*. Cambridge: Polity.

Lukács, G. (1971) First published 1923. *History and Class Consciousness*. Trans. R. Livingstone. Cambridge, MA: MIT Press.

Lyotard, J.-F. (1984) First published 1979. *The Postmodern Condition: A Report on Knowledge*. Manchester: Manchester University Press.

Mahmood, S. (2012) *Politics of Piety: The Islamic Revival and the Feminist Subject*. Princeton, NJ: Princeton University Press.

Mair, J. and Frew, E. (2018) 'Academic Conferences: A Female Duo-Ethnography', *Current Issues in Tourism*. 21(18): 2152–2172.

Mavin, S. and Grandy, G. (2013) 'Doing Gender Well and Differently in Dirty Work: The Case of Exotic Dancing', *Gender, Work and Organization*. 20(3): 232–251.

Mavin, S. and Grandy, G. (2016) 'A Theory of Abject Appearance: Women Elite Leaders' Intra-Gender "Management" of Bodies and Appearance', *Human Relations*. 69(5): 1095–1120.

McDowell, L. and Court, G. (1994) 'Performing Work: Bodily Representations in Merchant Banking', *Environment and Planning D: Society and Space*. 12: 727–750.

McNay, L. (1999) 'Subject, Psyche and Agency: The Work of Judith Butler', *Theory, Culture and Society*. 16(2): 175–193.

McNay, L. (2008a) *Against Recognition*. Cambridge: Polity Press.

McNay, L. (2008b) 'The Trouble with Recognition: Subjectivity, Suffering and Agency', *Sociological Theory*. 26(3): 271–296.

Merleau Ponty, M. (2013) First published 1968. *The Visible and the Invisible*. London: Routledge.

Merleau-Ponty, M. (2002) First published 1946. *The Phenomenology of Perception*. London: Routledge.

Milroy, T., Cutcher, L. and Tyler, M. (2019) 'Stopped in Our Tracks: From "Giving an Account" to an Ethics of Recognition in Feminist Praxis', *Gender, Work and Organization* (online early).

More, K. (2016) 'Judith Butler on Transsexuality: An Interview by Kate More (1999)', in K. More and S. Whittle (eds.) *Transsexual Grammars at the Fin de Siècle*. London: Bloomsbury, pp. 285–302.

Morison, T. and MacLeod, C. (2013) 'A Performative-Performance Analytical Approach: Infusing Butlerian Theory into the Narrative Discursive Method', *Qualitative Inquiry*. 19(8): 566–577.

Nentwich, J., Ozbilgin, M. and Tatli, A. (2014) 'Change Agency as Performance and Embeddedness: Exploring the Possibilities and Limits of Butler and Bourdieu', *Culture and Organization*. 21(3): 235–250.

Nussbaum, M. (1999) 'The Professor of Parody: The Hip Defeatism of Judith Butler', *The New Republic*. 22: 37–45.

O'Shea, S. C. (2018) 'The Girl's Life: An Auto-Ethnography', *Organization*. 25(1): 3–20.

Ortlieb, R. and Sieben, B. (2019) 'Balls, Barbecues and Boxing: Contesting Gender Regimes at Organizational Events', *Organization Studies*. 40(1): 115–134.

Page, T. (2017) 'Vulnerable Writing as a Feminist Methodological Practice', *Feminist Review*. 115: 13–29.

Parker, M. (2002) 'Queering Management and Organization', *Gender, Work and Organization*. 9(2): 146–166.

Perry, G. (2018) 'Arts Essay', *The Guardian*. 10 February, pp. 33–34.

Povinelli, E. (2002) *The Cunning of Recognition: Indigenous Alterities and the Making of Australian Multiculturalism*. Durham, NC: Duke University Press.

Povinelli, E. (2011) *Economies of Abandonment: Social Belonging and Endurance in Late Liberalism*. London: Duke University Press.

Preston, J. (2019) *Grenfell Tower: Preparedness, Race and Disaster Capitalism*. London: Palgrave.

Pullen, A. and Knights, D. (2007) 'Editorial: Undoing Gender, Organizing and Disorganizing Performance', *Gender, Work and Organization*. 14(6): 505–511.

Pullen, A. and Simpson, R. (2009) 'Managing Difference in Feminized Work: Men, Otherness and Social Practice', *Human Relations*. 62(4): 561–587.

Rajan-Rankin, S. (2018) 'Invisible Bodies and Disembodied Voices? Identity Work, the Body and Embodiment in Transnational Service Work', *Gender, Work and Organization*. 25(1): 77–90.

Rhodes, C. (2017) 'Ethical Praxis and the Business Case for LGBT Diversity: Political Insights from Judith Butler and Emmanuel Levinas', *Gender, Work and Organization*. 24(5): 533–546.

Riach, K., Rumens, N. and Tyler, M. (2014) 'Un/Doing Chronormativity: Negotiating Ageing, Gender and Sexuality in Organizational Life', *Organization Studies*. 35(11): 1677–1698.

Riach, K., Rumens, N. and Tyler, M. (2016) 'Towards a Butlerian Methodology: Undoing Organizational Performativity Through Anti-narrative Research', *Human Relations*. 69(11): 2069–2089.

Rubin, G. and Butler, J. (1994) 'Sexual Traffic: An Interview', *Differences: A Journal of Feminist Cultural Studies*. 6(2–3): 62–99.

Rumens, N. (2018) *Queer Business: Queering Organizational Sexualities*. London: Routledge.

Rumens, N. and Tyler, M. (2015) 'Towards a Queer Politics and Ethics Within Organization Studies', in A. Pullen and C. Rhodes (eds.) *The Routledge Companion to Ethics, Politics and Organizations*. London: Routledge, pp. 447–461.

Rumens, N. and Tyler, M. (2016) 'Queer Theory', in R. Mir, H. Willmott and M. Greenwood (eds.) *The Routledge Companion to Philosophy in Organization Studies*. London: Routledge, pp. 225–236.

Rumens, N., de Souza, E.M. and Brewis, J. (2018) 'Queering Queer Theory in Management and Organization Studies: Notes Toward Queering Heterosexuality', *Organization Studies*. 40(4): 593–612.

Sang, K. and Lyon, C. (2017) 'Editorial: The Women's March and Trump', *Interdisciplinary Perspectives on Equality and Diversity*. 3(1): 1–4.

Sayers, J. and Jones, D. (2015) 'Truth Scribbled in Blood: Women's Work, Menstruation and Poetry', *Gender, Work and Organization*. 22(2): 94–111.

Schilt, K. and Connell, C. (2007) 'Do Workplace Gender Transitions Make Gender Trouble?' *Gender, Work and Organization*. 14(6): 596–618.

Scott, J. W. (1988) *Gender and the Politics of History*. New York: Columbia University Press.

Sedgwick, E. K. (2002) *Touching, Feeling: Affect, Pedagogy, Performativity*. London: Duke University Press.

Segal, L. (1994) *Why Feminism? Gender, Psychology, Politics*. Cambridge: Polity.

Segarra, P. and Prasad, A. (2019) 'Colonization, Migration and Right-Wing Extremism: The Constitution of Embodied Life of a Dispossessed, Undocumented Migrant Woman', *Organization* (online early).

Spicer, A., Alvesson, M. and Kärreman, D. (2009) 'Critical Performativity: The Unfinished Business of Critical Management Studies', *Human Relations*. 62: 537–560.

Spivak, G. Chakravorty (1993) *Outside in the Teaching Machine*. New York: Routledge.

Thanem, T. and Wallenberg, L. (2016) 'Just Doing Gender? Transvestism and the Power of Undoing Gender in Everyday Life and Work', *Organization*. 23(2): 250–271.

Tyler, M. (2019) 'Reassembling Difference? Rethinking Inclusion Through/as Embodied Ethics', *Human Relations*. 72(1): 48–68.

Tyler, M. and Cohen, L. (2010) 'Spaces That Matter: Gender Performativity and Organizational Space', *Organization Studies*. 31(2): 175–198.

Varman, R. and Al-Amoudi, I. (2016) 'Accumulation Through Derealization: How Corporate Violence Remains Unchecked', *Human Relations*. 69(10): 1909–1935.

Velicu, I. and Garcia-López, G. (2018) 'Thinking the Commons Through Ostrom and Butler: Boundedness and Vulnerability', *Theory, Culture and Society*. 35(6): 55–73.

Weick, K. (1995) *Sensemaking in Organizations*. Thousand Oaks, CA: Sage.

Wickert, C. and Schaefer, S. (2014) 'Towards a Progressive Understanding of Performativity in Critical Management Studies', *Human Relations*. 68(1): 107–130.

Wittig, M. (1992) *The Straight Mind and Other Essays*. Boston, MA: Beacon Press.

Žižek, S. (2000) 'Class Struggle of Postmodernism? Yes Please!', in J. Butler, E. Laclau and S. Žižek (eds.) *Contingency, Hegemony, Universality: Contemporary Dialogues on the Left*. London: Verso, pp. 90–135.

Index

Note: page numbers followed by 'n' refer to notes.

9/11 141, 196n8

abjection 39, 62, 67, 69–74, 89,
    157, 160, 164n6, 174,195n2, 202;
    corporate 163; and death 143;
    and exploitation 155–156; and
    organizations 98–9; see also
    de-realization; Kristeva, Julia
accounting 11, 25, 73, 109–139,
    153; and hailing 113–117; and
    politics 117–121; and recognition
    135–138; and work 121–135;
    see also narratives
Adorno, Theodor 73, 76, 117–118,
    120, 169, 185–187, 195n7,
affect 77, 83n10, 104, 126,
    134, 152–153, 171–172; and
    dispossession 145, 151–155; and
    solidarity 171–172, 175–176,
    178–179
affective recognition 154–155
agency 30–32, 34, 47–48, 50–51,
    98, 153; and endurance 134;
    and organization 78; and power
    72; and recognition 37–38; and
    subjectivity 10, 13–15, 18–19, 37,
    58n8, 59n13, 67–68, 85, 115, 120;
    and vulnerability 179–183, 185,
    200–201, 203–204
Ahmed, Sara 21, 37, 46, 50, 59n12,
    83n10, 84n11, 94, 98, 131, 170-2,
    176
AIDS 67, 163–164n4
alterity 16–20, 22, 30, 44, 62, 94,
    192; see also encounters with
    difference; exclusion
Althusser, Louis 9, 21, 52, 59n11, 86,
    107n1, 110, 113–116, 118, 121,

124, 127, 138n2, 195n1; see also
    hailing
ante-narratives 138n4
anti-narrative research 103–105,
    122–125
appearance 22, 37, 79, 99, 148, 167,
    177–188, 196n9, 202; of autonomy
    74; of gender 93; of substance 34,
    40, 47, 62, 68–69; space of 153,
    176, 178–179; see also Arendt,
    Hannah
Arendt, Hannah 26, 148, 153, 155,
    167, 176–178, 181–182, 184–185,
    202
Aristotle 82n2
assaultive speech 97–98, 109
assemblies 11, 132, 153, 167–170,
    175–177, 180; organizations as/
    and 188–195, 200–203; see also
    bodies
Austin, John L. 5–8, 13–14, 31, 57
Australia 127–131, 138n5, 139n9

Benhabib, Seyla 12, 32, 50, 58n3,
    59n10, 91
Benjamin, Jessica 20–21, 27n3, 89,
    94, 107n4
Benjamin, Walter 196n11
Berlant, Lauren 134, 156, 164n7;
    see also damaged futures
Bhabha, Homi 196n11
bodies 23, 35–39; 61–84; and
    assemblies 10–11,167–189;
    and breastfeeding 78–79, 137;
    categorization of 44–45, 69–75,
    58n4; gendered/sexed 3–5, 27n4,
    30, 33, 40–45; 89–90, 93–93;
    managerial 52–56; maternal

38–39; and matter 60–64, 63–64, 77, 82n1; menopausal 78; and organizations 98–100; and schemas 82n2; and substance 83n3; *see also* ideals, bodily
body work 23, 150
Borgerson, Janet 3, 33, 76, 96, 123
Brown, Wendy 152, 180

call centres 79–80
capitalism 141–144, 147, 195n1; and precarity 154–155, 158
categorization 69–75
chrononormativity 103–107
Cixous, Hélène 38
Coca-Cola 158, 160–163
community arts workers 53–54
compulsory heterosexuality 35,42, 96
corporations 19, 23–24, 50, 62, 75–77, 84n11, 87, 99–100, 102, 113, 143, 157–163, 204
corruption 135–136, 139n10
cosmetics 107n3; *see also* Escape the Corset
critical discourse analysis 5
critical performativity 27n6, 56–57, 126
critical theory 30, 33, 51, 173, 196
cultural translation 62, 189, 196n11

damaged futures 156–157, 164n7; *see also* Berlant, Lauren
death 19, 22, 88, 141–143, 196n9, and precarity 132–134, 148; *see also* grief
De Beauvoir, Simone x, 1, 16, 30, 37–39, 44–46, 64, 72, 90, 93, 99, 174, 195n3
dehumanization 44, 67–68, 162, 143, 156, 192
dependency 144, 168–170, 172, 176–179, 182–183, 203–205; *see also* interdependency
derealization 148, 154, 163n4, 164n6; and accumulation 158–162; and indigenous people 158; and whistleblowers 135–137, 156–158; and violence 160, 162–163; *see also* abjection
Derrida, Jacques 6–7, 18, 21, 31, 33, 46, 148; and iterability 21
desire 8, 16–19, 27n12; as male prerogative 35, 41–42; politics of 153, 155, 182, 186; for recognition xi, 4, 8–9, 15–16, 19–21, 24–26,

29–33, 46–47, 54, 61, 77–78, 88–107, 110–116, 140–142, 164n5, 167–171
de Souza, Alexandra 65–66, 83n7
destruction 18–21, 95, 167, 175; self- 133
determinism 14, 40, 44, 66
differentiation 2, 22, 71–73
Diprose, Rosalyn 78, 92
discourse 2, 5–10, 14–16, 49–54, 58n5, 62, 84, 94, 112–113, 128, 138n4, 146, 192–194, 200; corporate 84n11, 137, 158–162; and healing 138n6; leadership 59n13; organizational 98; scientific 43; and vulnerability 145, 163; *see also* critical discourse analysis; leadership; management, discourse
disposability 155–158, 167–176
dispossession 25–26, 144–163, 170–183, 195n4; institutionalized 128–131
diversity 27n10, 37, 113
doing 32, 85–88; and gender 46–47, 89–96; ontology 4–17; and organizations 96–98; and/as organizing 98–103; and recognition 88–89
double negation 143
drag 10, 18, 27n4, 47–50, 59n10, 65, 68, 167

ek-statis 17–19, 22–26, 88, 111, 114, 140, 175, 182; and affect 151–155; and recognition 187; and signification 76–77
embodied ethics 168–169
emplacement 149
encounters with difference 62–63, 66; *see also* alterity
Escape the Corset 107n3
ethical life 117, 124, 182, 188; *see also* Hegel, Georg Wilhelm Friedrich
ethics: and accountability 116, 117–121; embodied 168–169; and politics 142–143
exclusion 66, 69–70, 73, 96, 105, 114–115, 157, 169, 171–172, 191–192, 195n2
exploitation 130, 144–145, 156–157, 164n5, 176, 185–186, 195n3

Facebook 197
Fanon, Franz 152

feminism: difference 12; and
    emancipation 12, 58n3, 89, 95–96;
    and subjectivity 36, 38–43, 91; and
    subversion 38–47; *see also* post-
    feminism
field of appearance; *see* appearanace;
    Arendt, Hannah
Ford, Jackie 33, 57, 123–124
Fotaki, Marianna 26n1, 31, 194–195
Foucault, Michel 6, 12–13, 15, 27n8,
    27n9, 34, 51, 58n8, 82n2, 85, 93,
    117, 129
Fraser, Nancy ix, 26n2, 28n13, 84n11,
    95, 103, 123, 165–166, 179, 199
Freud, Sigmund 51, 83n9, 164n5

gender 58n7; and bodies 35; and
    doing 46–47; and lawyers 78; and
    matter 61–62, 66–67; and office
    space 81; organizing 98–103; and
    parody 49; as property 27n7; and
    sex 43–44; and spaces that matter
    80; and work 97
gender performativity 3–4, 7–8, 9,
    30–33, 58n5; and abjection 72; and
    appearance 178; and girling 83n10;
    and organization 99; and un/doing
    90; and workspaces 55–56; *see also*
    performative acts
girling 83n10
Goffman, Erving 13–14, 49, 59n10
Grenfell Tower 143, 160, 163n3
grief 141–143, 159
Guantanamo Bay 160

Habermas, Jürgen 20, 107n4
hailing 9, 11, 21, 22, 86, 107n1, 109,
    113–117; *see also* Althusser, Louis
Hancock, Philip 27n11, 33, 77–78,
    101–102, 168
Hanlon, Bigali x, 127–131, 139n8,
    139n9
Harding, Nancy x, 8, 16, 26n1, 31,
    33, 51–53, 59n11, 123–124
Hart Island 163n4
healing 138n6
Hegel, Georg Wilhelm Friedrich
    x, 12–13, 15–23, 24–26, 26n3,
    28n13, 41, 86, 92, 141, 164n5,
    198; and bodies 64–66, 77, 169;
    and inter-subjectivity 85–87,
    94–95, 116, 118–119, 154; and
    organization theory 27n11; and
    recognition 29–30, 90, 101–102,
    107n4, 111–113, 140–142, 144,

150, 170, 195n4, 196n8, 205n2;
    and self-consciousness 85; and
    servitude 164n5; *see also* ethical life
hegemony 72, 83n6, 120, 132, 195n1;
    gender 68; organizational 91
heteronormativity 8, 29, 33, 40–41,
    48, 65, 80, 103, 105
heterosexual hegemony 83n6
heterosexual matrix 3, 8, 19, 27n8,
    33–35, 40–43, 46, 48, 83n6,
    102–4; and abjection 70–71;
    and bodily ideals 64–65; and
    chrononormativity 104; and desire
    35; and workspaces 54, 102–104
Honneth, Axel 20, 28n13, 126, 146,
    150, 161, 167, 172–173, 175, 177,
    195n7
Horkheimer, Max 195n7
humour 48, 108n5, 190

ideals 1, 27n4, 66, 77, 146, 171,
    178; bodily 77–78, 107n3, 150;
    emancipatory 95
identity work 79–80, 99, 121, 122,
    124, 126
ideology 114–115
illocutionary force 6
inclusion 28n14, 28n15, 84n11, 146,
    150, 152, 169–172, 175, 183–184,
    191–192, 195n2; *see also* tolerance
incorporation 19, 28n14
India 79, 158–162, 164n8
indigenous people: and accounting
    121, 127–130; and de-realization
    158; and healing 138n6; and
    language 138n5; and narrative
    138n7; and wages 139n9
intelligibility 8–9, 16, 19, 32, 35, 41;
    bodily 62, 67–68; gender 46; grid
    of 27n8; and legitimacy 67, 90,
    120, 131–133, 198; and normative
    regimes 25, 47–48, 70, 76, 87,
    98, 104–105, 111, 119, 121, 160,
    195n6; organizational 59n13, 157;
    risks of 146–147; schemas of 82n2,
    120; signs of 33
inter-corporeality 77–78, 86, 141,
    145, 151, 169–170, 181; and
    vulnerability 191–194
interdependency 141, 176–177, 179,
    181–184, 188, 195n3
interpellation 9, 59n11, 83n10, 104,
    114–119, 177, 174; conditional
    150; and subjectivity 85, 107n1 *see
    also* hailing

inter-subjectivity 15–16, 26n3, 118–119, 150, 195n4, 199
Irigaray, Luce 38–39
iterability 6–7, 21, 32; sedimented 70, 82n1

journalists 55

al-Khawli, Mariam 132–135
Kelan, Elisabeth 3, 33, 56, 58n5, 97
Kenny, Kate 14, 23–24, 33, 123, 135–137, 139n10, 154–157, 162, 191, 205n2
Kirby, Vicki x, 1, 22, 29, 37, 39, 41, 50, 63–64, 71–72, 81–82, 82n3, 86, 98, 107n1, 107n2, 116–117, 121, 138n1, 166, 195n1
Kristeva, Julia 38, 69–70, 73–74; *see also* abjection

Lacan, Jacques 51, 82, 96
language 6, 12, 14, 26n2, 32, 34, 40, 50–51, 81–82, 98, 166; and assemblies 184, 190; emancipatory 165; indigenous 138n5; and power 109, 128–129, 160, 180; and subjectivity 12, 65, 114; *see also* assaultive speech; hailing; name calling; speech acts
lawyers 78
leadership 52, 59n13, 99; *see also* discourse, leadership
Levinas, Emmanuel 92, 111, 116–118, 174, 191–193
LGBTQ people 191–194; and accounting 121, 124–125; and chrononormativity 104–106; and politics 11–12; *see also* queer; trans people
liveability 19, 48, 100, 87–88, 166–167; and ethics 174, 187, 193; and relationality 179–180
locution 6
Lord and Bondsman 15, 17, 23–24, 45–46, 85, 94–95; *see also* Hegel, Georg Wilhelm Friedrich
Lloyd, Moya x-xi, 8, 12–13, 16, 21, 23, 27n5, 27n8, 27n12, 31, 37, 39, 47–48, 55, 62–63, 74, 87, 98, 109, 140–143, 172–175, 188, 191, 196n11, 197–198

management 52–53, 136, 150, 154, 161; aesthetic 102; discourse 201; and performativity 15, 27n6,

52–53, 56–57, 59n11; of resources 196n10; of subjectivity 27n11, 123
marriage vows 7, 83n7
masculinity 8, 46, 55; heteronormative 41, 100–101; organizational 75; and subjectivity 68, 93, 99
matter 60–64; and bodies 64–69, 82n1; categorization of 69–75; and organizational 75–82; and power 83n5; and vulnerability 150–151
media 75, 202; global news 133–134; social ix, 107n3, 108n5, 190
mediation 64, 76–77, 102, 163n1, 177, 187, 202
men 42, 45, 98–100
menopause 78
menstruation 55
Merleau Ponty, Maurice 12, 35, 40, 168–169, 181–182
migrant workers 156–157; *see also* refugees
misrecognition 16–17, 28n13, 73, 77–80, 89, 142, 144, 174; *see also* negation
modernity 52, 195n7
motherhood 38–39, 79, 137
mutual recognition 1, 16, 19, 64, 77, 88, 154; and assemblage 169–171, 177; and ethics 193; politics of 183, 196n8; *see also* recognition

name calling 14, 65, 115; *see also* hailing
narratives 10–11; and accounting 110–113, 117, 121, 138n4; and chrononormativity 103–107; and dispossession 144, 156; organizational 56, 123–134; *see also* accounting; ante-narratives; anti-narrative research
natural womanhood 58n1
negation 16–18, 20–22, 27n12, 58n3, 66, 78, 87, 94, 105–106; and dispossession 142–144, 157–160, 162; and assembly 192; *see also* misrecognition
non-performatives 37, 46
non-violence 192–194, 197–205; *see also* ethics

Occupy movements 187, 191, 200, 202; Occupy Gezi 200
oppression 28n13, 43–45, 158, 195n3
organizational mattering 75–82

organizational un/doing 96–98
organizing 1–3, 8–9, 13–15, 19–21,
  24, 98–103, 171; and assemblage
  177, 193, 200–201, 205; processes
  33–35, 39–44, 58n8, 61–63,
  70–74, 81, 103–105, 128;
  schemas 87

Page, Tiffany 132–135, 137
Parker, Martin 13, 52, 57, 123
parody ix, 29, 33, 45–51, 59n9
passionate attachment 154, 164n5,
  174, 202
patriarchy 36, 39, 42–43
performative accomplishment
  9; gender as a 33–34, 62;
  management as a 52–53; the body
  as a 68
performative acts 7–8, 10, 31–32,
  59n11; and gender constitution 2,
  34–35; and phenomenology 36–37;
  see also gender performativity
performative agency 15, 51, 203
performative labour 31, 171, 195n6
performative reflexivity 56–57
performativity 2, 4–7, 7–8, 13,
  27n6, 30, 59n11, 165–175,
  191, 197; and accountability
  120; and organization 177–188;
  organizational 51–56; and precarity
  144–145; and queerness 48; and re/
  assembling 175–177; and speech
  acts 13–14; and work 75–76;
  see also gender performativity;
  speech acts
perlocutionary effect 6, 13
Perry, Grayson 108n6, 196n14
phenomenology 5, 16, 30–34, 36–37,
  76, 89, 96, 150–152
plural performativity 165–175,
  199; and re/assembling 175–177,
  180–184
politics 12, 117–121, 142–143
post-feminism 59n9
poststructuralism 11, 30, 33, 50,
  58n5, 164n5
poverty 134, 145, 156, 161, 162,
  164n8; *see also* precarity
Povinelli, Elizabeth 133, 146, 172
power 2, 23–24, 85; and matter 83n5,
  96; and politics 12; and schemas
  71; and speech acts 14
powerlessness 161, 200
precarity 11, 17, 25, 33, 140–144,
  175, 205n2; and assembly

167–171, 175–188; induced
  10; and interdependency 188;
  and organization 144–154; and
  vulnerability 134, 198–202, 205n2;
  of women 164n8; at work 154–163
public assemblies 11, 167, 175,
  197, 204
Pullen, Alison 98–100

queer 12–13, 38–39, 180–181,
  192–193, 202–203; futures 194,
  200; and parody 48; politics
  12, 107n5, 112–113, 202, and
  recognition 180; theory 2, 11–13,
  38, 48, 191; and un/doing 97–98;
  see also LGBTQ people; queering
queering 67, 192 *see also* queer

racism 37, 145, 156
Rana Plaza 143, 160
rape 101; *see also* sexual assault
re/assembling 175–177
recognition 1, 8, 15–23, 26n3,
  28n13, 30, 195n4; and accounting
  111–113, 135–138; alternative
  forms of 152; and appearance
  178–179; and assemblies 188–190;
  and communication 107n4;
  conditions of 40; desire for 93–97,
  164n5; and dispossession 146; and
  heteronormativity 103–104; and
  humanity 109–110; and matter 64;
  meditation of 187; and reflection
  101–102; and reification 172–173;
  and subjectivity 85; and tolerance
  145–146; and un/doing 90; *see
  also* desire, for recognition; mutual
  recognition
refugees 132, 134, 200; *see also*
  migrant workers
reification 2, 14, 18, 46, 113, 145,
  167–169, 172–173, 199; as
  forgetting 195n7, and gender
  34–35, 42–43, 45, 68; of grief
  143; organizational 77, 84n11, 95,
  100, 113, 130–131, 172–173, 191;
  and precarity 145, 149, 161; and
  recognition 112, 151, 203
reiteration 7–9, 13, 37, 59n12,
  67–68, 72–74, 148
resignification 30, 47–48, 53, 67–68,
  74, 83n8, 84n10, 95, 107n5, 144,
  152, 166, 190; *see also* signification
resistance 47, 50, 124, 132–134, 144,
  159–163, 164n8, and assembly

166, 169, 172, 176, 185–6, 190;
and gender 56, 91, 100; and
vulnerability 10, 199–204
Rhodes, Carl 191–192
ritualized repetitions 60–61
Rumens, Nick 12, 38, 52, 101,
191–194, 200

schemas 61, 71, 82n2; *see also*
organizing, schemas
Sedgwick, Eve 83n7
self-consciousness 17–20, 64, 77, 85
self-harm 132–135
sex reassignment 93–94; *see also*
trans people
sex trafficking 143–144
sexual assault 164n8, 200; *see also*
rape
sexual harassment 100–101
sex workers 102
signification 14, 33–35, 41, 47–49,
69–76, 81–82, 154–156, 167,
176–177; *see also* resignification
social construction 15, 34, 39–40, 46,
51, 69, 73, 96, 120
social justice 34, 165–166, 171, 190
space of appearance; *see* appearance,
spaces of
spectres 61, 71, 83n9, 113, 148
speech acts 5–6, 8; and marriage
vows 83n7; and name calling
65; and politics 13–14; and
reiteration 59n12; *see also*
assaultive speech
Stolen Wages Commissions 128–131
subjectivity 9–10; and agency 85;
as a process 51; and undoing 87
substance 18, 24, 34, 40–41, 51,
62–64, 68, 83n3
subversion: and feminism 38–47; and
parody 47–51

tolerance 145–146, 156–157, 171;
see also inclusion
transgendering 83n9
trans people 64–68, 101, 108n6, 179;
see also LGBTQ people
Trump, Donald 189–190

Tyler, Melissa 27n11, 33, 46, 54–55,
77–80, 101–102, 170, 172, 189,
191, 195n6

un/doing 10, 85–88; and accounting
122–127, 132; and gender 89–96; and
organizations 96–98, 103–107; and
organizing 98–103; and recognition
88–89; and trans people 108
utterances 13, 31–32; *see also*
speech acts

Varman, Rohit 158–163
violence 133–134, 141–143, 145,
157–160, 162–163; *see also*
self-harm
voluntarism 14, 62
vulnerability 14, 24, 86, 205n2; and
9/11 196n8; and accounting 132,
134; and dependency 169–170;
and dispossession 161; and
ethics 118–119; and exploitation
143–144; and interdependency
181–184; and LGBTQ people
191–194; and oppression 195n3;
and politics 92, 190–191; and
power 196n10; and precarity 141,
194–195; and resistance 185,
200–203; and violation 175

wages 127–131, 139n9
whistleblowers 135–137, 154–156
Wittig, Monique 40, 45
women: bodies of 79, 174–175; and
cosmetics 107n3; and feminism 36,
42–43; in masculine workplaces
100–101; and matter 61; and
precarity 164n8; and signifiers
81–82; and work 75
Women's Marches 189–190
work: and gender 97; and
immigration 156; and precarity
154–163
workplaces 53, 54–55, 143–144, 156

Yindjibarndi people 138n5

Žižek, Slavoj 2, 81

Printed in the United States
by Baker & Taylor Publisher Services